The Reading Room

writing of the moment

FIRST ISSUE

Published by

GREAT MARSH PRESS

New York

The Reading Room

writing of the moment

Editor	Barbara Probst Solomon
Assistant Editors	Julie Berman Jessica Moon Julie Obaso Sarah Yaw
Art Director	Julie Schwartzman
Advisory Board	Saul Bellow, Marianne Bruni, Stanley Crouch, Juan Goytisolo, Enrique Krauze, Jennifer Lyons, Don Maggin, Daphne Merkin, Larry Rivers, Corlies Smith, Barbara Probst Solomon, Carla Solomon Ph.D., Maria Solomon

First Edition
Library of Congress 99-091745
ISBN 1-928863-05-1
© 2000 by Great Marsh Press, all rights reserved.
The Reading Room is published three times a year by Great Marsh Press, PO Box 2144, Lenox Hill Station, NY, NY 10021. Website: www.greatmarshpress.com. Telephone for business queries and ordering information is 212-946-4522. Ingram Books is the US distributor: 1-800-937-8000. The Reading Room welcomes the submission of unsolicited manuscripts, but cannot accept responsibility of their loss or delay, or engage in related correspondence. Unless accompanied by a self-addressed envelope correctly stamped manuscripts will not be returned. All manuscripts should be sent to Great Marsh Press, PO Box 2144, Lenox Hill Station, NY, NY 10021. Letters should be sent to: Letters Dept., Great Marsh Press, PO Box 2144, Lenox Hill Station, NY, NY 10021.

Typesetting by Syllables: www.syllables.com. Printed in the United States of America.
Opinions expressed by the contributors are not necessarily those of the editors.

TABLE OF CONTENTS

Cover artwork: Larry Rivers

Wandering the World

L'Imperiale at the Georges Cinq

Stanley Crouch

L'Imperiale began with its sonata as Holiday ascended the stairs at the chateau near Fontainbleau that led to the bathroom, pausing for a moment at the first step and playing with the wooden mane of the roaring simba that rose up from the end of the railing. She stood there at the top and looked down on the party, her face perplexed, then melancholy, a smirk winging up the corners of her mouth, then a deep breath was exhaled and she was gone, the gold frames of the portraits seeming to cast brighter light as she passed them. Maurice began telling me how she had come to Europe with a modeling agency called Vogel and Tanner, but that Holiday hadn't been able to get along with them.

"They put her on a pedestal and she was the fashion angel of Paris, darling, the hottest thing out here. But you know how oafish these motherfuckers can get every now and then. Very oafish, dear, very oafish. I never got the details right, but when she fell out with them they told her she could forget it. They would put her career right to sleep. Well, you know *I* immediately got her everything I could."

"So the fashion world is like everything else."

"It just *has* to be. There are always squabbles when it comes to getting something noticed and sold. Let's not even mention *staying* up there once you get your thing going. Who could stand you if you did *that?* The fact of the matter is simple, darling: someone always wants to believe that the power to stop you is in their filthy little hands. But you know me: I'm a testy little son of a bitch, I'll throw a gallon of shit at the fan in a minute. Oh, oh, Andre seems to be coming out of his fretful little pout. Look at him loafing around the room like that, trying to get me to notice him first."

"Is that the same guy?"

"'Now don't you get cute. You know that is exactly the same one: the finest glowing boy in here. Excuse me, I just must attend to one of the finer things of life. If anything happens with you and Holiday, let me know. I don't think I would mind having another *vicarious* heterosexual experience before I go."

Then Holiday came down the stairs, iridescently sensual and moving through the party like a mist, hovering, floating, disappearing through the French doors that opened to the colonnade and the steps that took one down to the huge patio where the view went past the topiary bushes and the sycamore trees into the green expanse given pale majesty by the birch. It was near twilight and the sun, having not much more time to loll up in the sky, was making the last few passes of illumination on its way down, gold and red, seeming to melt the horizon into darkness. I followed her and began to hum Billie Holiday's version of *Easy to Love.*

"That's not bad," she said, turning to me.

I stared at her.

"I have perfect pitch you know."

"Is that so?" I said, looking at her as though she was saying something very, very intimate.

"It could be a nuisance," she smiled, "but I do all that I can to keep my ears cosmopolitan. You know those of us from the provinces should never ever allow ourselves to simply *become* provincial."

"You seem pretty slick to me."

"Ah, slick. Yes, slick. You are an American black aren't you?"

"You knew that already."

"That's true."

"I'm sure it is, pretty face."

"Yes. It is true, and it also causes me to remember some things I enjoy returning to in my mind."

I said nothing, preferring to let whatever pressure my presence had stand in for any words. Looking at her was good enough for now.

"I remember when I was back home in Nairobi, I used to just love to hear black Americans talk. A friend of mine and I would sometimes sit near tables where the American black people were and listen to them in awe. What a sound it was! They usually thought we were prostitutes, but we were no more than curious girls out having a time of it listening to American slang."

"What made it so attractive to you?"

"In all honesty, it was very exotic."

"That's a good one."

"It was. And the slang of the American black was very confident. After all, we Africans aren't so different. Who isn't attracted by confidence and mystery? And, of course, there is always a soul in a sound, even if it is a very ugly soul. It was that soul I found rather magnetic. And I will not even try to *imagine* what would have become of me if it hadn't been for Billie Holiday. Ah, Billie Holiday. She was my protecting goddess when I came to Europe, my *juok,* my power. I was a frightened person, very frightened, a gazelle, and Billie Holiday made me feel so much less lonely. Back home, there is a sadness to the bush music, too. It is the melancholy of nature: there pain and killing are never less than normal. But in the sound of Billie Holiday, I feel I...I feel she has captured the true honor and sadness of the city. In Paris, in Rome, in the different places where I have been hired to wear clothes, I have often felt very lonely and very afraid. This is *not* my world, but this *is* my world. Do you know what I mean?"

I didn't know why she was telling me all of this but I assumed it could have been the champagne, since I had often been places where people started peeling away their emotional skins until they suddenly stood there before you, spiritually bloody and full of self-pity. But her tone of voice didn't have that sound and the way she stood there looking at me inspired my resolve to run a few riffs at her that would connect back to the experience she and her friend had listening to some American niggers in Nairobi.

"I think a pot-bellied moon sitting fat up in the sky is the same everywhere. I think the warmth you learn from your mama is the same. I think when somebody's daddy is joking about how dumb his son is, that boy feels the same anywhere in the world. Oh, now some people like their food hot and some like it cold. They'll cover themselves different and somebody will always look strange at you if what you're wearing clashes with what *they* think it takes to be sharp as rat shit is."

"Sharp as rat shit?"

"That's sharp at both ends."

"Oh, I love the American slang! You mean very, *very* well dressed."

"Clean as an archangel's underwear."

"These phrases you use are such fascinating barriers."

"You have to believe in something beyond the barriers, like Ben Webster breathing his vibrato on the neck of Billie Holiday's melody, like the perfume of this night and the sweet sensation of your absolutely superb beauty."

As in a dream, we then began to talk another kind of talk, as if we were suddenly hurling that net of ego which snares the world itself and makes all seem no more than an extension of an infatuated couple's whims. Our feet moved down the steps, leaving the party above and behind us. We walked across the bridge into the woods, where we paused outside the transparent house that shone in the moonlight, those beams standing in for the sunlight intensified during the day by the glass roof and the glass walls which provided hot house cultivation for tropical blooms.

I felt suffused by the fumes of a romance almost operatic in its thick self-obsession and refusal to acknowledge anything other than transporting appetite, when lust is elevated to a position of cosmic disdain. I imagined our mood was invincible to doubt and that the sensual tension between us was backed up by plunger-muted trumpets and trombones, afro-brass out to coax forth tenderness and build tempestuous ardor, changing timbre and speaking through buckets that gave a guttural pulsation to the molasses tempo of the music. We were becoming tar babies to each other: where she moved I moved: when I turned she twisted with me.

A smitten audiophile, I wanted to put my diamond needle in the hissing grooves of this rare African record, sometimes bump up against a scratch and play one series of notes over and over, move on, get caught again, repeating some passage with even more delicious repetition. I wanted to twist her stereophonic knobs and adjust her volumes, or become a cat burglar listening to her tumblers groan as my fingers moved with the stealth of a safe cracker out to make off with the palace jewels. I wanted her laid out like some marvelous combination of fury and finesse, her ankle bracelets ringing just above my head, her legs supporting the roof of the skies, and her womb the inside of a fig-star or planet I rose toward.

Feeling like that, the helium of Holiday's beauty filled me and I floated up over the French night, hearing everything and nothing, knowing I could easily catch Hindenberg fire and fall in searing orange gusts, kindling the chateau and destroying the estate. Or perhaps from that elevation I would pursue Holiday through this glamorous jungle as the cannibals had Betty Boop's sidekicks. Bimbo the dog and Koko the clown, intent on serving them as long pig. The hunters were reduced to one cannibal whose round face filled the sky, a grimacing head in the clouds, bone through his nose and nostrils puffing steam. Then the cannibal's face turned from a cartoon to the handsome superimposed cinematic head of Louis Armstrong. Those clouds were probably reefer smoke sending him high up where his trumpet usually spoke of the constellations that fuse in rhythm and tune the twinkling light of heartbreak, desire, triumph, and the eerie, deep-breathing solitude that follows the whimpers coating the climax of erotic union. Smiling and leaning his head back. Pops, the father of the grand improvisational dream, was singing and mugging, throwing in asides to **I'll Be Glad When You're Dead, You Rascal You,** *looking forward to the day when no more fried chicken will you eat; or accusing: "You bought my wife a bottle of Coca-Cola so you could play on her Victrola! Ah, you dog."*

Now that I had walked with her and had seen her shiver, had smelled the alcohol and the cigarette smoke on her breath, had removed a bit of dirt blown into her eye by a sudden wind, and heard her apologize for a belch that walloped the air in the middle of one of her sentences, she seemed no more a goddess. Hearing her talk and clear her throat or seeing her sometimes rub her left shoulder, I felt the presence in the night of a woman who was more than the Rosetta secrets of the Sphinx I had fantasized, but who still embodied the call that made the love poetry the Arabs brought to Europe seem a prelude to just the two of us.

We looked inside the green house and opened the door, entering a world of flowers built by two extremely tall German gardeners who were not far beyond this glass palace of horticulture, drunk and seated by a golden fire over which they turned a rabbit on a wooden spit. Holiday knew German and told me that one of them was complaining about the fact that his wife was never satisfied with anything and always wanted to improve their home, the other was muttering about how the Japanese were trying to buy up France. When they saw us, the second German stood and spoke to us first in French, then English, asking if we understood what they were talking about.

"We understand you perfectly," Holiday replied, "but it would be more easy if you spoke in English."

"I am sure that you are both guests at the party."

"That's right," I said.

"There are more interesting things than what is said by two old gardeners having a poacher's meal here and getting a little drunk," he said, his great height and posture making him seem not an old man at all though he was probably in his middle sixties.

"I pride myself on speaking freely with all people," Holiday said to him, "and I am very interested in what everyone thinks of the Japanese."

"It is a difficult thing," he responded, his thoughts bringing him to attention, "a very difficult thing. We are now at a tactical disadvantage in economic terms. It is only because we in the West have manners and connect them to the business of economics that they are doing so well in the world right now. When it is pure, business is never below a gentleman's agreement. The Japanese have a different idea of this all. Now the banker has replaced the general, the currency now does the duty once done by the soldier and of the bomb and of the bullet. But what do I know of this? I am only a gardener who had too many bottles of beer."

Holiday nodded in the direction of the chateau and we began walking back.

I agreed with her when she said, "Those things he said were very odd. He was strange. I didn't like those men."

"I wasn't thinking about them."

"What were you thinking about?"

"What my father told me he said to my mother back when she had her nose so far up in the air she would have drowned if it rained."

"And what exactly did your good father say to your good mother?"

"My old man told me he said, 'If you were standing in a ring of fire and I was wearing a suit made of gasoline, I would *still* have to come after you.' My old man was serious."

"This walk has awakened me. The drink made me a bit sleepy. Let's go back and go into Paris. I think you and I are going to have a very good time tonight."

Night was preparing to peel off its black and rhinestoned dress in a few hours: the air started changing and the smell of morning quietly began to insinuate itself. At last, we were at what I hoped was the capital of passion, the George Cinq, where this lean African beauty who had become so spiritually thick right before my eyes and in my arms resided. So tired was I that it was easy now to understand what the long ritual of courtship dances had always done: prepared the man for the expression of tenderness by wearing down the brashness of his strength, limbering him, filing away the bristles of his touch, the egotism of an unempathetic attempt to tear that pussy up with a cruel, poling pronouncement of muscular erotic conquest, attacking the woman as though her vagina was the gate of some flesh and blood fortress, her pants, gurgles, and whimpers the soundtrack of submission. No, there would be none of that, even had I thought it earlier, for my feet were so tired

I could feel every toe, my legs felt as though they had been smacked with billy clubs, and my upper body seemed a roof too heavy for the walls that supported it. Yet everything had that clarity that arrives five days into a fast: all details were moving under my microscoping perception and there was nothing that could have been more arousing than merely looking at the long neck, the color, the face of Holiday.

"This," she said, after we had gotten off the elevator, and her long fingers had turned the key in the lock, "is where I live. But I must tell you something."

"I know."

"You know?"

"Yes."

"You are quite sure?"

"Quite."

"What do I have to tell you then?"

"That you're really a man."

"You are just so *crazy,*" she laughed, embracing me. "No, I am not a man but what I must say is important. Please listen." She moved away from me, opening the curtain of the pale blue suite and looking out at the morning star.

"I'm prepared."

"I live here with a man."

"He's not hiding behind a mirror looking at us now, is he?"

*My little joke was a reference to an experience I had had back just before I went South. My car had run out of gas and I was hitching a ride very early in the morning after getting the thumbs down from a nearly obese beauty who was majoring in linguistics at UCLA. We were smooching strong and I had wondered what she could do with all of that meat the color of crust on white bread. The mistress of a black comedian who later died from a heart attack after playing Idi Amin, she pushed me back, looked me right in the eyes and said, "I want everything whitey has. I want it all — the money and all the ass-kissing. I want **all** of it! And I'm going to **get** all of it. This nigger is going to marry me someday and he's going to make a **lot** of money. The nigger is funny, but he wants to be dramatic. Can you believe that? Dramatic my ass. That nigger needs to just keep these white people laughing. That's what he needs to do." She got up and showed me a coin that had Booker Washington and George Washington Carver on it. "This is* *going to be worth a lot of money someday. Two niggers on an American coin? Just wait. The story is that when the white people in the South, when those redneck whities saw that, they wanted to kill somebody. I don't know if it's true, but the Indian lasted much longer on the buffalo nickel than them two niggers. Oh, by the way, you will get none of this pussy, tonight, no parts of this pussy. Don't start telling me how much you love me. It will get you nowhere. You don't have enough money. You don't have **any** money. Now is the time to make my declaration of independence from fun fucking. I like you, but broke niggers will no longer probe this pussy."*

I was mad standing out there in Los Angeles thinking about what she had said when this Cadillac pulled over. The guy in it had a proposition. He wanted me to lay some on his old lady. My family jewels were aching so much from all that foreplay with that greasy beauty that I accepted the hundred dollars and hoped that I wasn't going to end up getting caned like old Booker T when I had finished my task, dying not because I was raising money as well as white thighs for the cause but because I would prefer slipping into some perversity to going home and angrily servicing myself. My sin was one based in a lack of self-reliance.

*He lived somewhere up in the Hollywood Hills and I felt somewhat reluctant until his wife came into the living room, her body shimmering under her negligee the way the water was in the illuminated pool you could see through the glass doors. She was almost as big as the one I had just left but she had a pagan atmosphere to her walk and her gestures that I didn't understand then. She took off the negligee and began dancing before me, lifting and rubbing large stretch-marked breasts, rolling her protruding stomach, turning her cellulite riddled bottom in my direction, and poking her tongue out the way a frog does when it catches a fly. Her husband went out of the room after putting on a Nat Cole record, and by the time Captain Midnight's smooth diction got to **Nature Boy,** she was pulling my clothes off and pushing me into the bedroom, where we got all the way down. Though greasy as a possum stew, she had the classic education of a courtesan and made love with a high physical idealism that transcended the spattered way in which we had encountered each other. As we started panting toward the finish line, I heard a third voice. It was her husband standing there next to the bed in the dark holding a pen light and masturbating.*

"No, Kelvin, he is not hiding behind the mirror. He is in Italy."
"Good."

"He loves me."

"Good."

"Are you disappointed?"

"Of course."

"This really disturbs you, doesn't it?"

"Very much."

"What can I do about this?"

"You could hypnotize me so I wouldn't know what you said."

"I am not a hypnotist, Kelvin."

"Well, I guess I'll just have to die right here of heartbreak."

"Oh, you are only playing with me again!"

"I'm not playing at all. I'm serious as AIDS. I believe what I said: you can't change pain."

"This actually makes you feel pain?"

"Yes, the beginning of pain, the first impression of something that will get much bigger as I fall in love with you."

"How do you know you will fall in love with me?"

"Because I'm like all the other men I'm sure you've captivated: the closer I get, the more emotion I feel. Seems pretty regular to me."

"Yes, many men think they have fallen in love with me," she said, her voice becoming hollow and fragile, a wet substance delicately filling it, "but they are in love with my image. I know this. It is this image they love. I am this *thing from* Africa they want to penetrate. I am part of their *apparel.* I know this is true, Kelvin. I *know* it. I am no *child.* I have almost forgotten when I was innocent. I am only an image. I know this. I know this because whenever I become myself and speak of my own life and my own heart, they grow *quite* deaf. All of the attention they have shown to my every word when they wanted to get me in bed with them goes away. The courtship is finished. They grow quite deaf. They always do, Kelvin. They always grow deaf. I have been in rooms with men, naked, and quite ready to talk honestly, and I have heard my voice echo as though I was in a canyon. And, Kelvin, it never mattered how softly I spoke. It never mattered. A man and I were together, and above all else, I was alone. Do you understand this?"

"Have you said anything to me that I didn't listen to?"

"No," she said, her voice becoming even lighter, "you seem to listen to me, you do."

"Can you tell what I feel increases as you speak, as I hear you better and feel you more?"

"I think so, yes, I think so."

"Could someone play past your image, not even think you were part of their wardrobe, and slowly feel you seeping into them like a mist through a screen?"

"I would hope you," she was very delicate now, her voice almost transparent, "I would hope so."

As we lay in the mellow throb that was the after-space of an exquisite erotic encounter...

Hold it: now you think I'm going to turn around somewhere and give you another sex scene, don't you? Well, you're wrong. You will not find out what Holiday and I did. Only my youthful sexual experiences will your eye balls roll across. My adult erotic experience is off-limits. If you don't like that, well, go read Henry Miller.

Later, as we lay in the mellow throb of the groove left by an exquisite erotic encounter, Holiday told me of Carlo, the Italian textile millionaire who rented the suite year round.

"Carlo is just so crazy. When he arrives here, I put a mosquito net over the bed and he always pretends to discover me after his plane has just crashed in the bush. Kelvin! Kelvin! Kelvin! Stop laughing. Oh, all right, laugh then. Have you finished?"

"No: I have about five more minutes to go."

"Take them then," she said, chuckling herself.

"So, you were saying?"

"Yes, perhaps he imagines that he is also Mussolini invading Ethiopia. I don't know. It is actually harmless, you know."

"I'm sure it is."

"Actually, it is."

"Right."

"You don't believe me?"

"Why shouldn't I?"

"How should I know, Kelvin? You might be one of these black men who hate a black woman when she is involved with a white man."

"Did I seem like I hated you five minutes ago?"

"No."

"There you are. I'm just curious, really."

"But, Kelvin, do you think a woman can trust a man only because of the way he is in bed with her?"

"You I know better than that. I don't care, baby, I'm stretched out all the way into heaven with you right now."

I kissed her and she rubbed my cheek with goose pimpling tenderness as we compressed the memory and pulled from the air the feeling of our first intimacy, using our mouths and tongues to recollect the way we had just been. We lay there then and just looked at each other. She was fine as they come, black satin full of cayenne pepper. Finally, she started talking.

"I must tell you about this suite."

"Tell me," I said, rubbing the mild hillock of her belly.

"This is the suite that Diahnne Carrol had when when she was in Paris making the film "Paris Blues." Carlo is in love with Diahann Carol. I am her substitute for him."

"You might be."

"I might, but I have my own dreams in this suite."

"I hope so."

"I do."

When she said that I wondered if those dreams squirreled up out of her head when she was with Carlo.

"Do you want to know what I dream, Kelvin?"

"Tell me everything, baby," I said, embracing her, "I could listen to that beautiful voice until the end of time, when Gabriel would get mad because you sounded better than his trumpet."

"Oh, Kelvin, this feels so good!"

"But come on, sweetness, peel the underwear off some of those dreams for me."

"I would like to. If you want to know me more."

"I want to know you even more than that. I want to know you so well I can read your mind."

She stared into my eyes and a smile so relaxed changed the shape of her mouth that I felt as though I was looking at her in a state few men saw. It may have been a self-serving illusion, but it sure did feel good.

"It will take a long time before you can read my mind, Kelvin. But, no matter. I want to tell you things. I just feel that I want to. So! This is very fascinating being in this suite. I have never loved a room the way I love this one. It is my haven. I have such lovely dreams here. I do. I know that when Diahann Carrol lived here, Duke Ellington wrote music above this room and

Louis Armstrong practiced his trumpet in the suite below."

"They did?"

"*Yes,*" she almost squealed, "they were right here in this hotel at the same time! But this is what thrills me when I am here alone. It is so wonderful. I come home and turn out the lights after I have taken a bath and put smooth lotion on my skin. I take my time with the lotion until I am oiled and shining, Kelvin. You will see me like that. That is when I look my best. I am no longer an image then. I am myself and I enjoy looking in my mirror. I almost become hypnotized looking at my form, studying my eyes, my forehead, my neck, and everything down to my feet. I think of those African feet and all the runways they have walked. I am proud of them. But then I begin to wonder if I am losing my soul in affection for my surfaces. I wonder if I am the same as those men I despise who want to enter my body but hate the idea of my having a soul. Confused for only a moment, I regain my sense of purpose and I walk into the bedroom very slowly and pull back the covers. I have put on a blue negligee because I know that blue was Duke Ellington's favorite color. Yes, I know this. Then I lie down. The windows are open and the air of Paris almost has a warm taste. I begin thinking of the honor Diahann Carrol had with these two great men so *close* to her. But I am not Diahann Carrol, I am *myself.* Then I begin to dream as I lie here awake. I dream that the great Duke is writing a melody. It is very, very seductive. It so slowly hammers against the strings of the piano and comes straight down through the ceiling into my body that is oiled and shining. It lingers there awhile and I feel that I have almost *become* this melody. Then it passes through me into the bell of the great Armstrong's trumpet. Rocking in rhythm between them, rocking very softly, Kelvin, very softly, I am able to sleep the deep sleep of the perfectly satisfied."

"Look at that," I said, acknowledging the evidence of how much she had aroused me.

"I see it."

"Listen, my African seductress of sweet, sweet, Ellingtonian melody..."

"Yes?"

"I think we'll have to do something about the state you've put me in."

"Yes, my conquering American black love," she smiled with magnetic satire, "we will definitely have to do something about it."

The Stork-Men

Juan Goytisolo
translated from *Las Semanas del Jardín*
by Peter Bush

I'm a woman into magical realism, an avid reader of García Márquez, the Allende gal and their high-flying disciples. I'm just wild about novels and stories seething with colourful characters and awesome incident: sage grannies, clouds raining blood, children on the wing, galleons mysteriously beached in lush virgin jungle. These 'romans de pays chauds', as a defender of anaemic, worn-out literary notions dubbed them, bring a new sap and vitality, a pinch of poetry into the prosaic confines of our lives. Consequently, when I heard my esteemed co-reader in the Circle tell the story of *The Thousand Nights Less One,* which referred to the storks' nest near Eusebio's little place in the Casbah, next to the mechouar, I recalled my compatriot Ali Bey's paragraphs on these long-shanked migrators whose company he enjoyed in Marrakesh thanks to a gullible sultan.

According to an old Moroccan tradition, Berber peasants think of storks as human beings who, in order to travel and see the world, temporarily adopt their birdly shape and who resume their original form on returning home. Thus, when I reached Marrakesh in pursuit of the elusive Eusebio, I decided to renounce my risky, fruitless investigations and, thanks to the gracious help of historian Hamid Triki, I headed toward the ancient hospice for storks adjacent to the mosque of Ben Youssef.

After much enquiring and promenading I came across Dar Belarx and its keeper. Encouraged by my generous tip, he produced a bunch of keys and led me through a side-door, along a gloomy porch, to a huge and magnificent yet filthy and abandoned courtyard. All manner of rubble and rubbish covered the central space, blessed with a fountain; beautiful arcades, mouldings in side-rooms, friezes of tiles firmly resisting the passage of time. There

were infinite messes of pigeon feathers and droppings, even a fresh corpse of
a member of the species, attracted like its confreres, by the benign silence of
the place. The hospice had been closed a century earlier, upon the death of
one of its founder's grandsons.

I mentioned the myth of the stork-men to my companion. To my great
surprise, he corrected my characterisation. It was no myth, it was the unsul-
lied truth. He himself had a neighbour who migrated to Europe and returned
home a few months later, after recovering his normal shape. He lived right
up that alley and, without more ado, I was introduced to him.

The metamorphoser — what better nomer? — was a calm, peaceful old
man, similar in looks to those attributed by colleagues to Eusebio, with intense blue eyes and an immaculate white beard, seated in the doorway to his
house, his right hand perched on the top of his walking-stick. To avoid vexa-
tious preambles, I'll give you his story straight, be it genuine or not, fruit of
an invention of his own harvesting, or borrowed from folklore.

'Forty odd years ago, my wife — may God preserve her in her glory —
got a permit to work in a French textile factory and emigrated in order to in-
crease our modest income, leaving me in charge of the children. To begin with,
she sent news like clockwork together with a giro representing her monthly
savings; but gradually the money turned to a trickle, without any comforting missive. Such a strange, lengthy silence, raising apprehension and troubling
questions, plunged me into deep melancholy. My letters went unanswered;
my request for telephonic communication likewise. I asked after her via a
neighbour, also contracted by a textile firm in the same region. Her laconic
telegram — 'well and working' — not only was not soothing, it stoked my
unease. If she was well, why so silent? Had she forgotten she was a wife and
mother of four? At night, I tossed and turned restlessly in bed. In the mean-
time, the possibilities of getting a passport had shrunk: the crisis and
unemployment in Christian lands closed doors on foreigners and the French
Consulate would not grant a visa to an artisan like myself: a humble cobbler.
They demanded bank statements and goodness knows what else. In a word:
I had to give up. But I dreamt and dreamt ever more vividly of making the
journey. And one day, while gazing at the storks nesting on the battlements
of the royal palace, I said in my heart of hearts, if only I was like them and
could fly to where my wife's working, to the distant sweatshop in Epinal. As
if fired by a premonition, I went to see my eldest brother: I told him I'd decided to go to Europe and handed my children over to him for their temporary

care and education. That anxious phase of my life was abruptly at an end

"The following day, I was aloft with a flock of storks in an ineffable state of bliss and delight. The world was at once miniature and immense: toy towns and landscapes, seas gleaming like mirrors, white mountains... My altitude, lightness and speed of movement granted me a feeling of superiority over humans, slow as turtles, tiny like insects. Intoxicated by our gliding in precise, purposeful formation, I flew joyfully towards the prosperous, enlightened continent whence the Christians had come apparently to educate us and offer us work while they were about it. They were weeks of freedom and pleasure, beyond frontiers and the stamping of travel documents. Without any papers we crossed compartmentalised territories, transgressed their mean-spirited laws, avoided customs and police controls, mocked the miserly discrimination of visas. Once over a great chain of mountains, snow-covered like the Atlas, the panorama changed: the fields were greener, the woods denser and more frequent, ochre-tiled villages gave way to grey-slate roofs. We followed a river valley, its sides lined with factories and cities. A few days later, after long days of flight and nightly stops on towers and belfries, I felt my energy waning, went out of rhythm with my companions, fell irrevocably behind, flapped my wings with difficulty. Unable even to hover, I plummeted and landed in a garden as best I could.

"My appearance surprised the owner of the house, a Frenchman in his forties, who was pruning shrubs and tidying up the lawn with his shears. "Look, darling Aïsha, it's a stork', he shouted. My beloved wife's name made my heart miss a beat. Who was that fellow and how dare he be so familiar? When she peeped out of the backdoor I almost fainted. I stared at her till my eyes were awash with tears. 'How incredible', she said in Prankish tongue, 'there are lots of them in my country. I'm sure that where she's from.' She walked over, didn't recognize me, gently caressed my plumage. 'How tame! She must have fallen ill and can't fly anymore. I'll look after her and feed her on raw fish. In our country they say it brings luck: a guest sent from heaven, whom we must respect and offer hospitality.'

"Aïsha's tender, welcoming words deepened, did not soften my grief. Her use of 'we' and friendly attitude towards the individual confirmed my suspicions: she was his concubine, shared his bed and table. Bewildered and bitter, I wondered whether they had children. I was afraid I'd hear a baby's cry and inspected the washing basket and fortunately saw neither nappies nor infant clothing. But the previous feeling of superiority and pride that had possessed me in the ether transmuted into impotent rage. Two steps away from my wife and her lover, with my clumsy shanks and grating croaks, I was unable to react against her adultery. Aïsha's maternally tender affections, the zeal with which she cared for me, chose my food, built a kind of nest on the roof of the garden-shed, diminished rather than enhanced my temporary birdly state. My appearance reminded her of her country, she showered me with caresses and treats, but at dusk, when they both returned from work — she from her sweat-shop, he from the branch of a big bank, — they shut themselves in their house and left me one-legged on my nest.

"After the first melancholy weeks, my spirits began to rise; I decided to take the offensive. I abandoned my nest of misfortune and without a by your leave slipped into the house. At first, the intruder tried to chase me out, but she stopped him.

" 'This stork's a blessed creature who reminds me of all I left behind. If she wants to live inside, she will. God sent her to us and her wishes will be met.'

"The guy oozed bad-temper: 'This is all very poetic, but who'll clean the shit up?'

" 'I will! Haven't I told you a thousand times it's a sacred animal?'

"Although he snorted something scornful about India and her cows, she shrugged her shoulders and imposed her will: henceforth, if I felt like it, I'd live with them night and day. "The new situation created by my wife's energy and determination favoured my plans for revenge. I took advantage of both their absences during work-hours and sniffed around the furniture and nooks and crannies of the house: I could see for myself how Aïsha kept photos of her children like gold bars, put her entire wages in a savings account, and regularly sent home part by postal order. The intruder paid for everything, the shopping, my fish and leeches, the gas and electricity bills. Such signs of provision for our future, added to the attention she paid me, strengthened my resolve: I did more of the business on the guy's personal items and clothes, made myself comfortable in his bed."

As I dallied there, the domestic rows and squabbles got worse. " 'You're not going to let her dirty the sheets?'

" 'If she soils the sheets, I'll wash them. The poor girl (she always referred to me in the feminine), after such a long journey and then falling ill, feels at home here, is part of the family.'

" 'I pretended to yield to the intruder's irritation, nobly left the terrain, waited till they put out the light and he began to stir and stroke her before I swooped on the bed and soiled it. Immediately he switched on the bed-side light.'

" 'That's enough playing around! I'll deal with her now! Enough is enough!'

" 'You so much as touch one feather and you'll be sorry! You just listen to me: I'm sick of your disgusting fiddling. Let me sleep in peace!'

" 'If you want to sleep, sleep; but not with her. I've told you a thousand times l can't stand the bird!"

" 'Well, If you can't stand her, clear off to the sofa! Personally, I don't intend to separate from her!'

" 'Anyone would think she was your husband! Ever since she came, you've been behaving like a loony. These manias and witches' tales come from your country, not from any modern, civilised nation!'

" 'Hey, my country is better than yours. This stork's mine and , if you don't like her, I'm off and Happy Christmas.'

" From that night on there were daily quarrels. I wanted to sleep in my bed, next to my wife, and the intruder finally conceded and migrated to the sofa. I felt Aïsha preferred me and was thinking about me. Sometimes she sat at the kitchen table and wrote letters home, to the address next to the hospice for storks founded centuries ago. She cohabited with the Nazarene like a dog with a cat. When she went out I flew to the shed awning and perched on the nest. I was afraid the intruder would slice my head off with a knife or club me to death. I was comforted by my victory and began to recover a taste for flight One day, after devouring my ration of fish, I bid a silent farewell to Aïsha. looked out for my flock overhead, flew up and headed back to Marrakesh.

" '1 recovered my human form as soon as I arrived. I turned up home as if I'd just left and hugged my children. My brother had diligently looked after them, they'd been to school and, when they saw me, they danced with joy. Underneath the clock in my bedroom was a pile of letters from Aïsha. They spoke of the stork's visit, of how she missed her country. She was still working in the textile factory to meet her savings target and to be able to buy a shop on her return. When she returned two years later, she beamed radiantly and arrived loaded with presents. I forgave her, of course, I forgave her: I forgot her infidelity and lived happily with her till God wanted her at His side and she was buried in Bab Doukkala.

" 'I never told her or anybody else of the truth about my visit, except for my neighbour and a gentleman of European origins whose friend from the Rif died in a traffic accident and who had lived ever since away from the world, writing verse and seeking solace every afternoon in the mosque of Ben Youssef. His name was Eusebio.'

"I remember he listened very carefully and then wrote down word for word the very same story I've just told you."

Master of the Crossroads

Madison Smartt Bell

Papa Legba, we were singing, *Attibon Legba, ouvri barye pou nou ...* We sang, and Bouquart, the big Congo maroon with the cross-shaped marks of his people in Guinee paired on his stomach, struck the Asoto *tambou,* there at the center of the *batterie* of three drums. He touched the Asoto drum with his left hand and a small stick crooked like a hammer in his right. *Papa Legba, open the gate for us. . . .* It was Bahoruco mountain where we danced, on a height above the mouth of one of the great caves, and when the drums played the cave spoke too in a drum's voice. The drums called Legba to open the crossroads, let the *loa* come up from Island Below Sea into our heads, and I, Riau, was singing too for Legba, not hearing my own voice any more than I felt the salt water gathering on my face. We call for blessed Legba to come, but sometimes it is Maît Kalfou who brings himself to the crossroads, the trickster, betrayer sometimes, *magouyé.*

Singing still, I watched Bouquart, his face sweat-shining, with a motionless grin gleaming as he drummed. The *fleur de lys* was branded on his left cheek, to punish him for running away, and for another such punishment his right ear had been lopped off, and for the same reason he wore on each leg a *nabot* the size and weight of a cannonball, welded around his ankles, and yet he had still run as far and fast as Bahoruco. If there had been a forge, I, Riau, might have struck the *nabots* off his feet, using the powers of fire and iron (for that Riau who was a slave had learned blacksmithing from Toussaint), and equally the power of my *maît'têt,* Ogûn Ferraille, but there was no forge at Bahoruco, only the voices, the drums, the low droning out of the caves, then silence with hands fluttering on the drumskins light and soundless as the wings of birds, their gray and white feathers shivering, and the scream that came from Riau's body, stripped the body from the mind, as the god came up from beneath the waters, through heels and spine to flower in his head.

It was not Ogûn who came, they told me after, not the proper master of my head, but Maît' Kalfou who took my body for his horse, though never before had that one mounted Riau. Jean-Pic told me it was so, when Riau came to himself again at dawn, the cool mist rising round him at the edge of the sacred pool. It was quiet then, the birds speaking softly, hidden in the leaves, and only a drum's echo beating slowly somewhere behind my head. Maît Kalfou, Jean-Pic told me, had walked among the dancers, his arms raised in the shape of the cross and his muscles trembling from their own strength, and had spoken in his wet croaking voice, but Kalfou's words belonged to the proclamation of Toussaint from Camp Turel.

My name is perhaps not unknown to you. But Maît' Kalfou must have already been recognized by the *serviteurs* there. . . . *I have undertaken to avenge you. I want liberty and equality to reign throughout Saint Domingue. I am working towards that end.* How such words must have sounded in the harsh damp mouth of Kalfou... on the morning after my throat ached from his shouting at them. *Come and join me, brothers, and fight by our side for the same cause.* . . .

Those words were heard before in Bahoruco. Maît' Kalfou had not been the first to bring them here. The words of Toussaint's letter had come from both sides of the border, from the whitemen of France and the whitemen of Spain, and on the same day that the French Commissioner Sonthonax declared that all the slaves were free. Toussaint had signed his letter *Toussaint Louverture,* a name that he had never used before that time, when everyone had called him Toussaint Breda, from the name of the *habitation* where he had been a slave.

I had not thought much of Toussaint's words when they first came to us, though I saw that he was trying still to use words to sway men at long distances (as Riau had helped him to do, before Bahoruco), sending the words that walked on paper as his messengers, teaching them to speak with the voices of others. But the name... he had invented it, so much was sure, unless it was given to him by his *mystère,* but Toussaint always claimed that he served only Jesus, not the *loa,* and no one had ever seen a spirit mount his head. After Kalfou had let Riau's flesh drop in the windfallen leaves beside the sacred pool, the understanding came to me, that in calling himself *Toussaint of the Opening* he meant to say it was Legba working through his hands.

But sometimes it is Maît' Kalfou who comes. . . .

"Go to the *cacique,*" Jean-Pic said, when I had spoken part of the thought to him. And I got up from the leaves and drank water from a spring nearby, and touched cold water to my face and the back of my head. Jean-Pic and I shared a mango he had picked. We went down toward the cave mouth where the *cacique* was, but the way there was not straight. Below where we walked the *villan* spread among the folds of mountain in and out of sight, the square *cays* built of mud and stick and sometimes fenced with cactus thorn, the corn plantings twisting to follow veins of good earth among rock ledges on the slopes. The path twisted the same way between the corn and the yards of the mud walled houses. All down the mountain the cocks were crowing and people waking to the day, stepping out upon their packed-earth yards. Farther down the gorges were the palisades of sharpened poles and the mantraps dug and hidden for attackers to fall into, or for anyone. Riau, I myself, might have been so taken, only that I came here with Jean-Pic who knew where the mantraps were dug. Under Santiago the maroons of Bahoruco had promised with the French whitemen to return escaping slaves for a reward of gold, but now Santiago was dead and by the words of Sonthonax there were no more slaves in the land, but still the maroons of Bahoruco mistrusted the coming of any stranger from outside.

The little crook-jawed pin-tooth dogs scampered and turned behind their cactus fences as we passed, but they did not bark or growl because they knew our smell. It was those dogs who gave the warning when the whitemen came, or anyone outside the *villan.* Outside one *cay* a young woman looked up from where she was pounding dried corn into meal to smile at us both as we went by, but there were few women here, and the men were not so many as the whitemen believed they were. They told, when Santiago went to make the peace-paper with the French white men, he brought one hundred thirty-seven grains of corn to show the number of the people, but that was trickery, there were more. Though not the thousands the whitemen believed, there were some hundreds there.

We walked the twistings of the path, worn deep in rocky earth by people walking, with a stream twisting beside it, lower down, until we turned the point of the ledge and came to the cave opening where the *cacique* was. Bahoruco was a cave of many mouths, and when too many of the whitemen soldiers come our people knew to run into one mouth and come out at another, far away. The caves were full of the Indian mysteries carved in stone, so that the whitemen did not like to go in, or maybe they were only afraid of the darkness. In times before, enough *blanc* soldiers came to drive our people from Bahoruco back to Nisao, and they burned the corn and wrecked the houses, but afterwards the people returned here, and the *bityou* had all been rebuilt and had been standing for some years.

The *cacique* had already come out to sit on the ledge before his cave mouth. He was old, with white hair hanging in flat strings, and the gold-colored skin of his face bunched in fine wrinkles. His belly skin was slack and loose and because of an illness he had to carry his balls in a basket when he walked. Now he sat, the basket folded in between his legs, and took the sun on his high cheekbones and his closed eyelids. They called him *cacique* not because he was truly a chief among the Indians but because he was the last Indian in that place. There was still blood mixture to be seen in the maroons of Bahoruco, in the angle of cheekbone, smoothness of the hair or slant of the eye, but it was sinking to the invisible, washed away in the blood of Guinée. Only the *cacique* remained with his Indian blood pure.

We had still the Indian-woven fish traps, the bows with their arrows almost as long as a man was tall, and some said even the gourd and bead *asson* which our *houngan* shook in time with the drums as the spirits came down, that the *asson* had first been given by an Indian *mystère*. They said the *cacique* knew those mysteries, who had made him wise. Sometimes he could speak in Kreyol, but today he spoke only his own language, high and quavering as it floated out from his mouth over the green gorges, and the sound of it gave me sadness for my language of Guinée, my mother tongue, which Riau had forgotten.

A basket of *loa* stones, *pierres tonnerres,* lay by the *cacique's* knee, and I sat down and lifted one, holding it in both my hands. It was black, cone-shaped, and heavier than any ordinary stone, from the weight of the *loa* who stayed inside. I did not know the language the *cacique* was singing over the hills, but understanding came to me. It seemed to come through the palms of my hands, which were both curved to the shape of the *pierre tonnerre.* I saw that Toussaint, when he chose his name at Camp Turel, would have known already what Sonthonax meant to say. He knew many whitemen and was known by them, so that he would have had this knowledge from their councils, before Sonthonax had spoken. He made his message then, choosing the same day, to show it was Toussaint, not Sonthonax, who would open the barrier to freedom.

I went away from the *cacique's* ledge then, to the *cay* I shared with Jean-

Pic and Bouquart and one other. There was no woman in the house, not one among the four of us. Jean-Pic had gone up into the corn-plantings, and the others were gone too, so the house was empty. I took from a hole in the clay wall my two pistols and the watch plundered from the body of a whiteman officer long before, also a box of writing paper and two packets of letters, one tied up with string and the other with blue ribbon- these last things Riau had taken when Halaou ran over a *habitation* in Cul de Sac, and also two long candles of white wax.

I lit one candle and wound the watch, then opened its face so I could see the thin black fingers counting away the bits of time like crumbs falling from a round cassava bread. With all these objects placed before me, alone in a house, I became perfectly like a whiteman, except there was no chair and everything lay on the floor.

Sometimes I would use pieces of sharpened charcoal to copy words and sentences from the letters, so that my skill in writing, which Toussaint had first taught me, would grow larger. By this copying I learned to compose each word with letters that properly belonged to it. Bouquart had interested himself in this art, and sometimes I would try to teach him, but he learned little. I was not such a teacher as my *parrain* Toussaint, who could train a horse and could train a man to train that same horse in place of himself, and who had given me an itch for words on paper which would not leave me, not when Riau first ran from Breda to join the maroons of the north, not when he ran from Toussaint's army to come to Bahoruco. When I copied the letters to the paper, I was altogether myself here, the words and paper there, and the whiteman language filled up all the space inside my head, but I knew it was an act of power. When I practiced this writing I gained more power than my *parrain,* for Toussaint himself did not know how to put the same letters into his words each time he wrote them.

Both packages of letters had been sent to the *gérant* who a whiteman sent out of France to manage the plantation. Those tied with string were from the owners of that *habitation,* who lived in France but wrote mostly complaining to their *gérant,* that too much of money was spent, too small of harvests returned, that the slaves cost too much in money and would not work long or hard enough, that they cost too much in food, and too many ran away to the mountains. The last of those letters, written after the slaves had risen in the north, complained more bitterly of the disasters. But the letters tied with ribbon were sweeter to the taste of eye and mind — they came from two whitewomen of France, the *gérant's* mother and another who sent words of love to him although she did not have his child. BonDyé had not joined these two together before Jesus but it seemed they wished it, though now the ocean was between them. Those letters spoke words of love to the *gérant,* and went on whispering his name whenever I opened them, though the *gérant* had been dead since that night we had all come to that Cul de Sac plantation with Halaou, and when I copied the words they spoke again. Sometimes I thought of writing such a letter of Merbellay, who had my child make the love words speak to her from paper. I could write *my son* to Caco, how the letters of the *gérant's* mother always began— *my dear son.* But I did not know if Merbellay was still with Toussaint's camp wherever it had moved to, or if she had gone somewhere else, but wherever she was, she could not read and had never thought of learning.

This day I wrote nothing, copied no word, but sat with my arms wrapped around my knees, looking across the candle flame at the glitter of the watch and the metal pieces on the pistols. In learning to use such tools as these, Riau might enter the mind of a whiteman. Of Toussaint and Sonthonax, which was the greater *magouyé?*

With Toussaint's army Riau was an officer of the rank of *captain,* wearing boots and a sash and cartridge box, with power to order lesser soldiers how to fight, but when he felt too much like a horse in harness, he stripped off those officer clothes and ran with Jean-Pic to Bahoruco. There we heard that Halaou, who was both warrior and *houngan,* as Boukman had been in the first rising in the north, was killing whitemen on the plain of Cul de Sac. Then I, Riau, I went to see this Halaou with my own eyes— ten thousands of men followed him then, all slaves risen from the *habitations,* so one more was not noticed. Halaou kept his camps across the Spanish border, some way north of Bahoruco, but would come out from his camps to kill whitemen on the plain, or fight against the *grand blanc* Frenchmen who had joined the English of Jamaica to make us slaves again. Halaou was a big man, and he went to the fighting like a *posseédé,* and at the ceremonies strong spirits stormed around his head, but at other times he went quietly, so that he was not much noticed, and he always carried in his arms a white cock, tenderly as one carries a baby. In the cluckings of the white cock he heard the voices of his spirits.

Halaou ran to every fight shouting out that the cannon was bamboo, the gunpowder no more than dust. I, Riau, had heard such words before, from the mouth of Boukman (which was lipless now, for Boukman's head was rotting on a stake on the dirt walls outside of Le Cap) and had seen men die because of them. This was not Toussaint's way of fighting. Toussaint was stingy with the lives of his men as a whiteman with his coins. But when Riau followed Halaou to the fighting, there was Ogûn in his head, and the joy of war and battle belonged to Ogûn, and no harm came to the flesh of Riau, though others died and went beneath the waters.

Then Sonthonax came south to Port au Prince with his party of the French who were called Republicans, who stood against the *grand-blanc* French, the old slavemasters, who were with the English at Saint Marc. The *grand-blancs* and the English wanted to take Port au Prince, where the Republican army was mostly colored men, and no one was certain how those colored men would fight, because many of them, too, owned land and slaves before the risings. Sonthonax did not have many whiteman soldiers fighting for his cause. But Halaou had heard that the slaves who were made free now called Sonthonax BonDyé, a god for their freedom, and the white cock clucked that Halaou must go to see this Sonthonax inside of his own eyes.

With ten thousands of his men Halaou went to Port au Prince, men beating drums and blowing conch shells and cow horns and trumpets made of metal, swirling bulls' tails around their heads and shouting the name of Halaou. Many were mounted by the *loa* on that journey, but I, Riau, walked with myself alone and saw. The Commissioner Sonthonax came out to the ditches around Port au Prince, wrapped in the colored ribbons of France, and kissed Halaou on both his cheeks. He brought Halaou for feasting in the Palais National, and Halaou sat at the table among whitemen and colored officers in their uniforms, himself barechested but for the *ouangas* that hung from his neck, and holding the white cock always on his left knee or in the crook of his left arm. Halaou's people had filled up the town, enchanted and shouting to see Halaou feeding the white cock from the Commissioner's table, but I, Riau, was silent in myself- I saw how we were many, but that the colored soldiers were better organized and armed in their small number. I understood such things from serving with Toussaint, and I saw how the colored soldiers looked at Halaou's men, fingering the locks of their muskets.

After the feasting was done, Sonthonax sent Halaou to make an agreement with the colored General Bauvais, who commended the Legion de l'Ouest at Croix des Bouquets. Riau went there also, to Croix des Bouquets, and stood with Dieudonné in the council room. Dieudonné had grown strong with Halaou, and the white cock trusted him, so that Halaou liked to keep

Dieudonné at his back. As for Dieudonné, he had come to trust Riau. We stood with our backs to the wall, on either side of the window, while Halaou sat at the table with Bauvais and two of his officers. Halaou held the white cock on the table, stroking its feathers with his left hand and preening under its neck with his right finger. He and Bauvais were speaking in voices too low for us to understand their words. Afterward some people claimed that secretly Sonthonax had told Halaou to surprise Bauvais and kill him, and others said that the colored men had all along intended to murder Halaou. I did not know anything about it, though I felt that something bad would come from our going to that place. Why did the white cock not warn Halaou away? Two sergeants of the Légion de l'Ouest broke in through Bauvais's office door already shooting, and they shot Halaou many times before he could rise out of his chair, but the white cock crowed and flew between us, out the window. Dieudonné and I turned over the table and went out the window, after the cock.

Then the colored soldiers began to kill the men of Halaou. We were many and they were few, but they had the better guns, and discipline, and Halaou's men were in terror because Halaou was killed and they had seen the white cock fly away, deserting them. They dropped their bulls' tails, which would no longer fan away the bullets, and threw down their *Lambi* shells and ran" many were killed there and thrown in the ditches of Croix des Bouquets, and the rest scattered.

After this had happened, Hyacinthe came out of prison, released by Sonthonax. Like Halaou, he was both warrior and *houngan,* and many of Halaou's men had been with Hyacinthe before, and went back to him now he had returned, but the colored men teased Hyacinthe to a meeting and killed him, as Halaou was killed. Bébé Coustard attacked Croix des Bouquets with men that had been with Hyacinthe and Halaou, and all the colored men were trapped in the church, but one of them came out alone to parlay and killed Bébé Coustard with his musket, and seeing him dead the men were afraid and threw down their weapons and scattered.

I, Riau, went with Dieudonné, who gathered some of those men who had run together again at *habitation* Nerrettes. Then the English and the *grand blanc* French came both in ships and overland to attack Port au Prince, and Sonthonax had no soldiers left to fight for him except colored soldiers who wanted to go over to the English anyway, so Sonthonax ran away to the colored General Rigaud in the south. When he stopped at Nerrettes plantation,

Sonthonax gave his ribbons and the big Commissioner's coin to Dieudonné, and said with this gift went all his powers that he had brought out of France, and he warned Dieudonné against the colored men, saying, *Do not forget, so long as you see colored men among your own, you will not be free.* But later on we learned that when Sonthonax came to Rigaud he gave Rigaud the command of the colony as he had given it to Dieudonné (though only Dieudonné had the medal and the ribbons).

A boat had come from France, bringing a paper of French government that said the slaves of Saint Domingue were free, but Sonthonax climbed into the boat and sailed away. If he was the BonDyé for our freedom, he was gone now, like Halaou's white cock.

Fok nou oué nan jé nou— we must see with our own eyes. Yet I thought it had cost Halaou very much to look at the face of Sonthonax, so I left Dieudonne then and went back to Bahoruco, where I sat inside the clay walls of the *cay* which shut out the sunlight, and looked at the whiteman things by the candle flame. Sonthonax had gone **away**. In the west wherever the English came they brought back the *grand blanc* French who had been slave-masters, and whatever the paper said there would be slavery under them. Rigaud might say he fought for the Republican French who wrote the freedom paper, yet he and the colored men with him had all been slavemasters before the risings. Whatever black leader put his head above the rest was cut down and killed like Halaou. Perhaps after all there was only Toussaint.

The whiteman must know a reason for each thing which he does, but with the people of Guinée, it is not so. I had a spirit walking with me, whether Kalfou or Ogûn Ferraille, and had only to go where the spirit would lead me, as Halaou followed the white cock. I stopped the candle and put the whiteman things back into the hole in the wall and covered them, and then went out of the *cay.* The sunlight was a shock to my eyes, so that I stood blinking. I had not eaten since I woke, but I was not yet hungry. I went up into the provision ground behind the *cay.* Butterflies floated over the flowers on the plants of *pwa rouj.* The beans were not yet ready to pick, but the corn tassels were turning brown. I picked some ears and piled them, and then dug yams with a pointed stick hardened in the fire, until I met Jean-Pic coming the other way along the planting. He looked at all the *vivres* I had gathered and then into my face.

"I am going north," I said. "Will you come?"

Jean-Pic looked all around, at the green trees hanging to the sides of the mountain, the red-earth cliff across the gorge, with terraces to hold up cays. He scratched the back of his head, and said, *"Sé cacique-la ki té di sa?"*

I lifted my shoulders and let them fall. The *cacique* had not spoken any language that we understood, which Jean-Pic knew as well as Riau, but maybe it was after all because of the *cacique,* or because of Maît' Kalfou.

"Men..." Jean-Pic scratched his head again, looking all around the *lakou.* It was still early-morning light, with the mist still lifting off the slopes around us. "Sé *bon isit-mêm,"* he said. It's good right here.

"Sé vre," I answered, and it was true, and yet I would go anyway. I lifted the *vivres* I had gathered and began walking down toward the *cay.* I had known Jean-Pic for a long time, since we were with Achille's band in the north, but Achille was killed in the first risings, and since then Jean-Pic and I travelled sometimes together, sometimes apart.

Bouquart came after me, out of the corn. He moved in a fast rolling lope, in spite of the two *nabots* fixed to his feet, and caught me with no great trouble.

"You are going," he said. "Why do you go? Was it the cacique who told you to do that?"

I lifted my shoulders. A whiteman might have answered it was because I hoped to find Merbellay and Caco again, or because of the thoughts in my head about Toussaint, or only because there were few women at Bahoruco. But Riau had no such thought. At other times I had left Dieudonné, and I had left Toussaint's army. I had left *habitation* Breda when I ran away to the maroons and before that I left Guinée to be a slave in Saint Domingue. Now I was leaving Bahoruco. Bouquart stood with a cane knife hanging from his hand, the flat of the blade against his knee, sweat shining over his scarred chest where his breath moved, and his smile uncertain.

"I will go too," he said, and lost the smile when he closed his mouth, watching Riau.

I looked at the two *nabots* on his feet, and at the muscles that swelled up from his ankles to his hips. Bouquart had told the story, how he had limped through his days in the cane field, after the whitemen gave him his *nabots,* but by night he had practiced walking, then running, in the secret dark by the river. Now he could run as fast with his weighted legs as any other man without. If ever the *nabots* were removed from his legs, Bouquart would run faster than a horse.

"Dako," I said, agreed, and Bouquart smiled more fully.

Together we made ready to leave, putting the corn and the yams in a straw sack. I carried the watch and pistols and the candle ends in a smaller straw *macoute* with a strap for my shoulder, and I put the empty writing papers in there too, but the bundles of letters I left in the wall, in case the whiteman words should twist in my sack to betray me.

We left Bahoruco before midday and travelled until dark came, then walked through the next day also, but after that we slept through the days, hiding in the bush, and walked by night, because we did not want to meet any whiteman soldiers. Because the English were at Port au Prince we passed on the other side of the salt lake at the end of the Cul de Sac Plain, over the Spanish border, and then climbed into the mountains toward Mirebalais. Neither Bouquart nor Riau knew who was holding the town that time, so we went around it on the heights until we came to the south shore of the Artibonite. The river was too deep for Bouquart— his *nabots* would have drowned him, and also there were caymans in the water, or might have been. We passed one day in cutting wood to build, a raft, and when we put it in the water we learned that neither Riau nor Bouquart had good skill to guide it, so we drifted a long way downriver before we could reach the other side, almost as far as Petite Rivière. On the north shore people told us that the English had come out from Saint Marc to build a fort at la Crête à Pierrot, above the town, so we went around Petite Riviere to the west, leaving the river, and kept following the mountains north toward Gonaives.

The Savane Désolé was there when we came out of the mountains, all cactus, dust and salt pans, with water too salt to drink. The road was flat and open but Riau was uneasy walking it— we could be seen from a long distance in that open country. While we were walking, a dust cloud rose ahead, toward Gonaives, so we left the road and hid among the cactus and *raquette* trees. The army was a long time passing, with many horsemen, and even more foot soldiers, and mules dragging cannons behind. When it had gone by, and the dust settled, we went back to the road. Some campfollowers were still coming along in the rear, women or old men leading donkeys packed with provisions. I called to a woman in a spotted *mouchwa têt* riding sidewise on a little *bourik* with a wood saddle.

"*Ki moun hi pose la?*" I said, "Who are the people passing there?"

"*Sé l'armée Toussaint Louvti yo yé.*" She threw her head back, grinning, and whipped the air with the little stick she used to drive her donkey. Yo *pralé batt l'anglais.* She rode on.

The army of Toussaint Louverture, going to beat the English. Bouquart
wanted to follow them, but Riau wanted to go north, out of the desert to the
green of the mountains. We rested through the high heat of the day in the
thin dry shade of the *raquettes,* and I gathered salt from the flats and put it in
a cloth bag I carried in my small *macoute.* When the sun turned red and began
to fall, we walked on along the road, and in the darkness we turned from
Gonaives on the trail toward Ennery. We rested and travelled through that
night and at dawn had come to the coffee trees on the heights of *habitation*
Thibodet.

Most of Toussaint's army had left that place, it was plain, gone to the
fighting at Saint Marc. There were some few black soldiers left to guard the
habitation and the camp, and sick or wounded men in the hospital, where Riau
had helped the whiteman doctor Hébert before I ran from Toussaint's army.
Many of the women had stayed behind the army, with their children, and now
they were coming out of their *ajoupas,* lighting cook fires and beginning to
grind meal.

I left Bouquart to rest in hiding in the bush beyond the coffee trees, and
I went down softly through the *ajoupas.* That *ajoupa* I had raised was still
standing where it had been, but the roof was larger now and someone had
woven palmiste panels to make walls. The *banza* I had made for playing soft
music hung still from the ridgepole where it had hung, and Caco, my son
Pierre Toussaint, lay sleeping on a straw mat, curled like a kitten. Merbellay
was standing just outside, working a long pestle up and down in a stump
mortar. Her arms were smooth and strong and she wore a blue dress and a
red headcloth with gold threads on the edges. I plucked a note on the *banza*
and she turned and peered into the shadows of the *ajoupa,* first looking to see
that Caco slept safely, then finding Riau's face.

"*M'ap tounen, oui,*" I said, no louder than a whisper. Yes, I have come back.
Her face went blank as the surface of the sacred pool at Bahoruco. A moment
passed, and then she smiled and came underneath the roof with me.

Riau slept afterward for a time, tired from the long night of travelling. I
thought Bouquart must be sleeping too where he was hidden above the coffee
trees. When I woke Merbellay was still by me, lying on her back with her eyes
open to the cracks of light in the woven walls. I spread my hand across her
belly and felt the hard curled shape of a new child.

Merbellay sat up sharply then, and so did I, turning my shoulder from
her. Caco had waked and looked at Riau with his bright curious eyes.

"Vini moin," I said. *"Sé papa-ou, m'yé."* Caco hesitated, till Merbellay clicked her tongue, and then he came to me quickly. He had grown very much— his legs hung below my waist when I lifted him to my chest. I carried him outside the *ajoupa,* kissing the short hair on top of his head. When he began to squirm I let him down and he ran away toward the voices of other children.

Merbellay came out from the *ajoupa,* with all her cloths adjusted. Our eyes looked every way but at each other. At last I kissed my fingers to her and began climbing the hill to look for Bouquart. Anger was rising up my throat, but if my thought went outside of Riau, it said that Riau had left with no word or warning and had been gone more than one year. Why would Merbellay not take another man? But the anger with its bitter taste was hard to swallow back.

Doctor Hébert had gone to the fighting at Saint Marc, I learned, and in the *grand'case* was his colored woman Nanon with her son and also the doctor's sister with her man, the gunrunner Tocquet, and the child who they had made together. When I studied the *grand'case* from the hill, I saw that the rotten places had all been repaired and much work done to channel the water to a pool in front. Grass began to grow there now, and flowers, where packed earth had been before. But I stayed away from the yard below the gallery of the house, for Tocquet was a man to know one *nèg* from another.

At night I came to Merbellay, bringing Bouquart with me under cover of the dark. She cooked for both of us, and we ate without much talk. That night I lay again beside her, awake for a long time listening to her breath in sleep, until the moon was high, and I went out, down behind the stables, where the forge was dark and untended. A brown horse hung his head over a stall door and whickered to me, and I saw it was Ti Bonhomme. This horse had belonged to Bréda before, and Riau had ridden him with Toussaint's army too. I went to him and gave him salt from the bag I had gathered in the desert, and felt his soft nose breathing on my palm.

During the next day, I carved a wheel for Caco and pinned it to a long stick for him to push and play with. In the night I lay again with Merbellay, but at moonrise I went out quietly and found Bouqart and led him down behind the stables. We fired the forge, Bouquart helping with the bellows, as I showed him. When the forge grew bright, some few people came from the *ajoupas* on the hill and watched from the shadows outside the firelight, but no one challenged Riau, I don't know why. When the forge was well heated

I made the tools ready and cut the *nabots* from Bouquart's feet, first the right and then the left. They fell in their hinged halves, like heavy melons, and when each one opened there was a sigh, from the people watching out of the darkness, like a breath of wind.

Bouquart looked up at me, his eyes shining in the firelight. He wet a finger in his mouth and touched it to a spot where the hot metal had blistered his skin. Above his ankles where the *nabots* had been his leg hair was all rubbed away and the skin was polished and shiny, with black marks on the tendon from chafe-wounds that had healed. Bouquart stood up. When he took his first step his knee shot up so high it nearly hit him in the face. He walked farther, then ran and leapt, so high he touched the barn roof with the flat of his open hand. Ti Bonhomme the horse whinnied from surprise and pulled his head back from the stall door. Bouquart landed in a squat, then stood up, smiling from one ear to the other. In the shadows the people laughed and clapped, and some began to come forward toward the light, the women's hips moving as though they would dance.

We stayed for many days at *habitation* Thibodet, I did not count how many. It was calm there all the time. In the daytime the women worked in the coffee or in the provision ground, while the few men who remained did soldier tasks and cared for the horses. All day I kept inside the *ajoupa,* sometimes playing the *banza* softly, with the heel of my palm damping the skin head so that the sound would not carry. Or I would go into the jungle with Caco. I had seen no man there I knew by name (except the *blancs* in the *grand'case).* Those Riau had known in Toussaint's army had all gone to the fighting at Saint Marc, and the whiteman doctor went there also, Merbellay had told me, or perhaps some had been killed, or run away as Riau had done before. But still there might be some man in the camp who would know Riau by sight.

I spent my days in the *ajoupa* or in the trees with Caco far from the camp, and by night I lay with Merbellay. We had not spoken of the new child coming, yet it lay between us whenever our bellies came together.

The news came that Toussaint's army was returning. The English were not chasing them but still they had come back to Gonaives. It was told that Toussaint had come into the town one time, but the English had sent ships with cannons so that he and his men were driven out again. It was told that a cannonball struck Toussaint in the face, but his *ouanga* was so strong the cannonball did not kill him, though it knocked out one of his front teeth.

Toussaint, it was told, had captured Fort Belair and begun to put cannons on Morne Diamant to fire into Saint Marc from above, but during the work a cannon fell on his hand and crushed it, and for this he had come back to Gonaives to wait for healing.

By afternoon more soldiers had come into the camp at *habitation* Thibodet, though not Toussaint himself, and not all of his army. From the *ajoupa* I heard the voice of the whiteman Captain Maillart and the voice of Moyse calling out orders, they who had been brother Captains with Riau before. All day I stayed in the *ajoupa*, silent, though Caco called me from outside, and I was glad of the woven walls which hid me.

After darkness came and the camp was quiet, I lay beside Merbellay again, but this night we did not touch. It seemed a long time before she slept. Then I got up quietly and took the small *macoute,* which I had made ready before. The moon had not yet risen so it was very dark, but before I had gone many steps from the *ajoupa,* Bouquart rose out of his sleeping place, whispering.

"You are going."

"Yes," I said, "but you can stay." I told him he had only to go to Moyse or the *blanc* Maillart to be made one of Toussaint's soldiers. I had seen his eyes admiring the soldiers in the camp.

"But you." Even in the dark I saw Bouquart's eyes turn to the *ajoupa*.

"Gegne problèm, " I said. There was a problem, more than one. Merbellay's new man would be coming back, if he was not killed in the fighting. Riau knew this, though she had not said it. Perhaps I would not have left only for that, but there was another thing I knew. Toussaint would kill a man for running from his army, *desertion* as it was called by whitemen and Toussaint. Riau had felt his pistol barrel against my head one time before, and that was only *petit marronage,* two or three days of hunting in the hills. A year in Bahoruco was *grand marronage.*

I followed Bouquart's eyes toward the *ajoupa*. "Say I will come back," I told him.

Bouquart's head moved toward me through the darkness. "When?"

"M'ap tounen pi ta, " I said. *"I will come back later. "*

The brown horse Ti Bonhomme had been turned out into a paddock. He came to the fence when I clicked my tongue, and I gave him salt from the bag I had gathered, and made a bridle of a long piece of rope. Holding his mane with my left hand, I swung up onto his bare back. I did not steal a saddle or a leather bridle, though I knew where they were kept, and I would not have taken the horse either except that I needed him to carry me quickly far away.

When the moon did rise it filled the forest with the light of bones. By moonlight it was easy to ride faster. My spirit led me to a tree where hung the skull and bones of a longhorned goat and the cross of Baron Samedi. Here I reined up my horse, and looked at the ground, the fallen leaves piled under moonlight. The grave had long ago filled in or washed away but still I felt a hollow. In this place Riau had helped Biassou to take the flesh of Chacha Godard from the ground and make it breathe and walk again, a zombi.

I felt fear in my horse's heart, between my knees. I let the reins out and rode quickly on. The night was warm, but a cold straight line was down my back, like death. I took a lump of the desert salt from the sack and held it on my tongue, my jaws shut tight.

Where the Lightning Was

Avi Dresner

*M*y first day in Europe had started normally enough. I checked into the only youth hostel I could find for less than eight pounds, dumped off my backpack and made it to Buckingham Palace in time for the noon changing of the guard.

It had looked so much more interesting in the American Express commercials back home and I wasn't the only one who thought so. As soon as the ceremony ended, the young boy standing next to me looked up at his dad from underneath his Chicago Bulls baseball cap and asked, "zeh ha'kol, Aba?"

Before his father could answer, I knelt down and said in Hebrew "misha-ah-mame, lo?" The kid giggled in approval.

"Yes, very boring," the father agreed with a smile. "Can you imagine if we had to do that kind of stuff back home? I mean guard duty's bad enough when we get called up for the reserves, but at least they don't make us prance around like idiots, ah?"

"Actually, I wouldn't know."

"What do you mean? Didn't you serve?" he said with more than a hint of disdain.

"I'm not Israeli. I'm American."

"Really? Where's your Hebrew from, then? Your accent's very good."

"My mom was Israeli, but I grew up in America."

"Well, technically, then you are Israeli. If your mother's an Israeli citizen, then that makes you one too," he said definitively, satisfying himself that he'd been right all along.

Though I didn't care for his arrogant know-it-all tone, he did make a valid point. I'd never really thought about it that way. She'd left so much else behind, I guess I always assumed she'd left that there too.

"Look! Look!" the boy yelled, pointing at a red, double-decker tourist bus looping around the traffic circle behind us. "I want to go!"

"Not now, Shai."

The boy sullenly assumed a stone-face and stiffened his body, trying his best to mimic the guard standing opposite us.

"I'm sorry. Where in America did you say you were from?"

"Brooklyn."

"Oh yeah? I know someone that lives there or, at least, I used to. A girl I was in university with, but I'm sure you wouldn't know her. I heard she became an ultra-Orthodox Jew and moved there about twenty-five years ago. She must have twenty kids by now."

Part of me wanted it to be her. Part of me didn't. The stories were similar enough and, though I knew there was almost no chance, I couldn't prevent myself from asking.

"What was her name?"

"Hava something."

I stopped breathing.

"Weiss or Weissman. Something like that, but I'm sure she has a different last name now, anyway."

"My mother's name was Hava Weisenfeld before she got married."

"Really? Well, like I said, I'm not sure about the last name. How old is your mother?"

"She died when I was eight-and-a-half."

"Oh, I'm sorry."

I could see that he didn't know what else to say. We stood there quietly for a few moments, and I think both of us were grateful when the kid started tugging on his father's briefcase whining, "Aba, I'm hungry. When are we going to eat lunch? Aba! Aba! Aba!"

I had never been allowed to use that word. From my earliest memories, I had always called him "Rabbi," and even my mother referred to him as that — not "my father," not "my husband" — just "Rabbi." I guess I had always assumed it was meant as a sign of respect and, perhaps it was, but that turned out to be the least of the reasons.

"In a minute, Shai."

"I've got a picture of her with me." I was already digging for it in my knapsack. "Maybe you could take a look."

"Like I said, I haven't seen her in more than twenty-five years. I'm sure

I wouldn't even recognize if it was her."

"It's an old black and white photograph, taken about 1967. Please, just look at it." I slid the top picture from the rubber band wrapped stack, and handed it to him.

In the years since I'd discovered them in a cardboard box in our Brooklyn basement after my mother's death, I had memorized every detail of every picture in chronological order. Starting with this first one of her in front of Big Ben and continuing on through the pictures of her standing in front of the landmarks of Europe — the Eiffel Tower, Notre Dame, the Coliseum . . . these faded black and white images constituted my itinerary. I would visit each of the places in them, and trace her footsteps to Prague where they ended in front of the most important landmark of all. In the final picture in the stack, she stood wrapped in the arms of a bearish looking man I had never met, the man I hoped was my real father.

This single photograph told me I had made an enormous discovery. However, it was the letters I found in the box with it, written in a language I had yet to learn. From that moment on, I lived with the hope that some day I would be able to follow in my mother's footsteps and confirm the truth of our pasts. It would take nearly ten more years of waiting for the opportunity to realize that hope.

Moti studied the picture for several seconds.

"It isn't her."

I didn't know whether to be disappointed or grateful.

"This was taken here, right? That's Big Ben in the background." Then he looked at it again. "She was beautiful."

She really was beautiful. That much I remembered. But it was hard for me to remember what she looked like before she got sick. And, even then, her true beauty was almost always hidden under frumpy brown wigs and dowdy, long button down dresses that covered every inch of her from neck to wrists to ankles. "The uniform," she used to call it when nobody else was around, which was almost never. "Just like back in the army," she would sigh wistfully. Just like in prison was probably more like it.

"Aba, I'm hungry!" the boy wailed again.

"OK, Shai. Can't you see Aba's talking?"

He started stamping his feet, crying, "Hungry! Hungry! Hungry!"

"I'm sorry. The master calls. I don't suppose you'd care to join us? It's on me." He extended his hand toward me. "I didn't get your name."

"Alex. Alex Lamb."

"Moti Bashan," he answered, shaking my hand. "And the little monster down there is Shai."

My last meal had been in New York the previous evening since I'd been too anxious to touch the breakfast they'd given us before we landed at Heathrow. The kid's tantrum made me realize how hungry I was myself, but the twenty pounds I had in my pocket, after checking into the hostel and paying bus fare, made the rest of the decision for me. If I was going to make my money last, I'd have to watch my expenses.

We found a fast food style fish & chips restaurant called the "Fisher King" between the stolid dignity of Trafalgar Square and the flashing neon of Picadilly Circle. Shai and I sat down at a table on the sidewalk while Moti queued up for the food.

"Speak English to him," Moti shouted from the line. "He's been practicing."

"So how old are you?"

"Coca Cola," he answered pointing at one of the flashing billboards across the street.

I asked him the same question in Hebrew.

"Seven."

"Oh, you're a big boy."

I asked him all the usual questions about brothers and sisters, school and sports until his father returned with two grease stained cardboard boxes stuffed with fish & chips, vinegar packets and cokes. He pulled up short, however, as he went to hand me mine, and eyed me suspiciously.

"You're not kosher, are you?"

"No, I fell off the wagon a long time ago."

"Yeah, me too," Moti laughed bitterly, sitting down across from Shai and me. "I grew up in a traditional home, got a religious education, knew all the prayers, and all that. Then my father was killed in the Yom Kippur War, just before my Bar Mitzvah. I stopped believing after that. I guess I never forgave God. The 'Kaddish' prayer for the dead was the last one I ever said."

On rare occasions, this prayer was said for the living as a way of signifying that they were as good as dead to all who knew them. It was a course of last resort, reserved for unredeemable sinners or apostates who had shamed their family, their community, or even their God. A father might say it for a wayward son, for instance, who married a "shiksa," a non-Jewish woman.

Never, in modern times, however, had it been said for a rabbi, much less a Chief Rabbi. To do so, required the convening of a special Rabbinical Court modeled on the Sanhedrin, the Council Of Sages of ancient times. Unfortunately for the Rabbi and for me, his behavior had warranted it. In the months following my mother's death, he had become increasingly erratic and, what was at first written off to grief could soon no longer be ignored.

Soon after her funeral, the Rabbi became obsessed with *The Book of Formation*, a mystical text containing instructions for the animation of inanimate objects. The great Seventeenth Century Kabbalist, Rabbi Judah Lowe, is said to have used this book to create the Golem, the mythical protector of the Jews of Prague, from clay. This obsession, in turn, led the Rabbi to the writings of one of Rabbi Lowe's spiritual descendants, the apostate Rabbi Chaim ben Chaim, author of *The Book of Life: A Guide to Resurrection*.

When the Rabbi began to speak publicly of his plans to resurrect his wife, the Council of Rabbis was left with no other choice. A special Rabbinical Court was convened comprising the Chief Rabbis of the various sects except, of course, for the Lvover Rebbe, who stood before the court with his only son to receive its decree of banishment.

"Unorthodox Orthodoxy" was the verdict of the Rabbinical Court that pronounced the "herem," the banishment, on the Rabbi and on me with him. The rabbis said the prayer for the dead over us, turned their backs and left the room. In that instant, the Rabbi went from Chief Rabbi, "The Rebbe" of all Lvover Hasidic Jews — as his father and his father's fathers had been for generations — to pariah, and I went from nine year old scion to outcast. He cut my side-curls the next day and burned my black coat and hat.

"So I guess we'll dispense with the prayer over the bread, then?" I suggested, forcing a smile as I saluted Moti with a vinegary piece of fish and a "bon appetit" instead.

"Amen," he joked.

While we ate, he explained that he was in London on business, but had promised Shai he would take him along. His work schedule permitted some time for sightseeing but most of the time, poor Shai stayed in the hotel with a British nanny, coloring books and the BBC.

"Do you have any plans for the rest of the day?" Moti asked me.

"No, not really."

Actually, I didn't have any plans at all. The closest things I had to a plan were the pictures, twelve hundred dollars in cash and travelers' checks, and a used *Let's Go Europe*, that I'd bought in the campus book store before I left.

"Great!" Moti said, "seeing as you don't have any plans and as you and Shai seem to be getting along so well, I was thinking — if you wouldn't mind, that is — maybe you could baby-sit him for me this afternoon? I have a very important business meeting at two o'clock that should be over by six or six thirty. I'll pay you, of course. Is fifty pounds all right?"

Monetarily speaking, fifty pounds was more than all right — it was almost a week's hostel money — but leaving his kid was anything but. I was a total stranger to this guy. For all he knew, I could be a murderer. Part of me couldn't believe he would ask somebody he just met to baby-sit for his son and yet, unfortunately, I wasn't too surprised. Nothing about abandoned children ever surprised me.

I wanted to tell the guy off, scream at him, something; but, after a moment's reflection, I realized it probably wouldn't do any good, and the next person he left his son with might not be so trustworthy. So I agreed to do it for the son's sake.

Moti explained it all to Shai, who was feeding the remainder of his fish to the pigeons that had gathered around the foot of our table. He told him that he was going to be leaving him with "Uncle Alex" for a while. Shai shrugged his shoulders indifferently. He was obviously used to this sort of thing. Moti wrote down the address and telephone number of his hotel and handed me the key to the room along with a bag full of Shai's things.

"Why don't you take him sightseeing?" he suggested. "Just make sure that he eats."

He took a hundred pound note out of his wallet.

"This should cover the expenses, and whatever's left over is yours. I'll see you around eight o'clock." Then he kissed his son good-bye and left.

When he ran out of fish & chips for the pigeons, Shai looked up at me for the first time since his father left. He was quietly crying.

"My father used to leave me alone with strangers and books, too," I told him, putting my hand on his shoulder. "Mostly just books. It used to make me cry too, at first."

He nodded.

"Some of the people he left me with were really nice, though, and they taught me a lot of things."

"Like what?" he sniffled.

"Like Science, Math, English..."

These were subjects that didn't get covered in yeshiva and, if it were up to the Rabbi, I might never have learned them.

Growing up in an ultra-Orthodox section of Brooklyn, I could be forgiven for thinking that Yiddish was the official language of America. Yiddish was the language I heard on the streets of my neighborhood, the language of instruction at the yeshiva, the language of the daily newspapers and the language my parents spoke to each other at home. Only my mother spoke to me in Hebrew. We didn't own a radio or a television set and, except for spending summer vacations in a secluded part of the Catskill Mountains of upstate New York, I never ventured beyond the twelve block radius of my neighborhood.

Each summer, however, we made our yearly pilgrimage to the mountains. Within a few hours, we were travelling on backroads through farmland and then pine forest until I heard the familiar crunch of gravel under the tires as we pulled up the driveway of our summer house. It was a modest, single story, red-stained wood cabin off a dirt road in the middle of the forest overlooking a private lake, but it was the antithesis of the asphalt and brick that filled the rest of my year.

In Brooklyn, we had the biggest brownstone on the block — a three story black painted castle where the great Rebbe held court until the late hours of the night. Followers would spill out of the antechamber outside his study into the living room, where my mother was expected to provide food and drink for them while they waited for an audience with the Rabbi. For this, Lvover Jews waited patiently outside the house from early morning to late evening. Sometimes, the line extended from the stairs outside our front door to the sidewalk and down the block.

The lake house, on the other hand, was always empty. In fact, until I was ten years old, and the Rabbi and I had already been living there for over a year alone, I never saw another human being there. When my mother was still alive, it was often just the two of us while the Rabbi was away on one of his frequent trips back to Brooklyn, or teaching morning classes at some of the many Orthodox youth camps in the Catskills that he considered too frivolous for his own son's education.

It took the local school authorities over a year to find out that there was a school age boy living in the house with the strange bearded man who emerged once every few weeks to buy groceries. How they found out, I don't know, but I remember a clean shaven man showing up at the house one day in winter and arguing with the Rabbi in that strange language that I had heard a few "goyim," the non-Jews, speak in Brooklyn. It was English.

Soon after that man showed up, the tutors started arriving. First, only one for English and then after a few months, others. The Rabbi would not allow me to be bussed to the closest regional school for religious reasons — unkosher cafeterias, mixed sex classes, etc. — and so he had the school come to me. After seven years of tutors, however, I had been transformed into a well-rounded "secular" student. Even more miraculously, those same tutors and his own deadening sense of loss had systematically worn the Rabbi down to acquiescing in my acceptance to a university upstate on scholarship as a dual major in Judaic Studies and English.

"English!" Shai echoed. "My Aba says I have to learn English next year in school. Can you teach me, Alex?"

"Some of the greatest English writers of all time live not too far from here," I said. "How would you like it if they taught you?"

That was all it took to get Shai to agree to go to Westminster Abbey.

We rushed through the Royal Chapels — past the tombs of too many dead Elizabeths, Henrys and Marys to keep straight in my head — on our way to Poets' Corner. Once again the Amex commercials had led me astray. I had always pictured the Poets' Corner as a verdant cemetery plot behind the cathedral reserved for the graves of England's literary giants. But, there were no tombstones there; only plaques in the floor of the Abbey forming a scrabble board, marble tile anthology of British Literature.

The names inscribed there — T.S. Eliot, Dylan Thomas, Lewis Carroll, Henry James, Lord Byron, Tennyson, and many others — meant nothing to Shai.

Chaucer was the only one in a three dimensional, above ground tomb - directly across from the others — and, since it seemed to offer the best view to a seven-year-old, when no one was looking, I stood Shai on the sarcophagus to have a better look.

"Where are the writers?" he asked.

"Under there," I pointed.

"Well why don't they come out?"

"They're sleeping right now, but they wrote some notes for us there on the floor. Do you want me to read them to you?"

He nodded.

I read the epitaph on top of Eliot's square: "The communication of the dead is tongued with fire beyond the language of the living." In my garbled translation, it came out something like "dead people's conversation french kiss fire past the tongue of lively people." Shai cracked up. He agreed that was very good writing indeed. I tried my hand at Dylan Thomas next and, judging by Shai's reaction, I was more successful with that translation:

"Time held me green and dying/Though I sang in my chains like the sea."

I took out the journal I kept in my knapsack with my mother's pictures and copied down the quotes.

"Boring," Shai moaned, obviously beginning to lose interest in his English lesson. He started fidgeting on top of the sarcophagus and whined, "So what are we going to do now?"

I didn't have a clue. Fortunately, he did.

"Look! Look!" he started yelling, jumping up and down on top of the sarcophagus in a display that might very well have woken Chaucer had I not snatched him off of there before one of the security guards saw us.

Mortified, I followed his index finger to another red, double-decker bus whizzing by one of the open double doors of the abbey.

"That's a great idea, Shai," I whispered, trying to shush him. "You want to take a bus ride?"

We walked back to Picadilly Circus on the advice of a security guard, and paid ten pounds for one adult and one child ticket on one of the buses that left the circle every half-hour.

Shai insisted we sit in the open-air top section, and I reluctantly agreed. I hoisted him onto my lap and gripped him tightly around the waist of his overalls. Before the bus pulled out, I made him turn his Bulls cap backwards and promise not to lean over the railing.

Most of the guide's explanations literally passed right through me. I had to simultaneously interpret everything he said for Shai and, as a result, I retained almost nothing for myself. Instead, I made mental check marks of some of the places I wanted to go back to, putting the British Museum at the top of my list.

We got back to Moti's hotel around seven, and Shai asked if I would read to him until his dad got home. He handed me one of the books from his suitcase, *Dani Din The Invisible Boy*.

The Rabbi was always reading to me or making me read, although not books like this. Every summer, while secular children were at camp or outside playing, I was inside the Rabbi's lake-side study learning Torah, discussing

Talmud and reading Jewish texts until it was time for evening prayers. I never thought I'd make it to that final "amen," the one that set me free but, somehow, it always came. Then I'd follow the Rabbi down to the lake for our near daily twilight swim.

Moti returned well after dark when Shai had already been asleep for over an hour.

"Sorry I'm late," he whispered when he saw the sleeping boy on the bed.

I nodded matter-of-factly. I'd expected no less from him.

"I hope he wasn't too much trouble."

"No, not at all. He's a great kid." *Too bad he's got such a shitty father.*

"Well, thanks again. There's a cab waiting for you downstairs. Here is my business card. Please call me if you are ever in Israel. Just don't mention the baby-sitting part to my wife."

"Don't worry — your secret's safe with me."

The following morning, I counted the number of steps in the picture and stood in what appeared to be the same spot my mother had posed on in the center of the grand marble steps outside the British Museum. As it turned out, the Poets' Corner wasn't the anthology of British literature at all; it was only the table of contents. The British Museum Library, inside the museum, was the awe inspiring anthology.

Nearly every glass and wood case in the library held another pillar in the temple of Western thought and culture: *Beowulf;* The *Magna Carta; The Canterbury Tales;* the *Gutenberg Bible;* the first edition of Shakespeare's *Collected Works;* Lewis Carroll's notes for *Alice In Wonderland;* not to mention the original sheet music of Handel's "Messiah" and the Beatles' "Let It Be."

"Have you read it?" a man's voice asked from behind me, as I stared at the *Gutenberg Bible.*

My life depended on a "yes." The Rabbi would not tolerate any other answer. From the time I could read, he assigned a book to me at the start of each summer. On our first day at the lake house, he would call me to his study in the back room, which was a near perfect replica of his study at the yeshiva, except for the lake outside the lone window.

The Rabbi would be sitting at his desk when I entered, which was cluttered as usual with four or five open books and countless piles of scribbled paper. He would look up from his work for a moment, then take one of the books off the desk and hand it to me.

"This is the book you will read this summer, Alexander. Now go begin."

"Yes," I finally answered tentatively to the voice without turning around, "but in the original."

A tall, slender, English gentleman stepped beside me facing the glass encased Bible. He wore an immaculate goatee, pince-nez glasses and an antique fob watch chain that arced downward from his vest pocket. I thought it was Freud.

"Impossible," he said. "The originals were printed over five hundred years ago and no one has seen them since. There are only forty-two copies of it in the entire world and most of those are incomplete. This beautiful specimen here is one of only a handful of complete copies."

"I meant the original original."

He looked puzzled.

"The Hebrew."

"Oh, the Hebrew," he laughed. "And I thought..." Suddenly he stopped chortling and began stroking his goatee thoughtfully. "The Hebrew, you say? You read Hebrew?"

"I'm a Ph.D. student in Bible Studies." I lied to save myself the explanation.

The truth of the matter was that I was supposed to be starting a Ph.D. program in Bible Studies in less than three weeks, which meant that soon the Rabbi would figure out that I wasn't coming back.

"Splendid, absolutely splendid! What a stroke of luck. You're just the man I'm looking for, then," the man continued.

"You see, I recently acquired a Hebrew text from one of my contacts in Petersburg and had come here to get Shaw to translate it for me, but it seems poor Shaw is dead."

I had no idea who the hell I was talking to, much less who Shaw was, and I didn't really care to find out in either case. There was something strange about this man, more than just his appearance or the questions he'd asked me. He didn't seem real in a way. He was more like someone who'd just stepped out of an old black and white photograph.

He must have sensed my unease, because he quickly proffered a card from his vest pocket and handed it to me. It said "Templer Antique Books" in plain black lettering.

"Witten Templer at your service."

"Alex Lamb," I said, shaking his offered hand.

"Yes, a mixed pleasure, Mr. Lamb. You see, Shaw, the dead man, was a close associate of mine."

"Oh, I'm sorry."

"Yes, as am I. He was eighty-eight after all." He sighed. "Ah, well, these things can't be helped. His death, however, seems to have put me in a bit of a predicament. You see, he was supposed to have a look at that manuscript for me this afternoon..." He looked away for an instant, then back at me as if he'd just remembered a forgotten item on a shopping list. "I don't suppose you'd be willing to have a go at it?"

Yet again, his question caught me off guard and, before it could sink in, he was already saying, "Just the first few pages, you understand. Just enough to know what I have. I'll pay you, naturally. Is twenty pounds a page agreeable?"

It took me a few seconds to catch up to him. He seemed genuinely harmless, and the request seemed too weird to be made up. Still, I hesitated.

"The book is in my shop, just around the corner," he added, sensing my reluctance. He took a ten pound note out of his wallet and offered it to me.

"Consider this an advance."

I declined the money, but decided to take a chance on the offer and followed Templer to an alley full of antique bookshops a few blocks from the museum. When I saw the sign, "Templer Books," stenciled in gold block capitals on the window, I instantly felt more at ease.

A bell rang as we walked through the door and a preternaturally thin young man in glasses and a worn, gray wool sweater rose from his spot at the counter to greet us.

"Back so soon, Mr. Templer?"

"Yes, James. It seems we're in luck. Alas poor Shaw's dead, but this is Mr. Alex Lamb from America. Hebrew scholar."

"Not exactly," I demurred as I took his fragile palm in mine and shook it as gently as I could.

"Would you mind the store a little while longer please, James. Mr. Lamb and I will be upstairs. We are not to be disturbed."

He led me through the labyrinth of shelves, crammed with brittle books, nineteenth century playbills and framed imperial maps. We walked up a wooden stairway behind the cash register and entered what Witten called the "la-BOR-a-tory."

It was actually more of a miniature version of the library we had just left in the British Museum. Heavy oak and glass display cases of books filled the room. After a brief tour of some original editions and first printings of Wordsworth, Herrick and Wilde, among others, Templer led me to a large, antique roll top desk and pulled out two pairs of gloves.

"The oil on the skin smudges the pages," he explained. "So we must wear these."

At first, it seemed strange but, when I thought about it, the gloves were no stranger than the silver pointer, or "yad," Jews use to read from the Torah. "Yad" meant hand in Hebrew, and the pointer was exactly that — a thin silver arm and hand ending in an outstretched index finger. The Rabbi used to pass it beneath the crowned, hand-inked letters of the weekly Torah portion as I read from right to left. The silver finger made a tiny imprint in the sewn lamb skin parchments of the scroll as it pointed my way through the text.

"It is a tree of life to them that hold fast to it," the Rabbi intoned each Sabbath after we completed the weekly reading and returned the Torah scroll to the simple, unadorned, pine wood ark he kept in his study at the lake house. Nor was this just rhetoric.

In fact, a Torah was more like a human being than a tree. Like a person, a Torah wore clothes — usually an embroidered cloth or velvet covering — and, like a person, a Torah could die. When it did, either due to damage or age that rendered its letters illegible, it received burial in a special cemetery for books called a "geniza." We had one in an unlit sub-basement of the yeshiva in Brooklyn and, occasionally, the Rabbi would send me down there alone to search for some obscure text he needed with only a skinny tallow candle to light my way.

I used to dread going down there. The dank smell of rotting books alone that wafted up the narrow wooden stairs leading to the geniza was enough to make me turn back. The breeze that carried it flicked menacingly at my candle flame as the floorboards at the top of the stairs creaked beneath my shifting weight. I would stand there for several agonizing seconds staring vainly into the blackness before I cupped my hand around the flame and descended the groaning stairwell. When I finally felt my foot sink into the soft dirt floor at the bottom, I knew I had reached my destination. I shuffled forward a few steps until I saw a wooden door in front of me and slowly pushed it open. The smell of dead books was unbearable.

In the light of my candle, brittle cracked book bindings cast tombstone-like shadows onto the cinder block walls of the room from their dusty wooden shelves. I had to hold the candle so close to them to read their faded titles, it was a miracle I didn't burn the whole yeshiva down.

Unbound stacks of parchment baled in twine rose like ghosts from the dirt floor beneath the shelves, their edges curling upward in the shape of gaping mouths. But the most terrifying sight of all were the decomposing bodies of Torah scrolls lying naked on concrete shelves recessed into the walls like burial vaults. It was in a vault such as these that the Rabbi discovered *The Book of Life*.

Templer led me to a draftsman's table in a corner of the room with filtered adjustable, overhead lamps and two high backed chairs that looked like bar stools. He then took a ziploc wrapped manuscript from one of the drawers and placed it in front of me.

"The book. Please do not touch it. I shall remove it for you and, if you require a page to be turned, kindly allow me to do it. Is that clear?"

I nodded. He then removed the book from its bag and I started to read.

"Door, Dar, Der...Without vowels it's hard to say. I don't recognize the word."

"That's all right, go on."

"Kong. Keng... This isn't Hebrew."

"What do you mean it isn't Hebrew? Those are Hebrew characters, are they not?"

"Well yeah, but these words aren't in Hebrew. They're in Yiddish."

"Yiddish! Of course. That idiot, Boris! I should have known. He found this book in Lithuania. How could I have been so foolish? Blast! I paid a hundred and ten pounds for it!"

He pushed himself back from the table in disgust and began pacing the room. After a few laps around the bookcases, he returned and sat next to me again.

"Can you read it anyway? I'm curious what we have here."

"Sure, it says 'Der Koenig Lear.'"

"Lear? King Lear?"

"Uh-huh."

"No, it can't be. What does it say next?"

"Far Villam Shekspeare."

"Oh my goodness. It is! Please, go on."

"Uberzetst."

"What does that mean?"

"Translated... un farbessert — and improved. "

"Improved?! King Lear by William Shakespeare. Translated and improved?"

"That's what it says. You want me to go on?"

"No, that's quite enough. It's certainly not what I thought it was," he laughed, playfully slapping the top of the table with his palm. "Still it is quite a curio, ay? I think I know just the right buyer for it. Well, in any case, Mr. Lamb, you have done me a great service."

He reached into his pocket and handed me a twenty pound note.

"Please accept this and an additional token of my gratitude."

He led me back downstairs and told his assistant to "let Mr. Lamb take the book of his choice."

I tried to tell him that the money had been more than generous, that I didn't need another book.

"Nonsense," he insisted. "You can never have too many."

The Rabbi had over seven thousand volumes in our Brooklyn brownstone and another three thousand in his study in the yeshiva. I know because I counted each one as he passed it down to me from the shelf and lay it on my arms in its proper order. When the stack threatened to cover my entire face, the Rabbi motioned to one of the growing piles on the floor, where I dutifully unloaded my teetering burden and quickly returned for more. So it went for several days and nights after the ban, at the end of which the Rabbi boxed the stacks and bound them with twine for me to carry to the waiting truck. One box escaped his binding, the one full of my mother's letters and photographs, which I managed to smuggle up to the lake house undetected amongst the rest. As for the Rabbi, only one book escaped his boxes. *The Book Of Life.*

In the months since my mother's death, this book had become the Rabbi's most constant companion to the point where, of the ten thousand, it was the only one that seemed to exist for him at all. As I would soon learn, this obscure Seventeenth Century Kabbalistic text was to hold the key to the desperate ritual we were about to perform.

The Rabbi called me into his study as he had done each summer before. Apparently, our first summer without my mother was to be the same as all the others. He was staring out the window when I arrived, and I stood there silently for several moments before he swiveled around in his chair to look at me. I'm not sure now if he was crying or not, but I'd like to think that he was. He picked up the cracked, veiny brown leather text from the top of his desk and handed it to me. It bore the unmistakable smell of dead books.

"This is the book you will read this summer, Alexander. Now go begin."

He had to have known I would never be able to understand it at nine or, for that matter, at any age. The words, if they could even be called that, were incomprehensible to me; just Hebrew letters arranged in no apparent order, like some form of code I could not hope to break and never would. Nevertheless, I tried each day, afraid to admit to the Rabbi that I could make no sense of it.

It was a typical day. I had just finished my lesson and prayers with the Rabbi, and we were getting ready to go to the lake. He used to say that the solitude of being in the water at sunset helped him get closer to God. My mother never liked the idea of swimming so late, but she wasn't around to object.

It was the last day of August, only four days before the one-year anniversary of her death, and he'd gone the whole lesson without even mentioning the book.

On the walk down the rock path to the shore of the lake, he finally asked, "What did you think of the book, Alexander?"

"It was very interesting," I stammered. "I learned a lot from it."

He looked pleased. I thought I was home free.

We stripped down to our trunks on the rocky shore and waded into the shallows.

"Let's swim the whole lake today," the Rabbi suggested. "You're ready for it."

It was more than half a mile long, and the most we had ever done together was maybe half of that and, even then, I had to rest several times, using the Rabbi as a floatable dock as I caught my breath. We started with a slow breast stroke, as always, with our heads raised above the water so we could talk.

"So tell me about the book, Alexander."

"What do you want to know?" I asked nervously.

"Summarize Chapter 10 for me."

"Which one was that again?"

"The one about the destruction of the first temple," he responded sternly.

I hesitated for a few seconds before I offered a barely audible "I forgot."·

"Summarize Chapter 5 then."

"I forgot that one too."

"Chapter 1?"

"I forgot."

"Did you read the book, Alexander?"

I put my face into the water, opening my eyes as if searching for the answer on the murky bottom of the lake.

When I looked up again, the Rabbi was already well ahead of me, swimming much faster than normal. I kicked as fast as I could in an effort to catch up.

Suddenly my left leg cramped from the strain, and I sputtered to a dead stop on the waves. I began to flail my arms and right leg in an effort to tread water. The Rabbi kept going.

I cried out, "Aba! Aba!"

He stopped and turned to face me.

"My leg hurts, I can't swim anymore!"

He started to breast stroke towards me, but stopped about five yards away. I stared at him confused. He treaded water calmly for several seconds before he answered.

"Will you read the book?"

Bewildered, I cried out more desperately, "I can't swim anymore!"

But he just stayed there, treading water, and repeated, "Will you read the book?"

My leg was a useless knot by then, and my shoulders were burning. I knew I couldn't stay afloat much longer, nor could I make it to shore on my own. Panicked and terrified, I shrieked "I'm drowning!" But he didn't make a move to help me. Again he repeated his question, which by now had become a demand.

"WILL YOU READ THE BOOK!"

In that instant, I realized that my father would not save me. I understood that he loved a book more dearly than his only son and, when my mind grasped that my father had quit on me, my body did too. My arms stopped flailing, and I went under. I screamed as I went down, swallowing a mouthful of water. I saw my father swim towards me. There was hope. My eyes were still open, and I could see him with the setting sun at his back looking down at me. The arm would come through the surface any second. But the only thing that pierced the waves was the sound of a garbled question that seemed to take years to reach me.

"Will you read the book?"

It was the last thing I remember hearing before the world went upside down, then purple, then black.

When I opened my eyes, tendrils of welcoming moss were waving gently to me from the bottom of the lake. A vision of my mother emerged from behind a stone, her long dark hair flowing in concert with the moss. She held out her arm to me and whispered,

Do you want to come with me?

"YES!" I screamed as my lungs filled with water, and the arm shot through and pulled me to the surface.

I awoke on the beach with the Rabbi's bearded face bending over me. He handed me a towel and we walked back to the house together in silence. Three days later, I finished the book, whose words now made sense to me; not literally, but intuitively.

"You had to be imbued with the power of water, first," the Rabbi explained.

"It was the only way."

He then made me memorize the letter combinations I would need to chant at the resurrection ritual. The day after that, we returned to the lake to raise my mother from the dead.

I pretended to survey the rows of antique books while I waited for Templer to retreat into his laboratory. Then I quickly thanked his assistant and left. As the door closed, I heard him shout after me, "You forgot your book."

Several days later, after making my pilgrimage to the rest of my mother's shrines, I found myself back at my room at the youth hostel, now nearly empty as students made their way back to their respective countries and universities for the start of the fall term. I decided it was time for me to go as well. There was only one more thing that remained for me to do. I removed the journal from my backpack, and tore a blank piece of paper from the center of it.

Dear Rabbi,

By the time you get this letter, the school year will have begun and I will not be there. I myself don't even know where I'll be other than somewhere in Europe. Do not attempt to look for me. I do not wish to be found. I am sorry if this causes you pain.

Say Kaddish over me if you like.

Your son and student,

Alex.
Or, at least, his student.

Again, I took out the picture of my mother in the arms of the man, and studied his bearded face. Even if he turned out not to be my real father, he had known my "real" mother, the one who had died before I was even born, when she became Orthodox and married the Rabbi. The man in the picture had loved my mother and she him; her letters attested to that. But that was all I knew of them. The chance to learn who he was, and who she had been before, was the reason I had crossed the ocean and, now, I was about to do so again for the second time that week.

I dropped the letter in one of the red London postboxes on my way to the train station, where I bought a one way ticket to Dover for the ferry trip to Calais on the northern coast of France.

The famed white cliffs of Dover jutted defiantly above the roiling, teal Atlantic. I stared at the cliffs for nearly an hour as they receded into the horizon, sinking slowly into the sea. Their whiteness was soon indistinguishable from the white caps of the waves pulling me towards the continent like tiny flags of surrender.

Lucy in the Sky

E. M. Chakkappan

As Prashant Panicker followed his wife up the stairs from the platform at Ernakulam's South Junction, he admired her bum. Its even sway, first to the right, then to the left, each silken sweep punctuated with a bounce as her foot planted her weight, was immensely satisfying. *Nobody climbs quite like my Lucy,* he thought. She spread her hand over the pleats of sari covering the firm roll of her stomach, pulled herself over the topmost step, and turned toward him. The morning heat had creased her neck and made wet blooms out of the scent of her perfume. *How good to be home,* he thought.

"Did you and the Gellars enjoy Ooty then?" Lucy didn't know why she asked the question. The hill station was just in the next state, and the Panickers often took weekend trips to their time-share to escape the heat in Kerala. But at the moment she had no interest in Prashant's and his American associates' opinions of it. She had made the half-hour trip into the city with Krishnan, their driver, to meet Prashant's train and take him back to their home in Fort Cochin, only because it was expected of her.

"They had a grand time. Full of praise for the weather and scenery." Lucy saw the success of his business partner's annual visit to India spread over her husband's face like melting butter. The corners of his mouth slid up into his cheeks, and his eyes lost their crisp, inspecting rims. "Are all the preparations made for the party tonight?"

Before she could respond, a coolie, laboring under an aluminum trunk, yodeled roughly past them and almost knocked her over. She lost her balance and thought she saw the tracks, far below, fly toward her face. Prashant quickly reached out to steady her, wedging the heel of his palm into the cleft of her moist back, but he wished he hadn't noticed the way she bit her lower lip and narrowed her eyes at the callused heels bounding away from them.

"Everything is fine," Lucy pronounced curtly, adjusting herself. Usually, she too enjoyed Earnest Gellar's visits and the chance to see their home through unaccustomed, appreciative eyes, but the past year had been draining and she still hadn't recovered her poise. Earlier in the morning she had had a phone conversation with her mother that had bothered her. But she continued, "Tereza keeps at me about the prawns for her curry. You said you would send someone yourself to the fisheries and we were not to go to the market?"

"That's exactly right." Prashant was determined to make the evening's party the crowning event of an already glittering itinerary. Set among the orchids and mango trees of his newly planted lawn, with an array of dishes inspired by his travels through Southeast Asia's newly commercialized capitals, attended by Fort Cochin's most prominent citizens, and with a special appearance by his father, the aging freedom fighter whose brilliant reputation ensured instant respect, it was bound to make just the right impression.

"So I will — " he began, but a spear of light struck his eyes. At first he couldn't see the trio of school children in cornflower blue uniforms climbing the stairs as they descended. The tallest, a girl, was swinging a stack of aluminum tiffin trays to and fro, in rhythm with the loud *squish* of her plastic sandals. Her dark, almost black face floated in a mist of white powder, and a heavy gold stud was embedded in her thin nostril. Prashant wondered if it was the lunch boxes or the preposterous jewel that had blinded him. Why do people still insist on clamping gold rings on their children, when they don't have dependable plumbing or a raised bed to sleep on? Yet there was something about the girl, she reminded him of someone, not any of his own children though. They would be driven to school, and Tereza, their cook, would feed them at noon, leaving the house with lunches still warm from the stove. "How are the children?"

"Sameer keeps glued to the cricket matches on TV. Sonya no longer eats rice. Your father found an error in Smitha's history textbook and is convinced that the next generation will forget their roots," Lucy gave him a fatigued look. "He wants to arrange a meeting with the children's headmaster and the Minister of Education."

Prashant laughed, "Aaaah ... some things are dependable. My family and their ailments." Whatever unease might have plagued him a moment ago disappeared. The innocence of these complaints fully restored his sense of homecoming.

Lucy was suddenly furious. She hurried down the stairs and crossed the platform toward the station exit. Only when she was convinced that she had put enough distance between herself and Prashant's patented joviality, did she stop. She searched the crowd for their driver. She was tall, and could see above most of the men, women, and children — even in the flat sandals she always wore so that Prashant would not feel uncomfortable with the inch she gained over him in heels. The crowds of people, with their powdered faces and pressed clothes, already appeared as worn and dusty as the railway cars they were rushing to fill. Their movements grew more antagonistic, bony elbows branding naked stomachs, taut veins cutting reedy necks, as they shoved and threatened to secure enough space for babies and belongings.

Lucy snapped the gold clasp on her pocket book open and shut. She couldn't find Krishnan, who had walked ahead with Prashant's bags. What if they lost him? Neither Prashant nor she had keys to the car. What if they had to roam the station for hours looking for him? At that moment she couldn't think of anything more necessary than the smell of worn leather baking in the sun, or the grumbling and fretting of the engine and air conditioner as the car sprang to life. Why was she so desperate? Krishnan was probably in front of the station, already waiting in the Benz.

It was Arvind, she realized. Her mother wanted her to obtain a favor for her sister Valsa's son, and she did not see how she could do it. As Krishnan pulled the car up and she settled into the backseat with Prashant, who squeezed her arm and commended her for arranging things so efficiently, the events of the past year of the boy's life ran through her mind. Both his parents had died and he had suffered mentally, dropping out of the local college. There had even been dirty rumors that he had gotten involved with a fast set and taken drugs. So Lucy's mother had coerced him to spend a couple of months at a charismatic retreat. Lucy was disappointed in the current trend among Christians in Kerala, which required attendance at prayer meetings where the holy spirit induced a believer to speak in tongues. As a dutiful and emotionally aloof Catholic, she had always been proud that their religion had never been tainted by the fanaticism that, as Prashant liked to say, was "the ruin of this country." But, apparently, the charismatics had helped Arvind. At least according to her mother, who took credit for his complete change, his adjusted personality. During the past few months he had managed to complete a course in computer science. He was currently applying for positions abroad, but with little luck.

Her mother had whispered shrilly into the phone about the efforts Arvind was making, the letters he was writing, and the expensive subscriptions to foreign trade magazines she had bought for him. Lucy had cut her off before the list expanded to include the now familiar chant of special seminars, tailoring bills, preparatory tutoring … Though her mother liked to give the impression that her involvement was dutiful and wearying, she couldn't hide her pride in mastering the details of Arvind's exciting future. The words, *hardware, software, telecommunications, Silicon Valley,* tumbled out of her mouth with relish. Lucy felt that her mother was giddy in the role she was playing in these novel, modern matters, and had put too much faith in the instant fortunes they promised. It embarrassed her.

But, even more worrisome was the message that she, Lucy, was the only one who could help her poor sister's only son. And didn't she owe it to him? After all, hadn't he accomplished as much as he could, considering his tragic circumstances? Wasn't it only natural that she should be his champion as he embraced progress, just like her husband and his forward-thinking family? Wasn't she in the position to help him, with her proximity to such powerful foreigners, who had so much pull? But Lucy was painfully aware that Arvind, even with all the improvements, did not cut much of a figure. He lacked something. What, exactly, she preferred not to think about.

The day before Prashant and Earnest left for Ooty, she almost had brought the subject up, but hastily reconsidered. They had driven to Earnest's hotel, on the island between the city and Fort Cochin, for a late lunch. The hotel's four dining rooms were built along its western wall, which faced the Arabian Sea, and each reflected a different Asian culture in its cuisine and decor. The three of them had decided on Cantonese food and found a table near the windows, as Earnest desired. Prashant had suggested a late lunch, after the zenith of the day's temperatures, so Earnest's seating choice was not as uncomfortable as usual.

During their meal the conversation turned quickly to business. Earnest's staff had weeded through countless queries for a managerial post at their Los Angeles plant. "It's all a matter of luck," he had shrugged. "You can only tell real potential when you meet a person face to face. A lot of loose cannons hide behind good-looking papers." Despite the sun drenching their table, Lucy had felt the small hairs on her nape grow feet and stand up. At that moment she realized that Arvind was and always would be, with or without good-looking papers, a loose cannon.

"We'll send the car for Earnest and Joan later tonight — their plane is arriving from Madras only this afternoon." Prashant's words interrupted her thoughts as the Benz skimmed the island's main road. They were almost home now. The worst of the city traffic was behind them. Though Wellingdon Island contained their busiest resort, the naval base, and the airport, it usually offered a smooth drive. Lucy imagined the island received its sense of order from the British statesman it was named after. She examined the brightly colored billboards over the thatched straw and palm huts. They were the only distraction on the otherwise vacant, grassy stretch and showed young, blue-jean clad men and women driving scooters and smoking cigarettes. Suddenly she felt another surge of anger toward Prashant, who was far too comfortably settled into his side of the back seat. Just who did he think he was, with his nostrils flared to the wind and his paunch hanging over the too-tight pants of his khaki suit? How dare he raise his elbows like that? One on the seat back and the other on the window ledge, like some new-edition-viceroy?

She remembered the first years of their marriage, when he couldn't decide if he wanted an American wife or an Indian wife and his every gaze was one of probing criticism. A check for flaws in the way she lined her eyes, or matched pieces of jewelry to her saris, or served herself at buffet dinners. And then the corrections. "That's not quite right, Lucy." "Lucy, there's something gaudy about that combination." "You'll get a pimple if you have another one, Luce."

After their first anniversary, Prashant decided that she had put on a few extra pounds, and he was not ready to accept a wife with an expansive waist line. So he started an exercise regimen for her. Every morning he would make her run laps on the beach. She could still see him standing there with the wind whipping his hair into shiny, bryl-creamed coils as he counted down her progress by striking the spot she started with a long palm frond each time she passed it. As it turned out, the reason she had put on weight was because she was pregnant with Smitha.

Just what had she subjected herself to? Just where had those years gone when she should have been carefree and adored, like those girls in the advertisements? She could not decide who had been more backward: her, for meekly cowing to her confident, westernized husband, or him, for leaking unexamined ideals, like a torn sack of rice. When Krishnan pulled up in front of their gate, she bit her lip and vowed that those days were long past: loose cannon or not, her nephew would certainly find a position abroad. Even if his only foolproof credential was that his aunt had decided to enforce a whim of her own instead of acting on one of her husband's.

Nothing pleased Prashant more than the stroll he took around his house and the surrounding grounds after returning from a trip. It was one of his favorite activities. It reminded him of what he had achieved, not just materially, not just mentally, but aesthetically. Because aesthetics, Prashant believed, revealed both pursuits. The house he had designed, built, and decorated disregarded the kind of ostentatious facades and interiors that were popular among Fort Cochin's wealthy residents. He had spent a fortune of rupees to create the unconventional impression of simplicity. Believing that this image was best represented by the more muted East Asian cultures, his house was built above ground-level like a Japanese farmer's abode, but with a dipping, red-tiled Indian roof and encircling verandah. The inside of his home was carefully littered with dishes, urns, rugs, paintings, and large, glossy art books that explained things like brush strokes so masterful they had to be accidental, just excess ink shaken onto the canvas and forming a tree branch. Outside, he had pushed back the natural vegetation of bamboo, plantain, and coconut trees, and the grasses that were long and sharp and independent enough to slice off a running girl's flying plait, with a low wall of granite rocks fitted together like puzzle pieces. Wanting a lawn, not the vermilion dust kicked up with every step, or the seeded grasses that inevitably appeared ersatz, he instructed the gardener to experiment with various creepers. One finally took horizontally, and the grounds were now covered in a net of diamond-shaped leaves.

But today his stroll did not take him further than the living room. A crude hunk of metal had appeared in front of the delicate legs of the hand-crafted bamboo table. A square-mouthed porcelain vase covered in a perfect glaze of obelisks and pagodas rested on the table's glass-top. At its base was an unblinking gold beast on an unfamiliar rug.

"Lucy," He shouted.

She came running out of their bedroom.

"What is *this?*" he asked, pushing the thing's snout with two fingers.

"Prashant — the fawn — it arrived yesterday."

"The fawn? What fawn?"

"The one we saw in the brass shop in the city."

He cut her off, "But what is it doing here?" What he really wanted to ask was. *Is this my home or All Baba's?*

"Prashant. You admired it — I bought it."

"*You* admired it."

"*We* decided —" Her expression changed, "You forgot?"

"*No* — I —" He had forgotten. But now, cramming his fingers behind his elbows and examining the thing again, he remembered. They had spent an afternoon browsing in the new shopping complex on Marine Drive, in Ernakulam. It had seemed to him that the shops were as repetitious in their wares — brass puja lamps, coir rugs, teak footstools — as they were in their construction, unpainted concrete shoeboxes stacked one on top of the other. But Lucy, wrapped in a sari the color of dark grapes, her arms and shoulders bursting out fair and curved in pleasing contradiction, had been impressed by the display of local crafts and handiwork, as well as the oily smiles of the bespectacled, marionette-like shop keepers, and she had made a regal, sumptuous procession, from shoebox to shoebox. He might have followed her anywhere and agreed to anything. But he had never imagined the piece in their home. Nothing could be as perfectly mismatched with the rest of the room. And on the day of the party! It had to go. Lucy was looking at him, her curly hair loosened from its knot and frizzing around her face, her unbuttoned house-coat hanging shapelessly from her shoulders. He wondered how someone so beautiful, even in such a state, could have such bad taste. "Where is the rug from?"

"A salesman — he said the Gulf."

"Mmmmm . . ." He squatted down and picked up a corner, the one farthest from Lucy's fawn.

"You don't like it, do you?" she inquired. There was a note of doubt in her voice, "The colors?"

He quickly picked up the cue. "And the weave ..." He would not insult her, but less directly, and more graciously, enforce his own point of view.

"Oh Prashant, do we have to be bothered with it today? Can't we fix it later?"

He was silent.

"Fine — if it bothers you so much I'll ask Krishnan to wrap it up and store it away in the car porch."

"Lucy what would I do without you?" He raised himself, planted his hands firmly on her cheeks and tickled her lips and nose with his mustache, humming, "*Lucy in the sky ...*" as he made his way to her ear, "*with diamonds. Lucy in the sky...*" It was their trusted make-up ritual. When they first married he would insist that the only reason he flew back from California to meet the girl his father had found was that her name matched his favorite song. He had cultivated the idea of a cool, world-weary American bachelor in hip-huggers and wide collars, committed to living the carefree life of a Berkeley graduate, innocently lured back home by an Indian girl with the name of a popular Western song. He believed his thirteen-year marriage was the perfect blend of tradition and romance. After his time abroad, all his decisions, commercial or intellectual, public or private, monumental or trivial, similarly combined East and West. Old and new. Poetry and precision. Weight and lightness. All his decisions were aesthetically sound.

He continued humming the tune that had changed and changed back, picked up inflections and innuendoes, evoking the spirit of those early years when they had been shy of words and needed to communicate deep longings and petty fantasies, all the while gently guiding his wife's steps back into their bedroom, where he could finish his entire welcome home ritual. She smelled of lilacs, but not as pungently as at the train station, and of the rice powder that she so often pressed over her skin. She sweat the stuff. He sniffed it out of the soft folds behind her neck and ears as he squeezed the flesh on her hips and felt it escape from his fingers, slowly. Wanting to feel all of her like that, soft, heavy, retreating, he leaned her against the credenza and unbuttoned his pants.

"Prashant."

How good to be home, he thought.

"Prashant — I think the curtain just moved."

He kissed her, full on the mouth. "How beautiful you are."

"Oh, Prashant," she moaned, surprised by the look on his face and in his eyes, like a traveler's, dazed by countless flying images.

Then he finished. He withdrew, let his pants drop to the floor and started to vigorously unbutton his shirt, all the usual curl and punctiliousness returning to his features. "You know, when I first met you, you could have gone either way," he said, tweaking her nose. And over his shoulder, in front of the bathroom door, "beautiful or wasted."

Beautiful or wasted. She repeated the words to herself as she straightened her clothes. What did he mean? She walked to the mirrored vanity next to the bathroom, the door to which Prashant had left open, and examined the reason for her husband's belated warning. *Beautiful or wasted.* Did he mean that he was —? That their marriage was the proof her beauty hadn't been wasted? How dare he presume such nonsense? As if— but it was no use, she knew that sometimes she had the same thought.

How could the idea that her looks entitled her to something better not have entered her mind? When she was a child, upon her introduction, aunts and uncles would immediately twinkle and look for presents to bestow, later, sweet vendors and ticket collectors would excuse her inability to produce correct change and offer their goods or services for free. Even now, she could win favors from her servants or her children's school teachers with just a few well-chosen words. It was her luck, "Lucy's Luck," She could barely remember a time when she hadn't felt it, felt that there was something better in store for her. *But better how?*

Even her father, preoccupied lawyer that he was, had unknowingly encouraged this feeling. It might have been the year after her twelfth birthday when he developed the habit. Saying he wanted to smooth her curly hair, he would pull her face toward his own for just a moment each morning before he left the house. The whole family knew it was uncharacteristic attention from the reserved man who kept communication with his wife and children to a minimum. Lucy was always thankful for the chance to look directly at that powerful, usually distant face and find it not so stern, just lined and slightly worn, like an unmade bed. When she followed her father out to the front verandah and watched him stroll over to his rikshaw, quite grand and impervious in his flowing black robe and white wig, she would try hard to remember the comfort of his face when it was close to hers. But she never succeeded until the next morning when, there he was again for just a second. *Why must someone else always choose the moment? Something better when?*

"Prashant," she called out.

"Luce," he answered from the bathroom, "they forgot to put clean towels in here." His usually wavy locks were dripping over his face.

After she had found a towel for him she tried again, "Prashant there's something — *Ammachi* called this morning — "

"What is it Luce?"

"It's Arvind — she's worried —"

"I thought the Arvind Reformation Project was going quite well." In front of the mirror, he began to towel his head. "Computer classes, foreign tuition masters —"

"Not foreign tuition masters, *foreign magazine subscriptions,*" she corrected him, though she knew he would find her tone unflatteringly sharp.

Prashant balled the towel with one hand and dropped it on the vanity.

"Well it's not important," Lucy continued, thinking that for appearances' sake, the boy was family, after all, her husband could show some interest. But

Prashant picked up a comb and leaned into the mirror to inspect the length of his mustache hairs. "It's not important because in spite of all that he's not been able to find anything," She burst out with what she felt was her last bit of resistance, "Prashant — I think we should help him. It sounds as if there are many posts at the plant in Los Angeles —"

He walked toward their adjacent armoires, "Lucy — Arvind?"

The way Prashant pronounced the name was enough. She felt her forehead grow very warm and her lips, her lips began to feel like the clasp on her pocketbook, opening and shutting. "I just feel something might be done,"

"Certainly." Prashant wiggled into his underwear and snapped its band across his stomach. "I feel the same,"

As Prashant's assured stride carried him out of their bedroom, Lucy saw her face again, reflected in the mirror inside her armoire. *Wasted, completely wasted,* she decided.

When Prashant turned the corner to his father's apartment he saw Tereza making her way down the path.

She had been his ayah when he was a baby. It seemed right that she was still by his side, feeding his wife and family. She wanted to know if he had sent his assistant to the fisheries, because if he hadn't yet, she needed to change the order to twelve kilograms of prawns. Prashant assured her that he would tell the fellow the new order immediately. As she walked toward the gate he noticed the tiffin trays she carried, tied together with a red and white checkered towel, they held the children's lunches. Following the path to his father's rooms, he wondered vaguely why the sight of those lunches was not comforting, though this morning the thought of them had been.

As he neared Augustin's apartment, Prashant could hear a British voice grow increasingly authoritative. He knew his father was lying on his bed with the short wave radio balanced on his broad, boat-like belly, tuned to the BBC. When Prashant began to suspect that Augustin Panicker, a veritable legend throughout Kerala, was not getting the respect he deserved in the family home he shared with his brother and sister-in-law, he insisted that he move in with his son. So Augustin's rooms had been added to the house hastily, interrupting the flow of Prashant's design. The entrance was behind the children's rooms and in front of the servants' quarters. Of course Prashant had not intended it to be that way, but it couldn't be helped. His father's stipulations had been privacy and a view of the plantain trees. "Your new home will no doubt be quite something," Augustin had complied. "But this late in my life the best views are those that remind me of my youth. And the best rooms are where I can quietly contemplate those times."

Since Augustin's work with the Congress Party during India's freedom struggle had led to a long and distinguished career in the State Legislative Assembly, and since Prashant had insisted on paving his own way financially, Augustin's brother had inherited the family's shipping business, as well as the ancestral home. "It is only the custom," his father would tell him — even when Prashant discovered that Augustin had been forced to share a room with his grand-nephew. "This is where custom ends," Prashant had announced. But as he pushed aside the leaves hanging over Augustin's doorway and saw the clothes-line the servants had erected behind it, he wondered how someone who had been so passive in his brother's home had become so demanding in his son's.

"Acha," he called out as he entered the room.

Augustin's shivery palm, inscribed as deeply as the bottom of a cooking pot, halted the rest of Prashant's greeting. After a few moments, when the broadcast died into static, Augustin propped himself into a sitting position and switched it off. His thick eyebrows, which looked yellow in the middle of his dark, potato-shaped face, almost covered his eyes.

Prashant could not help but think that this old man, with his weak movements and sackcloth odor, hardly matched his vita.

"Still the only ones who understand the situation," Prashant heard him mutter, then ask more clearly, "Well — did the Americans pay homage at the summer capital of the British Raj?"

"They were impressed by the history as well as the natural beauty of the place."

"Don't let them fool you Prashant. If not for the history, they would not be here to see the natural beauty."

"Come, *Achen,* let's not bite the hand that feeds us. And besides you've known Earnest since we were in college. Surely, he's more than a tourist to you by now."

Augustin took in his son with a swift glance. Despite the slowness that seemed to have settled on his body, Prashant thought of the way ants covered a piece of bread, his eyes were still quick. In fact the perception and energy that gleamed there could often be frightening. "So do I hear there's to be a party tonight?"

"A small gathering. Some family and friends." Prashant knew that the best tactic would be to sound casual, Augustin disapproved of displays.

"Your brother, Gladys Levi." She was one of the last members of Cochin's White Jewish families, most of whom had emigrated to Israel after the end of British rule. Her presence would cheer Augustin, who had known her all his life through the families' common shipping connections, as well as impress the Americans with living proof of Cochin's diverse, even cosmopolitan, history. "Some of the fellows from the club might come along with their wives —"

"Local history. Natural beauty."

"Acha"

Augustin interrupted him by picking up his transistor radio again, "Do you know what's brewing, Prashant? In the Punjab?"

Prashant wasn't keen on discussing politics with his father. He hadn't had a chance to look at a newspaper in the last couple of days but had no doubt that twenty-four hours was sufficient time for the circus of opportunistic crooks running the country to start another dumb show. He also had no doubt that his father would never dismiss their antics as easily as he did. Augustin would, of course, see a pattern in their actions, a pattern that should be analyzed and understood, and he would never cede the only point Prashant could make passionately: that the corrupt, witless political scene was bad for India's international image, and, therefore, bad for business. But at the moment it seemed like a safer subject.

"Hasn't Indiraji settled with the Kalistan faction?"

"Settled? Storming the sun temple is settling?"

"Extreme situations call for extreme measures. Perhaps they will buy a measure of moderation for the rest of us."

"And what about democracy, Prashant, your generation's inheritance?" Augustin's question was directed at his son, but his tone had grown milder.

"What about democracy for all of us?"

"Speaking of democracy," Prashant recognized the opportunity, *"Achen,* what's this I hear about you and Smitha's history master having tea with the Minister of Education?" Despite their clashing viewpoints, Prashant deeply needed his father. The whole anachronistic picture, from the wanton plantain trees to the cement-floored room, with its four-poster rope bed, lumpy cotton mattress, and Anglo-Indian style mahogany desk on which the latest installment of his memoir sat, was essentially linked to his son's own identity. Even Augustin's disappointments were valuable. Prashant considered them a vital part of his inheritance. Since they existed, he could guiltlessly attend to other things. And then it struck him, the best idea he had had all day. "Did you know that the Minister is married to Rajesh Gobi's sister? The textile merchant from the club? And he mentioned that his brother-in-law was visiting the family house this week."

Augustin said nothing but returned his transistor to its shelf.

Prashant was not deterred, "Why don't we invite both of them to the party — the Minister and Smitha's history master?"

"Fine, Prashant." Augustin rose from the bed and sat down at his desk. "I'll be there," he said as he put on his spectacles and picked up his manuscript.

"I'll do it right now." He reached for his father's phone, and the thought echoed in his mind, *how good to be home*. "With both of them there you will be able to start a democratic discussion about the syllabus sooner than you hoped."

"But Prashant —" he called out, after his son pulled off his feat of social finesse and was walking out the door. "Is it right? A party? Less than a year after the tragedy?" He was referring to Lucy's sister and her husband, but Prashant didn't know what to say. He had never thought of it. After a moment of embarrassed silence Augustin returned to his papers, "Aaah well, it's not our house — and there's your business to consider."

Of course it wasn't their house, Prashant reminded himself. Official mourning was being observed in his mother-in-law's house, where Arvind was living. Nevertheless, his father's last words disturbed him. That early morning feeling of arrival and satisfaction was beginning to evaporate. During the train ride into town he had envisioned walking through the day like the Greek king who had turned everything he touched to gold. But Prashant had not desired Midas' wealth, just his ability to preserve forms, to preserve moments. Frozen in the right form, at the right moment, he generously felt, people could be exquisite. But as he stopped on the lawn to supervise Krishnan and the gardener, who were setting up tables and stringing the outdoor lights, he wondered if he had acted out of greed.

No, that was impossible, he decided as he entered the house. He had only brought Lucy around to her better judgment, regarding both the fawn and that Arvind business, only helped his father forward his own ideals, while enlisting his aid in the evening's event. *But — what was this? The fawn? Still in his living room? And only the rug removed?* "Lucy —"

Lucy had missed her henna appointment. When Prashant left their bedroom she had remained standing in front of her mirror, wishing she had a different face, a different life. Perhaps if she had looked more like Valsa ... *Her life had certainly been different.* When she and her sister had been young girls, they would push their heads in front of their mother's small mirror in order to examine their faces. First the eyebrows, which were almost too straight, like a crow's flight under high, wide foreheads, then their eyes, then cheeks, right down to pendant-shaped chins. Lucy remembered a time when she had only seen different distances between the same features, distances which were mutable and lawless, like emotion or girth or anything else the body possesses. It had been Valsa, the elder, she realized, who had seen something else and begun to call it "Lucy's Luck." Until Lucy had started to believe it too.

And wasn't she being a bit melodramatic? Didn't she have much to be thankful for in her life with Prashant? Hadn't they achieved so much together? How could he have chosen Valsa to be hostess to his foreign business partners? Or his escort on trips abroad? Even if her looks were ultimately somebody else's advantage, Lucy knew she was confident and poised and could move easily in any milieu. That's what really mattered, she decided. And her looks had bought her the time and forgiveness to cultivate these traits, which were not innate, like intelligence or optimism. Whereas Valsa had been meek when she was unsure, loud and over-eager when she was accepted, and had never sought to better herself. But what about the procession of overbearing girlfriends and wives Earnest had brought to India with him? Without the slightest trace of shame on his part? It was different for Americans. People felt they knew them, or at least their movies, their music and their ads, so they accepted them, however they behaved, curious to compare the image to the reality. *But it's not the same for the rest of us.*

Beautiful or wasted. She scoffed at Prashant's superficial remark. He knew not one thing about either state. She would encourage her daughters to be independent women with their own careers, but she doubted whether anything would really change, whether a career would really bring them what a modern society demanded. *What had Valsa's job teaching biology at a girls' school brought her?* Her daughters would have to learn for themselves, like she did. Why couldn't her mother understand that times had changed? She couldn't help Arvind just because he was family. Maybe during her mother's time families had led the same lives, but in today's society there were only individuals who rose and fell by separate standards. Lucy unscrewed the back of her earring. The coral fell into her palm and she closed her hand tightly around both pieces. They felt like the pebbles that her youngest daughter collected during their walks on the beach.

Remembering that Valsa had admired them, Lucy unlocked the drawer inside her armoire to see if her sister had ever made a copy. Her mother had entrusted her with storing Valsa's gold in a safe deposit box at the bank, but she had not yet found the time, and she really didn't think that the entire collection was worth much more than what she regularly took out of her own locker, to have on hand, at home. With Lucy's traveling and active social life she had collected a dazzling assortment, from Chinese opals to South African diamonds to silver from the American Southwest. Over the years Valsa had often looked to Lucy for clues for jewelry patterns. The unusual settings inspired Valsa to confer with her goldsmith and imitate the designs, invariably changing them, in order to suit her own tastes and means.

Lucy knew the story behind each of the pieces in the sandalwood box, the necklaces, the bangles, even the earrings she held in her hands. They had five little gold chains looped around strings of pearls, and were inspired by Lucy's pair, which only had three and were a gift from Earnest after his visit to Syria. Oh Valsa and her extravagances! Those chains had been so heavy they had begun to stretch her earlobes. She found the coral studs as well. Lucy giggled thinking of how Valsa used to manipulate her husband's savings account in order to hide the money she spent on her jewelry. When Valsa's goldsmith was working on a commission, the two sisters would speculate daily about her husband's near discoveries of her budgeting tricks. Since Valsa and George didn't have a telephone, Valsa would call from her neighbor's, "Don't scold me Lucy. It's an investment, no? Something you can touch. Not like one of those schemes George would waste it on. Something of value for my daughter-in-law — for my granddaughters. Something small," she would laugh, "We can't all have Lucy's luck."

But Valsa never had anything to fear from George — his affection for his clever wife, his smartest investment, was immeasurable. His only smart investment, Lucy remembered. Everything the two of them had accomplished had taken manipulation, stretching, some sort of creative bookkeeping. They had just barely pulled it together on George's meager engineer's salary from Tata, Inc., Valsa's teaching dues, and much ingenuity: a little bungalow in the new development where Lucy and Valsa's mother lived, college entrance fees for Arvind, excursions to Thekkadi and Ooty, the jewelry, the scooter — that bloody scooter. For a couple in their forties to be driving around on a scooter.

If you couldn't afford a car at that point —

When the pain finally came it was almost like love, an ecstatic ocean, a feeling that had grown and grown until she could contain it no longer. Sobbing, Lucy clutched at the bed, at all the pieces of her sister's life that had fallen there, trying to find something she had lost or something she had never had.

Orange balloons dotted the ceiling of his daughters' room. No, there were none there at all, it was only the afternoon light. Prashant remembered saying goodbye to his father once when he was very young. Somewhere above his head Augustin had explained the gravity of the demonstration, of answering Gandhi's call. But Prashant had pressed his face against the scratchy cotton of his father's pant leg and refused to let go. Outside the open doors of their ancestral home, the world had been filled with the same light, more like a sound than a color, low, throbbing. Augustin had not returned from that demonstration until six months later. The newspapers had reported so much violence, not just by the British, but Hindus, Muslims, the country had turned into a bloodthirsty zoo. The whole family was sure he had been killed. But he had been thrown safely in jail along with the other *satyagrahas*. Augustin always joked about it: "Have you ever been arrested Prashant? At least once in his life, every man should go to jail. It is an education, I tell you." While Augustin was being educated, Prashant's mother had become weightless and remote, from lack of sleep and appetite.

From the bed next to him, Prashant could already hear the even flow of Lucy's breathing. Maybe he had never been in jail, but he would never give his wife cause to lose sleep. He was not a man of extreme beliefs. At the party he would be sure to tell the person he was talking to, be it his business partners or the wives from the club, "I am a simple man. I know there is little I can impart to the world." He would admit it gladly. "So why not keep the little I can get?" He would make them laugh. "Now my father, he is another story. My father is a great man." He would also recognize weight and lightness, and it would make people trust him.

He yawned. It was true, that morning's golden optimism had gone, but something else was lifting too, little by little, with each delicate breath that streamed from Lucy's mouth, and he didn't regret it. The children would be home soon, and in a couple of hours the guests would begin to arrive. It would be a fine enough party. And he would do what he could to help his wife's nephew; he was family, after all. Prashant would discuss it with Earnest. Even if they couldn't hire him at the plant, perhaps they could arrange a student visa. Weight and lightness, he remembered. If he approached it correctly, it could work.

"Prashant — Prashant, wake up!" Lucy was shaking him frantically, "Prashant we fell asleep." It was dark outside and he couldn't remember what day it was or why he was in Smitha's bed. Close to him was Lucy's face, streaked black by her eye makeup. Then it returned to him, how he had found Lucy weeping on their bed, amidst Valsa's ornaments, how they had stumbled to their daughters' bedroom like survivors from a crash ... "Prashant, the guests will be here any minute, and Krishnan says the connections for the outdoor generator are down, and Tereza didn't get —"

A scream from the street cut off her words.

"Go dress. I will see to it. Go — don't worry."

He quickly strode out the front door, and Tereza approached him with a look of horror on her face. She pointed at the gate. A limp, bedraggled, puppet of a man was fighting with their driver. Prashant stopped in his tracks when he realized who it was. He looked at Tereza for confirmation. She nodded, bringing her thumb to her mouth by way of explanation.

He turned around and returned to the house. Lucy was sitting on the bed, the orange and gold sari she had planned to wear undone around her waist. Valsa's jewelry was still there. "Is it true? Is it really him?" she whispered, unable to pronounce her nephew's name.

He nodded.

"High?"

He nodded again. He hoped the Education Minister would not be an early arrival. "We'll wait here. Krishnan will take care of him." He wished he could be like his father, who would not be affected by these events, who was already beyond the evening's party, already resigned to the fact that the words and actions exchanged there would have no lasting consequences. But he couldn't. Prashant cared about it all far too deeply. Unlike Augustin, he had never known anything else.

"It will only excite him if he sees us," Lucy agreed.

"Aunty," Arvind's voice rose loudly, "Uncle," it beseeched, before falling away into the night. Prashant imagined the same sounds trapped between the glass walls of an aquarium. He sat down next to his wife.

"They will take care of it," she repeated. "The servants will manage it before the party begins." They had tried, they had really tried to do the right thing. Prashant had agreed to talk to Earnest, but now it was impossible, and all that mattered was that the party go as planned.

Prashant tried not to think. It felt like hours passed while they waited in the bedroom. He examined every feature of it again and again, the curtained windows which hid them from the front lawn, the custom-made armoires in the alcove, the stucco-style paint on the walls, the miniature Japanese prints. The rooms beyond the locked door unfolded in his mind. All of it whimsical. All of it meaningless. The mosaic tiles would age badly, he realized, already they were starting to yellow. But Lucy's fawn would remain.

He picked up one of Valsa's ornaments. There had been jewels at the beginning of the day too. The young school girl at the train station had worn one on her nose. She had blinked against the morning sun, just when he did. She sprung forward from her plastic sandals, bringing her sister and brother with her, with that quality, a certain dignity. It was in Lucy, when they were first married, he realized, that he had seen it too.

Outside the bedroom, the screaming grew louder, closer. There were sounds of a struggle and a violent pounding on the bedroom door, "Aunty, Uncle, you forgot to invite —" Arvind's cry was stifled, and the front door banged shut. Krishnan had taken him away. Prashant felt crushed by the heaviness of it all. There was nothing but extremes. Nothing. He had been a fool to believe otherwise.

In a final attempt to make sense of things, Prashant wished her everything, that young girl at the train station with the jewel in her nose, probably a chauffeur's daughter who lived in a house with thatched walls and kerosene lamps. He wished her good fish pickle in one of those tiffin trays and a window seat on every train ride she might ever take and first class marks on her public exams and many marriage proposals and kanjipuram saris for her trousseau and strong, bell-voiced sons, who would grow into men far better than himself.

Then a twinkling, like a far away city, shone through the curtained windows. The party lights — someone must have fixed the generator. Music flooded the house, *"Lucy in the sky..."* It was their song, *"with diamonds. Lucy in the sky . . ."* Prashant looked at his wife. She rose from the bed, dragging her sari behind her like an expensive net. Her face was twisted in anger and bitterness. "Can't somebody turn that bloody thing off?"

The Stricken Hour

Julie R. Obaso

*L*egends say that fish once grew out of the ground in Kisumu Town, spawned from the murky and fertile depths of Lake Victoria. Legends also say that Ramogi, god of the Lake, spoke to inspired fishermen of the Luo tribe, and regularly commanded the massive waters to become to each man a private, fecund vessel over which, with his net extending into a long, billowing arm inches above her shifting surface, he could cast his spell.

The water grips the lip of the rising sun, willfully staying its struggle to thrust up from the deep line of the lake's horizon. Morning listens, trembling on the cusp of an inevitable beginning, and must wait, until the red sun lifts from the water's tight hug. Lake spirits hurriedly gather their nightly shrouds and flee atop the glassy table. Their pale, ghostly eyes glance briefly back as they disappear into the mists clouding the distance: the tremulous light must not introduce them to their human companions, who stand chest-deep in the water near the bank, casting and re-casting their nets, before drawing them in, writhing with live *tilapia*.

Sebby Okoth looks on the wraiths merging with the winds in the weak light. The sun chases them over the Kenyan border into the world of spirits. Through the balmy air, fishermen and women hail each other as they haul their catches along the edge of the lake. Sebby staggers with the weight of the heaving mass in her hands. Wading out of the water, she deposits the contents of her net into a huge sisal basket. Her *suka* flaps wetly against her. With a small *adita* she scoops a portion of the fish and balances it on her head. The wind quickly dries her wet clothing. She begins the ten minute walk to the market. She will make the trip approximately six times, as she does once every week, until her entire catch is sold.

Walking down the sandy path to the open-air stalls, Sebby sees the annals of Lake Victoria extending into Kisumu Town. She remembers mornings as a child when she came to fish at this very spot with her father. He'd always said that four-thirty in the morning was the best time to catch *tilapia*: at this precise moment they became drowsy, lethargic. This, he surmised, was because they stayed up all night talking to Ramogi and his underlings. By the time the net was cast in the pre-dawn, they were too drunk with conversation to dart away. Young Sebby and her father caught mounds of drowsy fish at exactly that time every morning. Afterward, they trekked back home to the village, where she would fetch him water to wash while her mother prepared breakfast. Later, at the junction of the main road, he would branch off to the fields while she continued to the schoolroom. There, in the narrow path overhung with loquat bushes and heavy-scented frangipan, fish darted from underneath the bramble, jumping between her feet, their iridescent scales causing colourful patterns to appear on the skin of her legs, patterns that stayed all the way to school and to the end of class. Sometimes the designs would linger into the night, so that it seemed young Sebby wore a pair of colourful, reptilian shoes. It was in her eighth year then, when Second-Mother came to stay, that the patterns disappeared.

Second-Mother, or *mama matin,* arrived with Father one strange evening. The air was taut and feverish against a twilight that was unwilling to leave. Swallows swooped rapidly in weird, disturbing arcs, dark objects hurled downward by an unseen hand in the sky. Sebby and her mother stood in the yard outside the main house, squinting in the dim light. Behind them, the kitchen and shed formed a protective arm from the shadowy, somehow threatening advance of the two undefined figures. Father held the woman close to him, as if she could not walk on her own. They progressed in a slow, stately manner from the gate at the bottom of the compound. It took them several minutes to arrive at the cluster of buildings at the top of the homestead. A dog barked once and was quiet. The woman's green canvas shoes stepped gently into the yard. They were new, shiny, and made the earth look dull and hopeless. Sebby moved forward to greet the stranger, impressed by her tall angular beauty, her smooth, coal-black skin on an oval face elongated by a carefully draped head-wrap, a replica of the brightly patterned *suka* tied around her waist. The woman leaned forward from a far away height, bringing her eyes close to Sebby, who was suddenly rooted to the ground by something unknown. Her eyes looked familiar, frightening. Father stood behind her wearing his best shirt, and a determined expression. He stepped forward, his arm around her waist.

"This is Opanga. *Ero, akelo nu mama matin.*"

Sebby's eyes swung to Mother, who said nothing. Her face expanded into a frigid grimace. Sebby realized the woman's eyes were familiar because they moved like the eyes of the crocodiles swimming in the swamps of Lowo forest. Opanga smiled, showing brownish teeth, and did not say a word. Father's eyes would not meet Mother's. His lips pursed and he stared at the ground.

"Fix the room in the main house," he said gruffly, "and prepare some chicken and *chapat*. Opanga likes chicken."

Mother did not move. She stood plucking aimlessly at her hairline.

"Well go on woman! Don't stand there like an old tree!"

Her face searched his. A vein began to throb in his neck. Abruptly he turned and walked into the verandah, heavily scented by the frangipan bush growing beside it. Opanga stood looking around the compound with arrogantly raised eyebrows. Her whispery voice floated almost inaudibly through the air: *go on bitch, where's my chicken where's my chapat*. The swallows dipped lower. Mother turned toward the kitchen. A strong, sad heat emanated from her body, mingling oddly with the perfumed evening. Sebby moved closer to touch her, to absorb some of it, drain some of it. Her mother stared through Sebby, as if she did not know her. She pushed Sebby violently away. The ground rose up and struck her in the forehead. Sebby felt nothing, only the sharp stabbing hand of her mother knocking her down. She lay on the earth, feeling hundreds of little caterpillars crawl up her legs, onto her face. Mother's fingers kept tying and untying her head-scarf. Her mouth hung open, yet dared not speak, for the answer was in the stony, stubborn look in Father's eye that pierced her once, briefly. That was the time they stopped catching the drowsy fish.

When a Luo child is conceived, the ancestors convene a meeting to decide the day it will join the earth, and to assign it a spirit with which to walk until he or she decides to leave the world. Sebby wonders if *tilapia* have walking spirits. If they still reminisce with Ramogi. She sifts through the fish, mentally calculating how many shillings she might make if she sells all today. Her fingers neatly arrange them on sisal mats, almost as if they were her children she were putting to bed, almost as if their perfect ovaloid forms were ornaments from which she might fashion a skirt to tie about her waist. She lays the fish-filled mats on the wooden tables with the prettiest ones foremost; they might charm the early customer with their still-shiny skins, they might be the perfect fillet.

By noon the fish selling is over. Sebby quickly packs up her things and leaves. It was a good day for she has nothing left to take home. The early afternoon sun burns through her scalp as she heads to the bus-station by the north end of the market where she will catch a *matatu* back to Nyabera village. There is bedlam as people jostle for seats, and the strident "always room for one more!" cries of the *manambas* packing more and more passengers into the garishly painted mini-vans, so that every inch of standing space is taken. Somehow, Sebby finds a seat at the back of the van, breathing the fishy scent that pervades the humid, sweaty air. She leans forward to open the window, and catches sight of the scar on her leg. The cut is healed. Suddenly it tightens, and the wrinkled skin reminds her of the dried bed of an old river. The *matatu* begins to move, slowly navigating the pot-holed road out of town. The smell begins to wane as they reach the main road to the country. Ramshackle city dwellings fall away, replaced by the odd thatched mud house. People working their land wave at the passing vehicle and shout greetings. The terrain becomes sparse, eventually turning into flat plains interrupted by rock formations. Beyond that, the hills of Nyabera. And beyond those hills is the place she was born, the place from which she ran.

The *matatu* rolls steadily on. Someone begins to sing and others join in. Sebby is silent, with the singing of her thoughts. Memories come floating from the tops of thorn trees shimmering like mirages in the hot afternoon. The red eye of the sun already starting to lean West brings the sound of voices within its splintered light fragments. Her eye is red, red as the sun, and burns a hole through a crack in the wooden door of her mother's hut.

It was night. Father lay on the bed, and Mother sat on the edge, stroking his chest. She was naked. In the dancing light of the paraffin lamp her skin glowed like softly crushed nuts. Father's hand rubbed the outside of her thigh. The skin on his knuckles was rough and peeling. He cleared his throat, speaking to the roof. "There is a woman from Gem Location I want to bring here." A mosquito buzzed persistently nearby. "She can help you around the compound and on the farm."

Mother's fingers seemed to dig into his chest. "I don't need any help," she said quietly. "I have Sebby here every afternoon."

A strange look entered Father's face. He was silent for a moment, passing a hand over his face. He said, "I have to marry this Gem woman. We spoke to her people yesterday, and they accepted." His hand moved between Mother's thighs. "Tomorrow, after I deliver the dowry, I'll bring her here." Father's eyes moved from the roof and rested fixedly on Mother, who had turned into a beautiful *makonde* sculpture. Something entered the top of Sebby's head and gripped her entire body in an excruciating spasm, then released her just as quickly, rushing from the bottom of her feet into the earth. Slivers of wood pricked her eyelids.

"And if I do not agree?" Mother whispered.

Father was very still. Then he turned, grabbing her suddenly, savagely. His cheekbones stood out, and his eyes gleamed with parables of times past. The tribal markings on his cheeks blended lividly into the tired grooves around his mouth. In the flickering light of the oil lamp Sebby discerned a terrible, unfathomable expression on his face. His hand gripped Mother's breast, as if seeking a desperate salvation.

"I love you." His voice was hoarse. *"I love you."* In a quick movement he swept her on to the mattress beneath him. Mother looked dully at the wall behind his head as he moved on top of her. Her face was exhausted. Her lips mimed something.

"You cannot marry her," she repeated over and over, "Cannot marry her, can't marry her."

The walls listened. The bed creaked. A leopard coughed somewhere in the hills.

The singing has stopped. The van arrives at the junction of the road leading to the village. Sebby alights and begins to walk along the path, clouds of dust billowing and settling around her ankles. The long dark scar is an arrow piercing a soil as red and as brown as the day the cow kicked her.

The day the cow kicked her was the day Sebby was visited by her spirit-self in the form of a leopard. She'd had several warnings that week, like the calf born breech two days ago, and the memorable dream of Omuom the sorceror last night. She stepped out of her house that morning, the dawn light just bright enough to make her squint. Stared across the distance at the rows of wheat above which she could see her husband's bobbing head. The children were not awake yet.

In Nyabera, it is the season for weeding. New wheat ears cast a shimmery gold glow in the early morning light. Absently, Sebby observes her husband in the field. He tills in a steady rythmn, machine-like, monotonous. Digging and pulling. Plant by plant, row by row. She does not love him. Already, glistening sweat drops illumine his strong back. Her eyes travel to his worn trouser wrapped around bulging thigh muscles. She remembers the slick feel of them tensed between her legs earlier this morning, buttocks bunched, the loud groans as he drove hungrily inside her. She does not love him. Occasionally, with the back of his hand, he swipes the dripping sweat off his brow as if he were flicking the recalcitrant sweat from the middle of her breasts on one of those long hot nights. Now and again, he sips water from the flask at his hip. Soon she will take him his breakfast of tea and cassava.

Melancholy. She submits to its constancy, a gift, a necessary pain lingering, a thread, a hungry ream that cannot be assuaged. Her feet make a brushing sound on the earth as she walks across the yard to the kitchen. Brushing melancholy. Darkly, colouring her life. Her face, to her family, radiates a perpetual serenity, an inscrutable loveliness. Beneath it she bears her lesion-inflicted face, seeing in the laughter-creased faces of her children her unattainable face. In secret moments, smugly, she observes her family's unassuming faces, enjoying the deception, her affliction a coveted guest.

The mud room is dark and smoky. She is enveloped by its familiar dimness; errant cobwebs drifting from the blackened wooden rafters send a greeting across her cheeks. The dirt floor needs scrubbing. An array of black-bellied pots stand neatly stacked, on the left side of the room. To the right, sisal baskets in varying sizes house an assortment of nuts, grain and cassava. In one corner of the square room looms a huge clay pot in which fresh drinking water is stored. The pot is covered with an ancient crocheted mat that her mother-in-law gave her. Nobody knows she hates the mat. A nervous hand flicks spider strands from her skin. She looks up. *Webs.* Her chest is constricted. Standing on tiptoe she carefully picks off the sticky weave with her fingers. The constriction eases. Neatness cleanliness cleanliness neatness. Sometimes she detects her husband's bloated irritation, and at these times she watches him keenly, covertly, pleasurably.

Clad in a peculiar contentment, she arranges dry sticks in the three-stone stove at the back of the room. She lights the fire with a match. It is slow, so she blows it to life with a long open-ended pipe. Narrows her eyes against the acrid meandering smoke, that, conversely, coils a vague swirling unease lurking, a predator smarting, reddening her eyes.

Outside, behind the kitchen, aroused cattle stir restlessly, their udders heavy and tight with milk. Sebby decides to milk the new grade heifer her husband brought home yesterday. The cow is frisky, unfamiliar with its new surroundings. She drives it into the rude milking pen next to the cow shed, positioning its head on a wooden bar attached to two poles. Below this is a stack of fodder; the cow immediately begins to munch. She slips a metal pail at the cow's rear, beneath the pendulant mammaries.

Sebby begins to milk rythmically. Habit overtakes concentration. Her mind begins to wander. Thinks of mother. *Must've pulled too hard on teat.* The heifer rears its hind leg and kicks her hard in the left shin. Sound of a hoof crunching, tearing of skin and flesh. Something cracks. She screams, jumping up shocked, hobbling, knocking the pail *ka-plunk!* over. Milk streaks whitely into the muddy ground. Nothing bleeds at first, only sickly white patch of a gash turning quickly red. The cow, flexing its back muscles tautly, stamping lightly, preparing to kick. Again. Agony comes as a delayed explosion: she's slightly unhinged. Ache searing inside left side, cutting vision. She's immobilized. Gutteral sound from afar – moaning, vision blurred. The cow continues to munch fodder. The ground is visible, and a pool of blood in the dung and earth turning to reddish-brown mush. Mush, welling between her toes, like a row of brown mutant tumours. Blood, pumping freely down her leg.

Suddenly afraid, she staggers, spattering, back to her kitchen, ripping off her dress to staunch the red flow. The cloth is soon dripping. She falls by the fire, dizzy, scrabbling for ash to pack on the wound. Something moves at the corner of her eye, jarring the smoothness of the earth wall. She looks around, bleary eyed. A leopard sits in the shadows behind the fireplace, squashing the cassava she had placed to warm there. Swishing tail, scattering stray bits of wood back and forth. Sebby stares at the leopard and it stares back at her. It stares at her with yellow-eyed expressionlessness. *Dogs, frenzied, howling last night.* The hairs on her forearms prick her skin. *Should run out to the yard.* A surreptitious glance at the entrance, gauging distance. Then she looks at her leg and, *no.* He would be on her in an instant. She imagines his sharp teeth sinking into the wounded flesh, ripping her open. Worry creases her brow.

Schlish. She frets about the squashed cassava, ruined for breakfast. Studies Leopold to see if he's hungry. *Schlish. His persistent yellow stare.* A fly alights upon her leg, making her itch. One of Leopold's front paws lies at an awkward angle, bleeding. Relief floods her. *He's injured. Needs...help.* Beneath his fur she sees the steady heartbeat of him, she smells his basic animal smell. In his yellow eyes she sees her enlarged pupils, and it is strange, strange because she wishes to reach and touch his eyes, make them warm with feeling, with *something,* so empty those eyes, and it is strange. Strange because the emptiness makes her heart go limp; an alien softness comes washing over her, and it beckons, and it brushes away melancholy in a dark, melting liquidity growing into a thread of her heart that unfurls and latches on to the throbbing pulse of the other softness, the weakness opposite her, the warmness beneath the mottled fur, the speckled warm furry skin, beating.

And Leopold's blood flows, staining the floor of her kitchen. The stain spreads, soaked up by the cool earth. It reminds her of a former stain, an old stain she had seen on a different earth. This stain has grown legs, slithering stain legs, creeping toward her. Their blood must not touch. Her own marks the floor – soon they would join, and she didn't want that didn't want that...*should call for help.* The leopard lets out a sound. Startled, she thinks it is her voice. Yellow eyes flicker at her and as she looks dead into his eyes, the fire spits and cracks, she flounders, swims into a yellow inferno. Suddenly all around her flames of Yellow, flames of Eyes licking and singeing her flesh, and through the heat, she hears her name...*Leopold?*

"Sebby." *Coughing. Hurting.* Eerie voice waves, no particular direction, nor diction, obscenely strive for human tone. *"Sebby!"* Now the presence of the Animal crackles primitively in that still, dark room. Now, she tries to rebuff it, but it dominates her charged body. She tries to will it away, but she's smothered, absolutely. Terror seizes her...*can't breathe...*she must yield, and still cannot move. *Relent.* Her mouth works. Pain cramps her leg, jolts her head. Leopold's spots dance before her eyes. *Relent.* Stupefied, she sees the injured animal rise and shuffle toward her, his customary sleek prowl reduced to a shambling gait...*a cure for blood?...*his beautiful speckled skin shining expanding, enlarging, exploding,

And she remembers the day she killed a killer.

I was one with the stricken hour, I was one beating on the wings of steadfast Night.

On that day, when the late afternoon sun deepened on indigo, sending long shadows quivering across tree leaves. I trailed behind Mother, ploughing through wet undergrowth slapping on my arms. Stopping here and there to pick at wild bougainvillea and to inhale the heady scent of frangipan. I plucked wild berries, cramming them into my mouth, staining my fingers with pale yellow juice. I could not resist the sweet yellow guava I knew would have me running to the latrine early the next morning. From time to time, as she picked pieces of firewood, Mother urged me to hurry up, scolding me for eating too much wild fruit. I did not mind. The bundle of semi-dry wood on her back was slowly growing. Mine was not.

We reached the river near the edge of the forest. A sparrow sang sweetly and I was reminded of the dirge of the funeral harpist, of the sometime mournful sound of his woody strings bouncing off the cool surface of the water. But there was nothing sad here as I breathed the clean dung-fresh air, absorbed the evening sounds of bellowing cattle calling their young, the distant murmuring rumble of hungry herds. No sorrow, as the friendly red dusk enshrouded me in gentle violet tones of my mother's urging voice, and I followed the comforting up-and-down movement of her haunches. Across the river, in the huts on the other side, single dots of yellow light from paraffin lamps slowly appeared one by one. A whispering breeze flipped the dusky smell of burning firewood past my nostrils; the muted din of clanging pots aroused a hunger in me. I could hear other children scampering to complete their evening wash before dark; already, the taste of ghee-fried fish was on my tongue.

Like a sinister apparition, the man loomed out of the suddenly livid twilight, a hatchet raised somewhere high above the undefined border of his misshapen outline. I think Mother did not see him. He was a shadow, it seemed, conjured from some obscure depth of my imagination, yet I watched, instantly knowing the intent of the hatchet-man shadow. I watched mesmerized, as he slammed the weapon between her shoulder blades, at the place between her neck and where the bundle of firewood began. Mother uttered a strangled cry and fell heavily to the ground. Wood cluttered to the side, useless. The Shadow pulled the blade of the hatchet from her body. It came out with a sucking sound. As if it did not want to leave that warm place. My mother's blood jumped out, alive, a thick, red metallic-scented geyser. It leapt onto the leaves, which bowed under its weight. Leapt out, attacking the attacker with sharply aimed darts, some of which found their way to me and touched my face as soft slippery kisses, and I — I forgot to breathe. Befuddled, I stared as the man who felled my mother slunk through the sinister bush, the hatchet leaking grotesquely from between his hands. I was hardly ten feet from the blade. He did not see me; instinctively I had squatted beneath the heavy foliage. As if searching for something, he looked about. Fear clogged my throat. He seemed to look directly at me. But he was distracted by the sounds from Mother who was making a gurgling noise in her throat, like she did when she cleaned her teeth in the morning. In the gloom, rustling creatures halted their search for food. The distant mutter of hungry animals stopped. Childish titter faded. A terrible new reasoning welled prematurely in my chest, buttressed by grief, a void quickly filled with unfamiliar understanding. I breathed the wet leaves, the benign insects twitching in my hair, replicating the twitching of mother's body on that wet ground, on that July evening, when I thought, *Mother must not be dead.* Must not be dead. The man turned around and bent over, feeling her neck. As he did so, I recognized his face.

It was Opanga's lover.

Adrenaline of fear spurted in my stomach. Yet I was not surprised when Opanga's lover struck Mother in the back once again, nullified the indecent twitching. Silenced the mewling sounds issuing from her. He stood over her prone body, legs confidently planted astride. His face was determined, set in the deep lines of a task to be completed. My eyes were dry, but my insides ached. They ached. In a sudden flash, I saw myself living and dying in Opanga's house. I saw myself fading, bundled, dumped in a corner of her jurisdiction, becoming a fraction, a mere sliver of myself. I remembered to breathe.

Opanga was my second mother.

She had come to live with us two years ago at the instigation of Okello, my Father's younger brother. Uncle Okello had the kind of eyes that constantly shifted from side to side. Often, I found it difficult to concentrate on what he was saying because his eyes moved around so much. I never knew exactly what he looked at; he seemed to be looking everywhere. One day, I overheard Uncle say to Father: "My brother, you have no children. You need another wife." My mother, who was present at the time, moved her face muscles in a disconcerting way. She was silent. Uncle Okello gave no indication that he noticed. That night, seated in Mother's lap, absorbing the intimate smell of her soap, I asked: was I not my father's daughter? Mother hushed me, putting my head on her breast, telling me I imagined things. But I had seen the dark pain in her eye, and subsequently, I carried the darkness secretly with me wherever I went.

Now, I watched carefully as the Shadow removed a drinking flask from his hip pocket and took two large swallows. He sat at the base of a tree a few feet away. An odor of fermented brew wafted to my nostrils. Night crouched over the forest. I hunched down, too afraid to move, to scratch the itch in my thigh. I knew he was Opanga's lover. I often saw him leave her house in the early dawn, on my way to wash. The first time, I had surprised him at the door of the bathroom behind Opanga's house. I thought it odd that a stranger was in our homestead so early. He had hurried away, not looking back. I decided to mount a vigil. I noticed he would come very late at night on the days Father slept in Mother's house. One night, peering through a crack in Opanga's door, I glimpsed between them similar movements that Father and Mother sometimes made when they thought they were alone at night. I felt sorry for Father. The next day I looked at Opanga with cautious eyes.

I also knew that Opanga did not like me, nor Mother. I could tell from the way her lips curled behind Mother's back. I could smell her enmity in the rancid chunks of chicken she served when it was her turn to cook the evening meal, from the too-tight, hostile braids she made in my hair. As I sat on the short wooden stool beneath her torturous fingers, Opanga would say, in a shrill, loud voice, "Sebby, you lucky child! You know, when your mother was expecting you Omuom punched her six times: three times in the chest and three times in the stomach. Six times! You could have died, Sebby!"

Omuom, Omuom the sorcerer! Omuom whose name was whispered only by those who dared, in dark corners in dark places. Omuom the man, the legend who walked the abyss of the forest, wandering freely the hollows where spirits roamed undisturbed! And I would shrink further into the hard wooden seat, images of Omuom's red eyes floating around me. Opanga would jerk me up by the hair, calling me "Lucky Sebby." I never ate her food. Instead I would spill the soup into a corner and hide the stale chunks in my dress, throwing them to the dogs later. Opanga always commented on how fast I ate. And she invariably cooked Father's food in a different pot.

I was convinced of Opanga's hatred the day I saw her steal into Mother's kitchen, while Mother had stepped out for a moment. Suspicious, I followed, hiding in the shadows. I saw her carefully punch a hole into the steaming *kuon* Mother had just prepared for dinner. She poured a good amount of sand into the meal then patted it back into shape with a wooden spoon so that it looked untouched. Before I could warn Mother, Opanga quickly carried the food to the table, under the guise of helping us. Father, and Uncle Okello who frequently ate with us, were already waiting at the table. We all sat down, with Mother across from me. While Father launched into his usual sonorous prayer, I tried to kick Mother under the table to alert her. Instead, I kicked

Opanga, who pinched me soundly. Father finished praying, and Mother served steaming portions of stew. Father got the first helping of *kuon*. I held my breath, not daring to speak, as he dipped a huge dollop of the cornmeal in the stew and popped it in his mouth. Mother smiled, waiting for his usual compliments. He ground on sand and grit. Immediately, he spat out the offending meal. Mother and Uncle Okello looked on, amazed. An angry glitter had entered Father's eyes. He stood up, his agitation showing itself in the ticking vein at the side of his neck.

"What – what is this? This is – *what?* A joke? You j-jest with me?" He stuttered in anger, pointing a gravy-stained finger at the *kuon* that now flopped limply to one side. Bits of sand and meal and spittle flew from the sides of his mouth. "This is, t-this is, it's a nonsense!" I tried not to laugh.

Mother was perplexed. She put her hands to her head. "What's wrong? What is it? *What is it?*" Father was more infuriated. Large beads of sweat sprang on his nose.

"You don't know. You don't know, eh?" His brow furrowed thunderously. "You're trying to kill me, eh? Trying to poison me? Eh? Poison me, is it? Is that it?

By now I was vacillating between covert giggles, guilt and fear of retribution. Mother's shocked face moved from Father's threatening stance to Opanga's avid looks. Their eyes locked. Mother touched the cornmeal and the sand flaked between her fingers, spilling to the floor.

"Forgive me," she said in a thin, unnatural voice. "I'll prepare some more *kuon*, right away."

But Father would not hear of it. He barked at Opanga to prepare him some "real food," and walked out in a cloud of anger and mistrust. Opanga hurried to obey, her eyes gleaming with something I could not decipher. Father did not sleep or eat in Mother's house for a month.

I felt bad for Mother but there was nothing I could do. We accepted the injustice of the situation with customary resignation. My fear and dislike of Opanga grew and hardened into a brick that settled in the bottom of my stomach. I was always aware of it.

The man stood up and stretched, his job done. He gathered his belongings to leave, fidgeted, and put them down again. He picked a short stick and went crashing in the opposite direction, deeper into the forest. For a moment I wondered what he had gone to do. Then I realized he was looking for a place to use as an outhouse. Presently I heard the sounds of his ablutions. Now was my chance to run back to the village and sound the alarm. A fly-mushroom sprouted directly in front of my eyes, on the branches of one of the shrubs. Mother constantly described their ugly spotted nature, similar to that of dead flies stuck in mouldy bread. She warned me never to touch them. Deadly poisonous, it was said one ounce of fly-mushroom venom could kill an ox within moments. Blight from the past come to anchor, I saw a vision of Opanga's face in the mushroom, jittering amongst the spots of the fleshy plant, her breath spewing fetid and dreadful fumes. I grabbed two large leaves and broke off a chunk of the lethal mushroom, pressing it to a pulp between the leaves, carefully, to avoid touching it. I crept to the tree trunk near Mother's body, opened the Shadow's flask and squeezed the juice from the pulp into the drink. He was returning. Quickly, I replaced the lid of the flask and hid behind the tree. The Shadow reappeared, picked up his things, and started to leave. He took a swig from his flask. The result was instantaneous.

And I watched with grim ten year old eyes as Opanga's lover grimaced and convulsed in the quick throes of death. He jerked about like a headless fowl, hands grappling furiously at the tree bark. A sickly white foam dripped from his mouth and he groaned, vomiting copiously. The poison was ferocious. It gripped him in violent spasms. It became a shadow in the Shadow's veins, swelling and contorting his body. I sat still and crouched, waiting. Eventually he fell to the ground and lay still, the whites of his eyes staring palely in the darkness. When I was sure he did not move any more, I crept out and carried Mother away. She was heavy. The night was dense, death reeked the air. I hauled Mother bumpily along to a clearing in another part of the forest. I lay her down and arranged her limbs neatly about her. Tenderly, I covered her body with wet branches and sat a lonely wake there, laying my head on my mother's cold, stiff breast. Her face was calm and she seemed, in repose, just as she was moments before she awoke that morning, long ago. Lying on her back, the hatchet-wound did not show, the earth on which she lay welcomed her, and she was Mother of old.

I thought of Opanga and her lover and tried to imagine why she didn't like me. Who had told her of Omuom's six punches? I wondered why Opanga hated Mother so much that she had to send the hatchet-man Shadow to kill her. Would she one day send a Shadow to kill me? What did Opanga want? — I knew — she wanted me to be not there. She wanted Mother to be not there. My face was moist and I thought perhaps it was raining again, but there were no rain clouds that night. I prayed to the forest gods to forgive me for bringing Death in there, I prayed to the gods to look after my mother. Opanga wanted me gone and so I would oblige her. It was easy, I thought, easy — the forest would be kind to Mother. I knew that from the way the trees bent compassionately on the face of her grief, the way the coarse grass sprang close around her. I knew the forest would be good to her. I heard my sparrow sing again and my heart wrenched in understanding of the omen I had ignored. Her sharp, startled voice pierced the heart of a dark requiem. The frogs spat brackish swamp water from their flat mouths. Their hoarse whispering became a pillow cushioning the whispering of a thousand insect wings. Beneath it, the crickets' bewildered muttering struck up a humming ululation, and the staccato echo of an owl's moody call arched in the spine of an elegy sung for the unknown. At last, I stood up and ran, ran away, for I knew the forest would be good to my mother. And when Night grew too ominous for my eyes, I ran even further, slashing through the bushes into the open. Ran from the mushroom faces of Opanga and the Shadow, ran and ran, from Uncle Okello who said I did not exist. I ran from Father who perhaps was not Father; I ran away, and finally, when Night took its last gasp, arrived in Nyabera.

Nyabera was a cluster of packed-earth dwellings clutching the hem of a hilly formation. I climbed over the circular range that formed a wall around the village. At the bottom a river ran, hooded under the mists of the morning. From this high point, it was a shimmering line from which many paths branched into different homes. I came down the rocky face of the hills, and dipped myself in the water, washing the sweat that poured from my armpits in spite of the cold air. A woman sat washing clothes by the bank. I waded upstream, looking left and right, wondering which path to take. I came by the woman and stood watching her. Her hands dipped in and out of the water in graceful gliding motions. Her fingers scrubbed brownish linens that she lifted high out of the water so that they slightly obscured her face. She did not look at me. I moved closer and stood in front of her, the water up to my waist. I said nothing. Thin suds from her washing surrounded me and I flicked the muck with my forefinger. She looked at me silently. Her fingers never stopped their dipping and scrubbing motion. Below my chest, I was cold, numb. Rivulets of sweat flowed from my face downstream. The woman's black eyes studied me for a long time, as she slowly rose. She wrung the clothes, dropped them in a bucket, and began to walk up a path directly facing her. Activated by some mesmeric current, I splashed out of the water and followed her down the path that led to a small compound. My feet made a trail of dark indents on the moist earth. The grass growing wild on either side was shiny with wetness, and as she led me to the door of a large hut, the shininess seemed to light up the dank morning. The dawn cold was slowly being replaced by a weak emerging sun that lifted my sweat, yet drove the cold deeper into my bones. My teeth began a loud chattering. I was afraid the woman would hear. She stopped at the door and held it open. I paused, then stepped hesitantly into the dim room. A wood fire burned gently at the back. The smoky room was full of small figures spread casually on the dirt floor. They surrounded a large tray, from which they picked and ate pieces of cassava. As I stepped in, I felt all their eyes on me. Some, chewing suspended, rested briefly on my chattering countenance before continuing to eat. Others stared unwaveringly while their jaws went up and down. My face was suddenly hot. From behind me I felt the woman's insistent hand in my back. Her fingers were soft. I looked around the room. The fire was warm. The faces were gentle. Their eyes were my eyes.

I learned later that her name was Ruby. After I arrived, I just stayed and stayed there. I was unable to speak for a long time in the early years in Nyabera, and nobody pushed me to break a silence that could have been misconstrued as impertinence. Ruby was an enigma. Speaking to me through her silence, through her dark eyes that beat back the shadows of the night, I spent long moments holding tightly to the yellow and brown *suka* tied high around her breasts. Speaking to me through the constant and strong movements of her arms as she ground maize, pounded nuts; in the long months when my muteness tied me up in its twisted, bleak language, and evolved into an impediment so complete it could only be construed as imbecilic. In her eyes I saw no chagrin at the silence that trailed, like a marriage robe, wherever I went. Yet I did my chores, did what I was told to and what I was tacitly required to do — in silence. In the schoolroom in the church, I learned – in silence. Teachers and fellow schoolmates, at a loss for what to do, soon gave up on beatings, threats shouts punchings. I took it all in silence. And so after a time I became the Fool, relegated to the back of the classroom. And it seemed my muteness had indeed created an imbecile of me; but yet I remembered the darkness in my mother's eye, and it would not leave me, would not leave until it became a fifth limb, and eventually, I grew accustomed to my extra limb.

Years later, when the movements of Ruby's stout arms became a pattern fixed in my mind, and many mornings passed in a flurry of gestures no longer cryptic, I smiled. The smile wandered along, meandering its way to the corners of my mouth. That same day, Ruby's left arm, bunched into a fist, banged my chest as I choked on a chicken bone. The muteness which had lived there in a gnarled, dark core was knocked out with the bone, went rolling down the compound and out of the gate. It rolled faster, gathering dust around its knotted edges as we rushed out in pursuit, became a speeding, possessed ball churning down the path, and fell into the river which swallowed it in a loud, fast splash, then quickly returned to its customary smooth silence, as if nothing was ever there. People in the village later claimed they heard the river belching after it ate my muteness.

I began to speak in a voice husky with the unfamiliar motion. The imbecile was leaving. But always beneath the fugitive smile was the memory of soft slippery kisses. Sometimes my hands came away from my face with faint traces of lesions. I think only I could perceive the exact nature of these contusions, their peculiar tendency to appear disappear expand diminish in size, on every part of me, particularly my face. Except — Ruby. She would touch my face gently, as if she were seeking them out, observing the way they grew in the deepening dusk hours when it was their cue to wake. In those hours the kisses sought my attention, sought my attention, throbbed in thick ridges of skin beneath skin beneath unceasing dark ream of skin. They were alive. They were me. And in the daylight hours as they momentarily faded still I would not, could not let my kisses go. Soft feathery hand of my mother — did she think of me at all? Was she angry, that I left her cold and alone in the forest? Angry glitter of my father's eye, did he miss me, wonder where his non-daughter was?

She opens her eyes and looks into the faces of her children. Her husband is by her side, shaking her. "Sebby!" His anxious voice pours warm liquid into her heart. Her injured leg is tightly bandaged...*Leopold.* Her head is cradled in her daughter's lap. The boy holds cool water to her lips; she drinks.

A leopard sits by the fire, swishing its tail. Her husband hunches over and stokes the embers, bringing warmth into the room. His shoulders are magnified shadows moving squarely in the dimness. Something desperate lingers in the smoke coiling over her. She tries to hold on to its thin, grey tail, but it cannot stay, will not stay. It defects, crippled, wisping into the air, into nothing. The leopard is no longer bleeding.

A Second Look

Aesthetics on My Mind

Larry Rivers

The aesthetics of modernism now strikes me as having been a style of the time. Or if I want to be mean about it, a fad. At the time many if not all artists took this aesthetic as a religion governing the present and all of the future. To give an example of the power of this modernist aesthetic let me relate an incident that occurred during my student days at Hans Hofmann's art school. There was a nude female elevated on a stand, quite beautiful I thought, seated in front of our class of about thirty students. As yet I hadn't had too much experience sitting silently in a room with a nude female I didn't know, who had her legs wide open. The aesthetic, quite clearly, wasn't so much what you saw, but the use that you as an artist made of what you saw. You were not supposed to make notice of the fact that you were staring at a vagina. I obeyed its commands. You were now equipped with an aesthetic that governed the use you could put to what you saw. The use could be the marks you made on the surface of the sheet of paper in front of you, and the space and forms that this created.

I was carried away by this aesthetic that demanded I put the vagina to a use other than its usual one. It made me feel I was different from most people — perhaps superior — for here at Hofmann's there were other values that counted. What ended up on my drawing board, on the paper in front of me, was a charcoal drawing of three peculiar rectangles. The rectangles represented Hofmann's success as a modern artist and teacher in keeping me pointed in the direction of becoming a modern artist. It took about a week of looking at the model to take into consideration the other things I felt about her. I knew what Hofmann meant, I knew what we all meant, and how we were supposed to think. Hofmann and the art mood of the times dictated that we not recognize a personal sexual reaction as important — it became gos-

pel, because the other was old hat, Courbet had already done a vagina. I felt
it was courageous and revolutionary to live up to this modernist aesthetic.
What was more courageous and revolutionary than being modern? This was
the aesthetic milieu that we existed in. Still, there was a split in my feelings.
I didn't push my rectangles as much as I was interested in keeping the young
woman there. So that I would have another week to look at her.

To this day the modernist aesthetic has a strong hold. The art critic
Rosamond Krauze recently wrote a piece about Picasso changing from Cubism to Neoclassicism. According to Krauze Cubism was modern,
Neoclassicism was old-fashioned. She saw Neoclassicism as related to natu-
ralism and realism. And since those schools were part of the past, a return to
them inevitably lowered their worth. She considered Picasso's switch from
Cubism to Neoclassicism a betrayal. *Betrayal*...a word used about treason or
sexual cheating? In other words, if you make a choice of something from the
past over something modern you should be hung. When a known art critic
like Krauze makes a statement like that it carries weight and is influential. Her
point of view represents the climate, the received wisdom, that I grew up with
in art. Back then we were sitting there a generation or two younger than any
of these people. So they were like parents. They had authority, and children
for awhile really do believe what their parents tell them. Later they find out
that there was a lot of pressure put on them. Are you going to make art that
will betray their idea of modernity? Their serious beliefs? Are you going to
take away its high position in art?

Here is another example of the received wisdom that's been hanging
around for most of the century: the director of the Museum of Modern Art
Glenn D. Lowry, in a letter this fall to the New York Times, said that the real
problem with "Sensations", the show at the Brooklyn Museum that caused
so much of an uproar, is that the public won't accept the idea of modern
painting or recent new things. And to prove that this public disapproval about
modern art is an uninformed point of view, Glenn Lowry reminds us that
many brand new art works called modern and looked down upon when first
viewed by the public are now today considered to be wonderful things, and
terrific works of art — all the way from Duchamps "Nude Descending a
Staircase", to Picasso's "Demoiselles d'Avignon" up to the present, including
such works as Rauschenberg's "Goat and Car Tire", Roy Lichtensteins's paint-

ings based on comics and many others too numerous to go into.

I feel what younger artists have heard, and continue to hear and pay atten-tion to, is not so much the aesthetics of art: choices about style and subject matter, but rather the factors surrounding the artist's possibilities of achiev-ing recognition accompanied by success, and that has to do with disturbing what's left of public disapproval.

Mayor Rudolph Giuliani seems to know little about shows that exhibit the work of artists under 35. The Brooklyn show which so horrified him, though he didn't bother to see it, was "bad" like a bad boy: the works were ordinary, and as usual for younger artists, derivative. Art has always been a case of younger artists being "inspired" by accomplished older artists. Jenny Sayville in the "Sensation" show presented bigger and more repulsive paint-ings of nudes in the style of Lucien Freud's, who six years ago had a retrospective of them at the Metropolitan Museum of Art.

The work that was the most noticed and written about had a liquid squirted on it by a man later identified as a Catholic, who shouted blasphe-mies as he squirted his prepared concoction, was the least interesting of the exhibition. It looked like the painting of a primitive. It lay flat and still in a bed of easy to like yellows, oranges and red with an embarrassing stereotypi-cal depiction of an African face, the red mouth outlined in white, pop eyes and a wide flat nose. It really had to do with gaining success and using MOMA'S Glenn Lowry's hundred year old esthetic about frowned upon art works turning later into gems. Chris Ofili, the artist in the "Sensation" show, an African living and working in London, didn't have to work too hard. The title he chose for his work, "The Holy Virgin Mary" with the elephant dung in the vicinity, would produce the frowns for the "frowns-to-gems" formula. He is now known, and we are waiting to see what happens to him career-wise and art-wise, but we don't have to wait. The media news or grapevine is that he is working and selling everything he paints. Holy Virgins or just plain Janes.

Speaking of frowned upon work later turning into gems, I am reminded of John Cage, the composer mushroom collector and Zen Buddhist wit, who during his hay day in the 50's and 60's inspired lots of frowns. The jury is out as to whether his history of being booed and damned have turned what he did into gems. He was the Pied Piper of Modernist hope: here is one moment of John Cage in a music hall across the street from Carnegie Hall.

A man in black tie and tails walks slowly across a bare stage to an open grand piano. At the piano he bows long and low. He throws his tails into the air and sits down. He adjusts the height of the seat, fiddles with his shirt cuffs and jacket sleeves. Readies himself for the first piano flourish and stares straight ahead. Suddenly he gets up and reaches over the keyboard into the piano and plucks vigorously one of the piano strings. He straightens up, grabs something on the piano, brings it into his mouth and blows very hard, producing the powerful fluttering sound of a man passing wind, a sound that I knew as a kid as the Bronx cheer. Actually there was a little thigamajig that produced that sound.

The performer was David Tudor. He walks off the stage amid loud clapping. A moment later he comes back for the second offering of the evening. He sits down and performs John Cage's very famous piece "4 Minutes and 32 Seconds of Silence." The audience listens intently to the silence. For them he was continuing to live up to his reputation as the great proponent of the avant garde.

The jury is still out as to whether "7 Radios Playing at Once," another of his compositions, has become a gem. After twenty years the jury no longer is out without a verdict, they are presumed dead. I have not listened to or have heard of anyone listening to "7 Radios Playing At Once". Except for some polyphonic pieces composed in the 1940s John Cage did nothing "musically" until just before he left Mother Earth. But he did influence and broaden the possiblities for art and music. He did become a national guru. I think his love for the other do-nothing genius Marcel Duchamps was unfortunate. Well, Cage and Duchamps at least dumped very little into the already choked river of art.

I keep shifting my interests. I can have a few months when I have visions of the Holocaust, and then, the next few months I'm suddenly doing something that might be considered trite. Like fashion. Though I really can't make much sense of it, except for the continuation of the absurd in art. I go from this to that, and why be ashamed of it? It seems to me this is the human experience. I am talking about the mundane, the everyday Chekhovian stuff of life. Which we pushed away in our early days because we were looking at this blank screen called progress.

Citizen Proust: on Politics and Race

Barbara Probst Solomon

*O*n a wintry February day last year the French Minister of Defense Alain Richard unveiled a plaque at the École Militaire honoring Captain Alfred Dreyfus. It was the one hundreth anniversary of the 1898 publication in *L'Aurore* of "J'accuse", Emile Zola's courageous intervention (Zola was condemned to prison for it) for Dreyfus, condemned to Devil's Island on trumped up charges of treason. Almost forgotten was another courageous act. A twenty-seven year old unpublished novelist instantly organized a group of Sorbonne students and professors; the next morning *L'Aurore* published their support of Zola and Dreyfus. Though France was to go through political convulsions and a venomous wave of anti-Semitism over the Dreyfus Affair only two novelists chose to incorporate it in their fiction at the time it was happening. One was the twenty-seven year old unknown organizer, Marcel Proust; the other was the aging luminary star Anatole France, whom he had persuaded to sign his petition. Proust attended the trial, and his first attempt at a novel, *Jean Santeuil,* written during it, rather reportorially concerns the trial itself. In his eventual masterpiece *A la Recherche du temps perdu,* Proust chose to be less of a direct witness; instead he showed the effect of the Dreyfus Affair on French society.

Though Proust's novels and myriad letters to friends demonstrate his extraordinary political awareness, and his abiding concern with anti-Semitism, (and, as he put it, all the anti's, including anti-Protestantism and anti-Catholicism), Proust's political side has been given skimpy attention by snobby academic critics who have preferred seeing him through the prism of their abstruse literary theories.

Proust's reputation as a precious esthete is ironic: he loathed the fancy French literature popular in his youth and rebelled against the fusty hold the

French Academy had over the French language. He was the first major writer of the twentieth century to examine the roots of racial prejudice, to make it a central theme in his work. The older Balzacian interest in money transactions, in who inherits what, in who stole what, is replaced in Proust by transactions concerning race, and people's ideas about race. In this regard he was almost one hundred years ahead of his critics. In terms of official French culture he was subversive: in his literary imagination he was forever traveling to other countries. He admired George Eliot, Thomas Hardy, Emerson, Dostoevsky, and was an early enthusiast of Stendahl, who went through a long period of obscurity in France as did Melville in America. One can't read *la Recherche,* as many critics have done, as though the Dreyfus affair is a parenthesis about social customs, less important than the novel's loftier more aesthetic matters. The Dreyfus affair is the heart of Proust's aesthetic.

Proust's birth was the result of a marriage that in itself reflected amazing social and political changes. His father, Adrien Proust, the son of a petit-bourgeois who owned a grocery in Illiers (near Chartres) originally had intended to become a priest, did an about-face, became a man of science, then had a meteoric rise as one of France's most brilliant doctors. He played a key role in eliminating the cholera epidemics threatening Europe. He persuaded his friends in the top echelon of the government to adopt a policy of international hygiene, educating French political leaders to the importance of a *cordon sanitaire.* Proust's mother, Jeanne Weil, was the granddaughter of Baruch Weil, a porcelain manufacturer from Wurtemberg. After the Napoleonic wars the persecution of Jews in the Alsace was particularly bad. Baruch Weil joined the wave of German Jews migrating to France where they were granted full rights as citizens under the Napoleonic Code. Jeanne Weil married Adrien Proust in a civil ceremony on the third of September 1870. She refused to convert to Catholicism, though she agreed to baptize her future offspring. Her great uncle, Adolphe Crémieux, the President of the Israelite Alliance and a lifetime senator in the French government, was their witness.

Both sides of Marcel Proust's family owed their considerable political clout to the ideas of the French Republic, and both sides had considerable political clout. Doctor Adrien Proust belonged to President Félix Faure's inner circle. As Minister of Justice Crémieux was instrumental in abolishing slavery in the French colonies and capital punishment for political crimes. He also used his influence to intervene in the plight of Rumanian Jews.

We owe a debt to George D. Painter's and Jean-Yves Tadié's biographies of Proust, but some of their interpretations need modifying. Tadié argues that biographers are wrong in describing Adrien Proust as Catholic, that like many men of science at that time he was atheist. Perhaps he is right. But Tadié's proof, that Adrien Proust refused to enter a court room that had a cross hanging on the wall, only indicates that the very *républicain* doctor believed in separation of church and state. He was Catholic enough to want his sons baptized.

Tadié equates the Weil family's way of being Jewish as being the same as Adrien Proust's presumed atheism. This is mixing apples and pears. The Weils were part of the German Jewish middle class enclave in Paris (they had little, if any, connection to upper class French Jews) that was particularly vulnerable to charges that Dreyfus was a Jew spying for Germany.

Marcel Proust learned a tremendous amount about the Jewish religion from his great uncle Louis. As *A la recherche du temps perdu* indicates, he knew plenty about Rue du Temple and Kosher butcher shops. In his childhood he heard some Yiddish spoken; his Jewish references (a Yom Kippor break fast, a Passover meal) are less abstract than his references to Catholicism. His humor in describing the incongruity (which Baron de Charlus finds offensive) of Jews living in streets named after saints and cardinals is Jewish wit. Being Jewish transcends a specific religious ritual, it involves a permanent state of mind, and one can't imply as Tadié does, that because the Weils only attended Synagogue on high holy days and for family burials in the Jewish cemetery that they were the equivalent of an *homme de science* atheist.

The point is important. We go from there to Tadié's assertion, echoed by other critics including Edmund White in his campy biography of Proust, that Proust's involvement in the Dreyfus Affair had nothing to do with his mother's being Jewish. This is simply wrong. It leaves the door open for others (not Tadié) to falsely accuse Proust of anti-Semitism. The forward in the revised Random House edition also misleads in its euphemistic description of Jeanne Weil as being "of Jewish descent." The lady was Jewish.

In his letters to his friends Marcel Proust was clear on the subject: he acidly wrote to Robert de Montesquiou: "I did not answer the question you asked me yesterday about the Jews. The reason is very simple; while I am Catholic like my father and my brother, my mother is, on the contrary, Jewish...you could have involuntarily have hurt me in a discussion." Proust wrote the Comtesse De Noailles on the occasion of his mother's death: "Since when she married Father, she did not change from the Jewish religion, because in it she saw a refinement of respect for her parents, there will be no church service, only at the house . . . and at the cemetery."

Proust seems to have experienced being of mixed religion one way as a child and another way as an adult. The problem in the Proust household was not atheism or social ostracism, but religious confusion. Proust the child was profoundly alarmed that his mother's religion was different from his. There must have been a moment when he wondered — perhaps while gazing at his mother's portrait of Queen Esther confronting the wicked Haman — Esther's marriage to King Ahasuerus has to be one of the great intermarriages of all time! — who am I? What is my religion? From all accounts Jeanne Weil was not a particularly communicative person, but her family was the dominant influence in the household, and they were Jewish. The Weil side was richer, more cultured than the modest Prousts of Illiers. Proust was almost grown before he noticed a peculiar social fact: ironically, the humble Illiers side was mainstream, while the more powerful Weils were marginal. And how was Proust to assess his father's disjointed trajectory? The future priest married a Jew, baptized his sons, then left his Catholicism to one side and became *un homme républicain*. Was this a case of changed convictions? Or perhaps pragmatic ambition?

Due to both parents, the baptized Proust, along with his brother, was, so to speak, left out in the cold. One can easily intuit the anxious questions that must have tumbled about in his febrile imagination — did this mean he and his mother would have separate deaths? Burials? Separate heavens? Heavens and burials are a preoccupation of the Marcel in the novel. Proust the adult gave up his belief in heaven, but it had an awesome reality for Proust the child. In *Du Côté de Chez Swann* young Marcel's anxiety is caused by his mother's momentary preoccupation with her guest, M. Swann, yet Proust the author drags his readers into an unaccountable swirl of nameless sorrow that goes way beyond the separation which we find a few pages later will be resolved. In the novel Marcel isn't separated from his mother by religion (both are Catholic), so the reader responds emotionally (or is irritated) without quite understanding why, to the anguish of a separation that seems curiously vast. And for the young Proust so it was — for all eternity!

Jeanne Weil's explanation indicates, despite her possessiveness, a lack of understanding of the predicament in which she had placed her adored son. True, her filial devotion to her parents unified her to them, but where was young Proust in this equation? Her possession of a painting of the heroic

Queen Esther couldn't be of any comfort to a puzzled child. Proust's other great trauma, also related to death, was his severe childhood asthma, for which his brilliant doctor father could find no cure. Whatever Proust's later experiences were of feeling socially marginal, though I don't believe they were great, the pain caused by them was nothing when compared to the suffering in his childhood caused by his parent's lack of answers to crucial questions concerning his survival.

So, by the age of nine, the presumably pampered Marcel Proust, in regard to his body and ability to stay alive and his exploration of his true identity, was strangely on his own. He would grapple with his asthma in his odd personal monitoring of the disease, just as he seemed to have sought his own response to his mother's lack of one. She tended toward muteness, her son never stopped talking. In a subterranean sense Proust was an orphan on the lam navigating his own inner world. Far from being a whining invalid, he was as alert as any street orphan, any picaro, in his hyper-attenuated sense of physical danger and keenly honed ability to sight possible paths of salvation. His inability to chose one side over the other, his phobic fear of exclusion, translated into a need on every level, personal and artistic, to unify the universe.

Proust became interested in the ideas of John Ruskin while still a student. In 1897 (he was twenty-six) Robert de la Sizeranne's *Ruskin et la religion de la beauté* hooked him on Ruskin. Proust translated *The Bible of Amiens* into French though his knowledge of English was almost nil. Everything about the process was pleasurable: his mother, who had a good command of English, worked closely with him on the project. So did Marie Nordlinger, the young cousin of his lover, the composer Reynaldo Hahn — Proust loved exchanging opinions with her about Ruskin. The critic's theories on art provided him with a handy way of thinking about religion. He was especially attentive to Ruskin's examples of paintings which depict to the side of a canvass a broken wall or a pile of stones as symbolic of the exact moment when the ancient Jewish religion gives way to Christianity. The title *In Search of Lost Time* also relates to the "lost time" of the ancient religion. Proust could now put his churches in an abstract historical and architectural context, one in which the universe conveniently was unified through beauty, and the liturgy, the specific theological context of Catholicism could be circumvented. There is no scene of the young Marcel at the confessional, no instance where he grapples with his Catholicism. *La Recherche* is as significant for what is left out as for what so abundantly is put in.

During this same period the Dreyfus case exploded in France. Almost overnight Marcel Proust's longed-for bonding to his mother dramatically had fallen into his lap. As he later boasts to friends, he was (at least in his mind) the *first* Dreyfusard: he got the ball rolling by getting the French literary super-star Anatole France to sign the first public petition concerning the case.

In *la Recherche,* with every breath in his being, Proust obsessively entwines Jew and Christian, mainly through a series of intermarriages — he dare not see these religions as being separate entities if he is to bond with his mother. The Dreyfus Affair provided Proust with an engine and vocabulary with which he could externalize his allegiance to her, just as Ruskin's theories on art afforded Proust, ever the mediator (he had no desire to abandon his father), a non-theological bridge to retain the Catholic churches of his childhood. Proust's adaptation of Ruskin's idea of unification through beauty and his use of the Dreyfus case are twin engines that literally roar through *la Recherche,* The Jew, the prototypical minority figure, is removed from the static 19th century caricature and is given the same standing (for better **and** worse) as other characters. Proust's insistence on fluidity, on the idea of the Jew-in-motion, the Jew and non-Jew transformed through the effects of time as spelled out through the social cataclysms produced by the Dreyfus case, is at the heart of *la Recherche.* Willy-nilly Proust drags the novel out of the 19th century. In international modern lingo, in creating as central to his novel the questioning presence of the mestizo mind (no single English word conveys the cultural consciousness of a person of mixed blood and mixed religion), of complex and ambiguous rebellion, he plops the novel squarely into the consciousness and problems of the 21st.

In imagining oneself back to the time when Proust was growing up in the latter part of the 19th century one needs reminding that there was no American pop-Judaism, no Hollywood Yiddish slang, no smorgasbord varieties of assuming the identity: the Holocaust and the State of Israel were yet to come. One was Jewish through adherence to the Jewish God. You were either Orthodox or lapsed Orthodox. Modern habits of adapting religion to one's personal needs weren't available. Karl Marx and Sigmund Freud found their way out of this stony impasse into the modern world which was predicated on Christianity by developing their political and psychoanalytic theories. Proust did just the opposite. In that sense an outsider, he needed to find a verbal way into an allegiance with the Jewish part of his heritage.

Let's look at the madeleine scene in *Du Côté de Chez Swann,* the moment when Marcel the narrator eats the sweet cake dipped in tea, thereby discovering involuntary memory. Let's first examine the passage according to its medical content. Childhood asthma is something I know first-hand; mine fortunately was well-treated, but I can imagine the suffering of a child who didn't have access to modern medicine. What really mattered wasn't the madeleine, but the tea. It contains methylxanthines, a chemical related to theophylline used in the treatment of asthma which relaxes the muscles. The narrator describes a sudden change (whose origins he can't detect) after he drinks the tea and eats the madeleine. This physical change is followed by a physical feeling of well-being — the sensation of physical pleasure occurs just before the flood of involuntary memory.

Until recently the genetic and viral causes of asthma weren't understood. The 1950s psychoanalytic bent for seeing it as primarily psychological was a disaster. Proust's critics followed the psychological lead, thus assuming he had a willful control over it, or that it was imaginary, or a sort of literary disease linked to Dostoevsky's epilepsy. Proust observes (though he doesn't appear to know why) that the flood of memories released (probably due to the reassuring relaxation of his lungs) after the drinking of the tea is involuntary, quite different from a conscious remembering of the past.

The narrator Marcel drinks more of the tea to see if the sensation will be repeated. Proust is medically accurate in observing that it is the original drink that has the strongest effect, just as he is medically accurate when he describes the fumes emitted from the varnish on the staircase Marcel must take on the way up to his room to go to bed as poisonous. Varnish and glue are dangerous inhalants for asthmatics. If we assume this key scene to be somewhat autobiographical then Proust as a child had two very real problems to overcome. He must go up the dangerous stair case with its poisonous life-threatening fumes, and he must go to sleep, which in his mind was connected with dying, with the possibility of losing his mother for eternity.

Let's look more closely at the scene as he wrote it in the novel: the letter Marcel sends downstairs via the housekeeper Françoise to his mother contains an urgent message. The mother remains mute — she doesn't answer it. Proust, usually loquacious, never reveals what Marcel has in mind. Could it be the answer to his question: who am I? Why don't we share the same religion? The mother refuses to join Marcel because she is busy with M. Swann. I am suggesting that this is not the conventional Oedipal scene it generally is assumed to be, but the *ur* scene in which Marcel cannot reach his mother — not because she hasn't kissed him good night, but because *she can't answer his basic question because of her allegiance to a different religion.* This is the clear meaning of her being detained by the grandfather's close family friend, the Jewish Charles Swann, who is "the unwitting author of my suffering."

Critics generally have interpreted this scene as an Oedipal conflict — Marcel trying to wrest his mother away from his father, and asthma as a purely psychological disease fits in neatly with the theory. Well, maybe so — the Oedipal conflict is here to stay. But there's more to the story:

In the novel it is Marcel's father, in one of Proust's favorite gambits, a sort of mix-and-match-the-religion-of-your-choice, who is "standing like Abraham in the engraving after Benozzo Gozzoli which M. Swann had given me, telling Sarah that she must tear away from Isaac" who encourages the mother to spend the night in a bed in Marcel's room. In another scene Proust transforms Jeanne Weil's painting of Esther into a medieval tapestry in the church at Combray; he gives Queen Esther the features of an ancestor of the aristocratic Guermantes family and King Ahasuerus the features of a medieval King of France. Proust was obsessed with Esther — by my casual count there are at least eleven different references to her in *la Recherche.* But like much that intrigued Proust, he had no use for his mother's painting once he had mentally appropriated it for his work. After her death he casually offered it to his brother Robert.

After slamming the door on us so that we can't speculate on the real meaning of Marcel's traumatic relationship to his mother, Proust presents the theme of the mixed religions in another form. The two doors in Marcel's family home in Combray lead to the two ways to reach Méséglise. The French *Du Côté de Chez Swann* literally means on the side of Swann's house, which suggests family relatives as well as a path, and we know that Proust drew on his experiences both in the Weil family home in Auteuil and the Proust family home in Illiers to create his imaginary Combray. One road leads the young Marcel past Charles Swann's estate — he meets lurking off-stage the Baron de Charlus, Gilberte and other characters who will take center stage later on in the novel — the other goes past the estate of the aristocratic Guermantes family.

Painter rightly indicates the two roads symbolize: "the self we are born with and the self which we acquire." In Marcel's travels through time individuals and society continually undergo social and moral transformations. But doesn't the search for the self and lost time in *la Recherche* also include the Jewish self? Should we ignore that these transformations, brought about mainly through the Dreyfus affair and a series of marriages which unite the aristo Guermantes to the Jewish Swann more often than not involve two religions? In one of Proust's letters he alludes to God, then adds: "which God?" Proust said that in speaking the name of a place you possess it: spoken aloud Méséglise sounds like "my churches."

In his letters to the Duchess de Noaille and Laure Hayman (Laure Hayman, the chief model for the seductive Odette de Crécy, curiously, was first the mistress of Proust's favorite great uncle Louis Weil, then the mistress of his father Doctor Adrien Proust, and, finally, Proust's close friend), he emphasized that the Jewish burials on his mother's side following Orthodox custom were immediate. At the grave site. No flowers allowed. Yet in his Proust: *Philosophie du Roman* the brilliant philosopher Vincent Descombes contrasts the mourning customs in Marcel's family to those of the Guermantes and the provincial inhabitants of Combray, whose habits are more ritualistic, formal and socially inclusive, and include great banquets. "For in Marcel's world the word "mourning" does not designate all the public marks of grief and respect one owes to a relative who has died. Mourning is primarily sorrow, a completely inner state which it would be unseemly to manifest too openly."

Descombes has followed the text, and thus assumes that Proust is contrasting the habits of old society with those of the bourgeoisie. But this doesn't quite fly. What do I, as a modern New York Jew, who knows perfectly well that Proust is describing an Orthodox burial, do with this interpretation? Something is askew. Descombes, like many critics, has managed to write a dazzling exposition of *la Recherche* without ever mentioning the word Jew — but can one talk about jazz without mentioning the word Black, or analyze Faulkner without hearing the implicit rhythms of the South, the agony of the Civil War and its defeat, the agony of race? Should we ignore that in describing Rachel, one of the author's most chameleon characters, Proust alludes to Formentor Halévy's opera *La Juive* in which Rachel "pays the price of her joint Christian and Jewish heritage"? In *Jean Santeuil* there is a sad description of a lonely Christmas day. Jean (an early version of the young Marcel) buys himself a copy of *Echo de Paris* which has a story in it by Anatole France and a sprig of mistletoe which he puts in his room. "It's my little Christmas celebration," he nervously tells his mother.

Proust concealed in *la Recherche* the real nature of his childhood misery. Conversely, his youthful involvement in the Dreyfus case produced more of a personal high than one would assume from his depiction of Charles Swann.

Marcel Proust at twenty-three was hardly a lonely Jew inhabiting an exclusively Christian world when in 1894 Captain Alfred Dreyfus, the only Jewish officer in the French army general staff, was falsely accused of passing military secrets to the Germans and sentenced to life imprisonment on Devil's Island. One of the writer's most enduring friendships was with Genevieve Halévy Bizet Straus (the daughter of the composer Fromental Halévy). *Le Banquet* which published his early sketches was founded in her living room by Proust's school friends — the journalist Robert Dreyfus, her son Jacques Bizet, Daniel Halévy and Léon Blum. Culture in the upper middle class of that time, particularly among Jews, was frequently transmitted through family clans. Proust later entrusted Blum's younger brother René, who worked with Diaghilev (he died in a German concentration camp), with his most embarrassing delicate negotiation: to explain to the publisher Grasset that Proust will pay himself for the publication of *Swann.* Along with Leon Blum and Robert Dreyfus Proust also wrote for the remarkable *La Revue blanche,* founded by Thadée Natanson and his two brothers, sons of a successful Polish Jewish businessman located in Paris.

In 1898, when Emile Zola was convicted of defaming the French government with his manifesto *J'accuse,* the *Revue blanche* crowd immediately staged a protest performance of *An Enemy of the People.* The magazine became a center for Dreyfusards. Joan Ungersma Halperin in her excellent *Félix Fénéon Aesthete & Anarchist In Fin-de-Siècle Paris* quotes Jules Renard's journal:

"18 February. This evening at *La Revue blanche.* Everyone passionately involved in the Dreyfus affair. We would sacrifice, wife, children, even our fortune for it. Thadée, who brings us the news, is really becoming somebody."

But Proust's action had been even quicker. Painter points out in his Proust biography that the morning after *J'accuse* was published in *L'Aurore,* the newspaper ran the first installment of the "petition of the intellectuals" demanding Dreyfus's retrial. In *L'age d'or* Proust's friend Fernand Gregh (a founder of *Le Banquet),* described how the two of them corralled Anatole France at his home for his crucial signature. Supposedly his mistress, the wealthy Madame Arman (born Léontine Lippmann), visited him there every morning to make love. France grumbled that Proust would land them all in prison, Mme. Arman shrieked that they would become social outcasts, but the aging writer signed.

Proust masterminded the campaign strategies in defense of Dreyfus in daily meetings at the Café des Variétés with his brother Robert, the *Le Banquet* crowd, the Halévy brothers, Madame Straus's son Jacques Bizet, Robert de Flers, Léon Yeatman and Louis de la Salle. Once Anatole France gave his name they were able to rapidly obtain the signatures of half the professors in the Sorbonne, the manifesto signed by one hundred and four intellectuals jumped to three thousand. Proust's proudly claimed that he was the first Dreyfusard since he was the one who got France to sign. His four years of intense involvement in the Dreyfus case made him as much *un homme d'action* as the subsequent generation of French intellectuals who coopted the definition, whose actions frequently were more muddled and less useful.

Proust's father was furious that his sons had embarrassed him with their public meddling in the case, but Marcel eventually persuaded him to use his influence with the top French political brass to investigate Dreyfus's dangerously deteriorating health on Devil's Island — in insisting that his father attempt to cure Dreyfus physically, Proust was overcoming the sad fact that his father could not cure his illness. During "The Affair" Proust went from being an unknown writer whose talents were known only to a few friends, to enjoying a touch of limelight in the public sphere. Like his over-achieving father (also known for his brilliant medical books) Proust now had become a bit of a public player. More significantly, he brought home the gold ring to *Mama.* He was even better than a Jewish son — he was the numero uno Dreyfusard!

Proust's letters to his mother now make him sound very politically strategic. He peppers her with instructions for his brother Robert on ways to field the angers of the French government, he reminds her to enlist his father's medical help for Dreyfus, and tries to amuse her with a satiric rehash of the anti-semitic remarks that he has heard re: the case. The "Affair" becomes a family affair — it is now "we" against "them". Marcel Proust never forgave Henri Bergson (his cousin by marriage) for not signing his pro-Dreyfus petition. During his entire life he kept score of who did sign, who didn't, and when those who were anti expediently switched and become pro. In a letter to his mother written while he was on vacation he describes the anti-Semitic rantings of a friend's father. The man is furious that the Jews have invaded his territory, the luxurious Hotel Splendide. Proust characterizes him to his mother as an old man besotted by the *Libre Parole,* the anti-Semitic French rag later so useful to the Nazis. In *la Recherche* he transforms the rantings into the Baron de Charlus's diatribe against Bloch.

"... Were you ever formerly a Dreyfusard?" Proust wrote to his friend Sidney Schiff (translation Mina Curtiss). "I was — passionately ...nevertheless, since in my books I am absolutely objective it turns out that Côté de Guermantes appears anti-Dreyfusard. But *Sodome et Gomorrhe II* will be entirely Dreyfusard and corrective." To Schiff's wife he wrote: "I should like to reply to an objection of yours which moved me very much: 'I feel that I shall have many sorrows.' I think perhaps by that you mean, since you so graciously regard Charles Swann as a living person, that you were disappointed to see him become less sympathetic and even ridiculous. I can assure you that it has caused me great pain thus to transform him. But I am not free to go against the truth and to modify the laws that control the characters. The nicest people sometimes go through nasty phases . . . I promise you that in the following volume, when he becomes a Dreyfusard, Swann once more starts being sympathetic. Unhappily, and this causes me much sorrow, he dies in the fourth volume."

In the novel Proust describes the various stages of Swann's life: ". . . having come to the premature term of his life, like a weary animal that is being tormented, he cried out against these persecutions and was returning to the spiritual fold of his fathers... as a sense of moral solidarity with the rest of the Jews, a solidarity which Swann seemed to have forgotten throughout his life, and which, one after another, his mortal illness, the Dreyfus case, and the anti-semitic propaganda had reawakened. There are certain Jews, men of great refinement and social delicacy, in whom nevertheless there remains in reserve and in the wings, ready to enter their lives at a given moment, as in a play, a cad and a prophet. Swann had arrived at the age of the prophet."

There is a moment in the mind of every writer belonging to a minority when he/she questions: am I betraying my beleaguered people (or sexual preference) in portraying some of them as having morally bad breath? At being crooks, or greedy, or having an unappealing physical characteristics? No one would question Dickens's right to create Scrooge, or think that rule Britannica hit an iceberg because of his *louche* characters. But there is a well-warranted nervousness with which a Bellow, an Ellison has to proclaim they are not Jewish or Black, not merely ethnic, writers — Dickens and Hemingway needn't announce that they were not merely British, white or Christian writers, the subject doesn't come up. Proust didn't want to be labeled as Jewish, homosexual or even French. After World War One he shocked his intellectual friends by refusing to sign as too nationalistic a manifesto which called for a world federation of intellectuals under French leadership. He balked at the presumption that France was the guardian of the civilized world. One can't isolate, as has been done with Proust's portrayal of the Jewish Bloch and the homosexual Charlus, the tell-tale phrase that will reveal the writer as the betrayer of his own group. Proust based Bloch on Arthur Meyer, a specific Jew, whom he loathed. Meyer was a vociferous supporter of the most extreme anti-Dreyfusards and converted to Catholicism for opportunistic reasons. Proust never meant Bloch to be a Jewish prototype, but rather a betrayer of his people, and has been misunderstood on this point. Whether a portrait is a slur or humanizing depends on the writer's intent. The depiction of the volatility of human relations, Proust's *intermettences du coeur* — sex, jealousy, sado-masochism, hetro, homo — the lot — is fundamental to his literary aesthetics. The Bible is replete with bizarre sex, nutty passion and primitive cruelty. We don't grasp its fundamental meaning by reading each incident as representing a separate moral universe.

We judge Heidigger not only on his philosophy, but on his bad actions. We judge Sartre not only on his plays, but on his mistaken political beliefs. But, perversely, Proust's intelligent actions, the manifestos he signed, those he did not, and his moral reasons for doing both, are ignored by his admirers.

Proust's letter to the Marquis de Lauris, a liberal aristocrat who was surprised that Proust didn't agree with his championing of anticlerical laws, is illuminating: "I have no idea what you want. Is it to create *one* France? And you think that private schools teach their pupils to detest Freemasons and Jews...it is true that...Jews have no longer been received socially by those who come out of these schools, which in itself makes no difference to us, but which is an omen of that dangerous state of mind that fostered the Affair...[but] the clericalism which foisted anti-Semitism cannot be viewed as identical to Catholicism."

Proust's fears concerning the rise of a nationalistic anti-Semitic right were justified. During the German Occupation the *Nouvelle Française* critic Ramon Fernandez, one of the most gifted interpreters of Balzac and Proust, totally distorted the words of his former mentor. He surgically separated the writer from his Jewish conscience. Charles Swann is depicted as infected with the virus of Dreyfusism, the sickness of his race. Whether Fernandez felt forced to turn Proust's passion for the Dreyfus case on its head, or actually believed his scabrous anti-Semitic comments we will never know — he committed suicide before he could be tried as a collaborationist. How Proust's friend the critic Benjamin Crémieux would have answered Fernandez we also don't know. Crémieux died in Buchenwald after first being horribly tortured in France. Proust's friend René Blum also died in a concentration camp in Germany. Fernandez's critical work on Proust, a standard reference, remains uncorrected — just as it appeared during the Occupation. Sartre totally misunderstood Proust, dismissing him as an irrelevant bourgeois. André Maurois and Albert Camus had a more nuanced view of the writer. But to the degree that France's complicity in the Holocaust remains a somewhat unresolved issue, Proust's clear views on anti-Semitism also have been left in limbo.

In *Jean Santeuil* Proust wrote: "It comes to us therefore as a pleasurable shock to be able to enthrone henceforward an idea previously expelled and humiliated because we lacked respect for what we genuinely felt, when we read a letter written by Monsieur Boutroux in which he states that anti-Semitism is abominable, and the Jews are just as good as Christians, and hear Monsieur Bertrand say that if the juries had any breath of vision at all they would have acquitted Zola, [and] publicly pay tribute to the Scheurer-Kestners and the Trarieux [who defended his innocence]."

In his letter to the Marquis de Lauris Proust speculated that a Catholicism wiped out by laws rather than by lack of belief would produce an even more violently anti-Semitic society. He cautioned that a radical right with no religious beliefs curbing it would be extremely dangerous, ". . . if instead of restricting the freedom of teaching we could restrict the freedom of the press, (he had in mind the pernicious *Libre Parole)* we might perhaps lessen a little the ferments of discord and hatred, but an "intellectual protectionism". . . would have many disadvantages. But what about ourselves — have we the right to hate, too? A unified France would not mean a union of all Frenchmen, but the domination, etc. I am too exhausted to go on with it. . . . Let the anticlericals at least draw a few more distinctions and at least visit the great social structures they want to demolish before they wield the axe. I don't like the Jesuit mind, but there is, nevertheless, a Jesuit philosophy, a Jesuit art, a Jesuit pedagogy. Will there be an anticlerical art? All this is less simple than it appears . . . At this time, the socialists, by being anticlerical, are making the same mistake that the clericals made by being anti-Dreyfusard. They are paying for it today."

Proust's gaze seems to be going far beyond the First World War, the end of *La Recherche,* to the time after his death, to a France morally unmoored as the Dreyfus affair slides unstopped, almost imperceptibly, into Vichy and France's complicity in the Holocaust: "we shall pay tomorrow". The writer who had so magically evoked memory and the resurrection of the past was piercingly accurate in his assessment of France's future fate.

American Dreams

To Jewishness

Kenneth Koch

As you were contained in
Or embodied by
Louise Schlossman
When she was a sophomore
At Walnut Hills
High School
In Cincinnati, Ohio,
I salute you
And thank you
For the fact
That she received
My kisses with tolerance
On New Year's Eve
And was not taken aback
As she well might have been
Had she not had you
And had I not, too.
Ah, you!
Dark. complicated you!
Jewishness, you are the tray —
On it painted
Moses, David and the Ten
Commandments, the handwriting
On the wall, Daniel
In the lions' den —
On which my childhood
Was served
By a mother

And father
Who took you
To Michigan—
Oh the soft smell
Of the pine
Trees of Michigan
And the gentle roar
Of the Lake! Michigan
Or sent you
To Wisconsin—
I went to camp there—
On vacation, with me
Every year!
My counselors had you
My fellow campers
Had you and "Doc
Ehrenreich" who
Ran the camp had you
We got up in the
Mornings you were there
You were in the canoes
And on the baseball
Diamond, everywhere around.
At home, growing
Taller, you
Thrived, too. Louise had you
And Charles had you
And Jean had you
And her sister Mary
Had you
We all had you
And your Bible
Full of stories
That didn't apply
Or didn't seem to apply
In the soft spring air
Or dancing, or sitting in the cars

To anything we did.
In "religious school"
At the Isaac M. Wise
Synagogue (called "temple")
We studied not you
But Judaism, the one who goes with you
And is your guide, supposedly,
Oddly separated
From you, though there
In the same building, you
In us children, and it
On the blackboards
And in the books—Bibles
And books simplified
From the Bible. How
Like a Bible with shoulders
Rabbi Seligmann is!
You kept my parents and me
Out of the hotels near Crystal Lake
In Michigan and you resulted, for me,
In insults,
At which I felt
Chagrined but
Was energized by you.
You went with me
Into the army, where
One night in a foxhole
On Leyte a fellow soldier
Said Where are the fuckin Jews?
Back in the PX. I'd like to
See one of those bastards
Out here. I'd kill him!
I decided to conceal
You, my you, anyway, for a while.
Forgive me for that.
At Harvard you
Landed me in a room

In Kirkland House
With two other students
Who had you. You
Kept me out of the Harvard clubs
And by this time (I
Was twenty-one) I found
I preferred
Kissing girls who didn't
Have you. Blonde
Hair, blue eyes,
And Christianity (oddly enough) had an
Aphrodisiac effect on me.
And everything that opened
Up to me, of poetry, of painting, of music,
Of architecture in old cities
Didn't have you—
I was
Distressed
Though I knew
Those who had you
Had hardly had the chance
To build cathedrals
Write secular epics
(Like *Orlando Furioso*)
Or paint Annunciations— "Well
I had David
In the wings." David
Was a Jew, even a Hebrew.
He wasn't Jewish.
You're quite
Something else. "I had Mahler,
Einstein, and Freud." I didn't
Want those three (then). I wanted
Shelley, Byron, Keats, Shakespeare,
Mozart, Monet. I wanted
Botticelli and Fra Angelico.
"There you've

Chosen some hard ones
For me to connect to. But
Why not admit that I
Gave you the life
Of the mind as a thing
To aspire to? And
Where did you go
To find your 'freedom'? to
New York, which was
Full of me." I do know
Your good qualities, at least
Good things you did
For me—when I was ten
Years old, how you brought
Judaism in, to give ceremony
To everyday things, surprise and
Symbolism and things beyond
Understanding in the
Synagogue then I
Was excited by you, a rescuer
Of me from the flatness of my life.
But then the flatness got you
And I let it keep you
And, perhaps, of all things known,
That was most ignorant. "You
Sound like Yeats, but
You're not. Well, happy
Voyage home, Kenneth, to
The parking lot
Of understood experience. I'll be
Here if you need me and here
After you don't
Need anything else. HERE is a quality
I have, and have had
For you, and for a lot of others,
Just by being it, since you were born."

Easy Street

James Purdy

Mother Green and her faithful friend Viola Daniels, shut away as they were in their old four story brownstone, at the end of the mews, were unprepared for a sudden change in this unfrequented neighborhood. Big trucks with deafening sound equipment had moved in, men with bullhorns were shouting at other men up and down the street, and the whole area was roped off from access to the adjoining neighborhood.

Mother Green had recently celebrated her 96th birthday, and her companion Viola (she looked on her as a daughter more than an attendant) was some thirty years younger.

Their neighbors spoke of them as ladies in retirement who seldom ventured out into the great city beyond. At the unusual noise and tumult today the two friends stood at the windows in wonderment and incipient alarm.

Then all at once (it was July) a summer thunderstorm of unusual violence struck the neighborhood. Hail and blinding downpour and, as the newspaper called it, "dangerous and prolonged lightning" descended. The thunder was so loud no one had ever heard such peals. It reminded the older men of the sounds of battle and bombing.

The rain continued to come down in unpitying volume, interspersed with hailstones the size of duck eggs.

The two retired ladies drew away from the window and pulled down the blinds, but curiosity tempted them to occasionally peek outside.

What they saw was that all the men and the bullhorns and the trucks and the infernal shouting had ended. The disturbers of the peace could have been swept out to sea, who knows. Except for the unceasing downpour the street was as quiet as an uninhabited island.

It was then they caught sight of somebody seeking shelter from the flood. He was standing under their tiny front porch, drenched to the skin, his clothes so tight pressed against his body he resembled a naked drowned man, and such streams of wetness came over his face he appeared to be weeping in torrents.

Catching sight of Mother Green and Viola, the stranger made frantic gestures in their direction with his dripping hands.

"Open the door for him," Mother Green spoke to Viola.

Viola was taken aback by such a command, for Mother Green seldom if ever admitted anybody inside, and her voice now rang out like that of some woman preacher.

Viola hesitated only a minute. She flung open the door, and the drenched man staggered inside, and whether from being blinded by the torrent or through weakness, slipped and fell on his knees in front of the two ladies.

Streams of water flowed from his sopping vestments.

Meanwhile Mother Green was whispering to Viola that in the little closet off the parlor there was a man's bathrobe left from a roomer who had stayed with them some years ago, and a number of towels.

The stranger was given the bathrobe and towels and was ushered into the "little room" off the parlor. The two ladies waited uneasily for him to come out.

Many things crossed the two women's minds of course. Such as who, in fact, had she admitted to their solitary domain. What if he was dangerous or wanted by the authorities.

When their visitor emerged, Viola let out a short gasp, and Mother Green gave out a sound somewhere between astonishment and relief.

They saw the stranger was, like Mother Green, a very dark African, but he was also very young. His almond-shaped eyes betokened something very like benediction.

He sat down on the carpet and crossed his bare legs. He gave out his name which was Bewick Freeth.

"We were filming out there," he said, and he stretched his right arm in the direction of the downpour.

Neither then nor later did the ladies take in the word "filming." If it was heard at all, it was not understood.

But what made the impression now on the older woman was she heard in the stranger's speech the unmistakable accent of Alabama from where she had come so many decades ago.

Replying to her question if she was right about his speech, Bewick did not smile so much as grin, and all his gleaming white teeth reinforced his good looks.

It slipped out then both Mother Green and Bewick Freeth were from almost the very same section of Alabama, near a small lake, and the name Tallassee was mentioned.

Both ladies could now relax and smile.

Mother Green, at hearing the town named in a peremptory, even a slightly grand manner, urged Viola to go to the kitchen and bring some refreshment.

Bewick smiled at hearing her order and closed his eyes.

Mother Green liked the way he tasted the drink he was given, in small almost delicate sips, nodding his head with each sip as a kind of thank-you.

Yes, she saw she had not been mistaken in him, had not run any risk. And meanwhile the sound of Alabama in his speech brought back to her in a rush her almost forgotten memories of the South she had put behind her.

Looking at him closely, she wondered at times if she was not "seeing things." The terrible storm, his sudden appearance, their reckless admitting of a total stranger—Mother Green did wonder, but she knew she was right. She knew then she must have been meant to know Bewick Freeth.

Viola Daniels listened then as the visitor and Mother Green spoke. Viola Daniels was light-skinned and what Mother Green sometimes joked was that she looked almost more white even than an octoroon, while the more one looked at their visitor his very dark skin stood out deeper in hue.

Mother Green was easy then, not only because of his Alabama speech but the deep darkness of his face, as well as his long eyelashes, and she could sense the sweetness of his breath coming to her in waves.

Later, much later as Mother Green recalled his coming, it was as if they had been expecting him. He had walked in and they had spoken to him like he had been there before. No stranger. Even the glimpse Mother Green got of an earring in his left ear was no surprise to her.

They set aside for him the large front guest room up two flights of stairs. It had not been resided in for some years.

Bewie, as he asked to be called, one day after some time noticing Mother Green's limp, asked if she was in some discomfort from the way she walked.

Mother Green hesitated and fidgeted.

"She suffers from bunions," Viola informed him, and Mother Green stared reproachfully at her.

Bewie in a strange gesture clasped his hands.

"I know the very thing," he cried in the face of Mother Green's displeasure her affliction had been made known.

The next day Bewie instructed Viola to prepare a small basin of mildly hot water to which he added some herbs he had purchased.

Had he not done another thing, his bathing of Mother Green's painful feet would have insured him a refuge with them.

Only Viola looked a bit uneasy. More and more she had a kind of bewildered air.

"What is it, Viola, dear?" Mother Green wondered while Bewie busied himself with some self-appointed task in the kitchen.

"Nothing, Mother."

"You act a little put out," the older woman spoke almost in a whisper.

Yes, she saw perhaps Viola was hurt or maybe just jealous. And her almost white face between Mother Green and Bewie's fierce complexions may have been a cause. She felt in a way set aside. And she wanted more than anything to be close to them, important to both.

Mother Green patted Viola's hand and kissed her middle finger. "It's all all right, Viola," she whispered.

And so it began, their life together, Mother Green and Viola and this perfect stranger from Alabama.

He did not tell them what his work or calling was from outside. He only indicated that he would be out from part of the day and perhaps even some of the night.

"It's my present livelihood," he added, letting them know he would have to be absent every so often.

It all seemed unsurprising at least to Mother Green—as in a dream even the unbelievable will be perfectly believable.

He had come to stay with them and they were to respect his absences and his sparse explanations. "It's his livelihood," Mother Green repeated his words to Viola.

Then, as the stranger stayed on, Viola's uneasiness grew. Often she would go to the big hall mirror and look at her own face. She saw that not only was Mother Green closer to him because he spoke in an Alabama accent, but closer likewise because like her his face was the welcome dark color.

"You will always be dear to me," Mother Green said one afternoon when they were alone and she realized Viola was grieving.

Viola tried to swallow her pride and went about as before, caring for

Mother Green. In fact, after the arrival of Bewie she was more attentive and caring than before, if that was possible.

But Viola as if confiding to herself would think, "Bewie is everything to her. More than if he were her own flesh and blood."

One day Mother Green acted a little uneasy. "Where do you suppose Bewie goes? We don't as a matter of fact know much about him now do we," she reflected.

"We don't know nothin', you mean."

Oh Viola, who is he, yes, who is this Bewie?"

Mother Green then held Viola's hand tight in hers.

One thing of course they could not help noticing. Bewie hardly ever returned without he was carrying a heavy package or two.

At the ladies' look of astonishment, he sat down and said in a joking tone, "My wardrobe. In my profession, you have to look your best. And the film people of course insist on it."

Again the word *film* did not register with the ladies. And they were too shy to ask him outright what required so many clothes.

The clothes, or the *wardrobe* to use his term, intrigued Mother Green and Viola. They spent—yes hours discussing all the clothes he was required to possess because, yes, his *livelihood* made them a necessity.

The curiosity became too strong for Mother Green. One afternoon she told Viola she would like to go upstairs to see how he kept his room.

Viola frowned, "Those stairs are steep and rickety. And dangerous!"

"Oh you can come along then and steady me, Viola dear."

Mother Green was nearly a cripple from her bunions, but she must see how he kept his room.

It was more than a big surprise to her.

She opened the big closet door and stared at some brand-new three-piece suits, fancy cravats, big-brimmed straw hats, and shiny elegant high-shoes.

"All bandbox new!" Mother Green sighed and sat down on the easy chair Viola had brought from downstairs.

"What are you doing?" Mother Green exclaimed, for she saw Viola had brought with her the big thermos bottle.

"I fetched us some hot coffee."

Mother Green sipped the steaming brew.

"What did I ever do, Viola, to deserve a child like you."
A little sob escaped Viola, undetected probably by Mother Green.

So the mystery of Bewie deepened. Yes, who was he after all, and where did the expensive suits and shoes and ties and gold cufflinks come from.

Yet both Mother Green and Viola believed in him. He did not scare them. Even had he had no Alabama accent, he was one of them they were sure. He was not really a stranger in spite of his mysterious ways.

If only Mother Green loved me as much as she does Bewie, Viola would sometimes speak out aloud, knowing of course Mother Green's deafness would not let her hear.

It appeared to Viola Daniels at times that both Mother Green and Bewie had returned to Alabama to take up again their life in the South and converse in their unforgettable Alabama speech.

Viola sometimes thought about running away. But where could she go after all. She was no longer young. Who would want her. And beside all that she would never have the heart to leave Mother Green.

"Let her love Bewie more than me!" Viola would then say out loud. "What's you talking about over there," Mother Green would say in a joking voice. "I hardly know myself, Mother Green," Viola would say in a loud voce, and then the two ladies would both laugh.

It became if possible less and less clear both to Mother Green and Viola Daniels how and why Bewie had become part of their lives. It was especially unclear at times how he had appeared at all. Once Viola almost got the word out, "Like a housebreaker!" but she caught herself from saying it at the last moment. But it would have been true maybe to say an apparition. "We always knew Bewie," Viola said long afterward.

Something had been on Bewie's mind. Perhaps that's why he was so happy always performing so many tasks for Mother Green. He tidied the place up. He even washed the large front windows. And one evening he insisted on preparing a real Southern dinner for them.

But his presence in the house became shorter, less frequent. Sometimes he did not come home at night. Sometimes he barely spoke to them. He became sad, downcast...even tearful. Once Mother Green had heard this terrible sobbing in the front parlor. She didn't know what to do. It didn't sound like anybody she had ever heard. It sounded almost like a heartbeat. She opened the door ever so soft and there he sat slumped in the big chair just crying his eyes out. She closed the door as soft as she had opened it, waited a while, and then called out very loud, "Bewie is that you?" When she went in the front parlor his face was as dry as chalk, and he was composed and looked like always. Yes, as Mother Green kept repeating, "Something is on his mind. Something is worrying him."

Something too was on Mother Green's mind. She would start to say something to Viola, and then she would stop all of a sudden, or in Viola's words "clam up." She would clear her throat and relapse into silence.

"Do you remember Ruby Loftus?" the old woman broke her silence.

Viola said yes though she was not sure she did remember Ruby.

Mother Green smiled, lapsed again into a brief silence. Then she began to speak hurriedly, "She was what they call a psychic reader. She had second sight. Well, she often read for me. What she got for me was usually mighty interesting if not exactly calming. But what she told me one time happened years ago. Before your time, Viola. She "read" me, and lord how she read me. She told me that in my later years there would come into my life a wonderful presence, a shining kind of being who would bring me many of the rewards and fulfill many of the promises I had never thought would be mine. It would be harvest time."

Viola closed her eyes.

"That prophesy has come to pass," Mother Green went on. "My reward, my shining blessing has got to be Bewie Freeth."

Up until then Viola had never known Mother Green to offer her strong drink except in case of illness.

Tonight she asked Viola to go to the little cupboard in the pantry and on the first shelf reach for the whisky and then pour out two glasses.

Viola was even less used to strong drink than Mother Green, but she knew she must not disappoint her old friend after she had told her of the prophesy of the psychic reader.

And Viola was as sure as sure could be Ruby Loftus had told the undeniable truth. Sad as Viola was that Bewie occupied so deep a place in Mother Green's heart, a place Viola would never hold, nonetheless, Bewie Freeth, beyond the shadow of a doubt, as if foretold by an angel, had come into the old woman's life a late blessing and a special gift.

Mother Green was so happy when Bewie was around, Viola Daniels later remarked often to visitors. She never did seem to reckon it would all come to a close.

The first night he didn't come home, or rather the first dawn, Mother Green was calm.

"Bewie will be home soon, mark my word," she would smile.

But one day was followed by another. Mother Green would hobble up to where he had his room.

"He'll be back if only to wear his outfits," she told Viola.

"Maybe we should notify the police," Viola said one evening after several weeks went by.

It was the only time Viola and Mother Green disagreed.

"Don't never say police ever again in my presence, Viola Daniels. If you have to do somethin' get down on your knees and pray, but don't say we should call the law."

Mother Green relied on Viola Daniels in so many ways, but principally to keep her straight on time and events. Viola knew the old woman's memory had begun to show the effects of time.

Often Mother Green would inquire, "When was it that Bewie came to us?"

"Don't you recall. Mother. He come on that blusterous July night."

"Which July though?"

"Why, July last, dear."

But in a day or so Mother Green would ask the same question over again.

Viola choked up then with the realization her old friend was beginning to fail, and she could not restrain a tear. She knew Mother Green was only holding to life at all because of Bewie.

"He was her all and everything." Viola would tell of it some time later.

Another thing which worried Viola was that Mother Green continued to steal upstairs to Bewie's room despite the fact she had such a problem managing the rickety stairs.

At the foot of the stairs Viola would listen. She could hear Mother Green lifting up his shirts and muttering something like, "Why ain't you come home, Bewie, when you know we miss you so."

Finally though if Mother Green didn't guess at the truth, Viola did. The truth that Bewie Freeth was gone for good.

But yet, if he had gone, his duds and finery were left behind.

Viola herself could not help stealing up the stairs and going to his closet. She took down his silk underwear, his pure cotton shirts, and once while arranging his Palm Beach suit on a handmade hanger, something fell out of one of the pockets onto the floor. The slight sound it gave out falling frightened her almost as if it was a firearm going off.

Slowly she picked the object up. It was a newspaper clipping. And the clipping was rather recent from a Chicago newspaper. Its heading read: *METEORIC RISE OF UNKNOWN YOUTH.* Her eyes moved on the article! *Bewick Freeth who made hosannas ring nation-wide from his two previous films is now the undisputed charismatic idol of the hour. He has never been greater, his success unanimous.*

Viola let the newsprint slip to the floor and sat down heavily on one of Mother Green's upholstered chairs. She felt faint, she felt, yes, betrayed, perhaps even mocked. Here he had been with them and never let on who he was. Yes, he had deceived them.

At the same time she felt he had not really lied to them. She knew he must have cared for them, a little perhaps, but, yes, he had been happy with them. He had often said he never wanted to leave, that she and Mother Green were "home to him." And now the clipping.

Sitting with Mother Green that evening, she was gradually aware the old woman was staring at her.

"Yes?" Viola managed to say.

"You look like you seen a ghost," Mother Green said. When there was no answer from Viola the old woman clicked her tongue.

"You know somethin' I don't know, Viola. You know somethin' and you know you know somethin'."

"Maybe I have found out who Bewie really is, Mother Green. And how come he ain't here anymore I guess."

"If you know something Viola, let's hear it, all of it."

"Bewie Freeth is not like us, Alabama accent or not. He's a famous movie star. What he was doin' here with us, well who knows."

Slowly, unostentatiously, as if handing Mother Green something she had perhaps asked for, Viola handed her the clipping.

The old woman put on her spectacles. She read and reread the article from the Chicago paper.

To Viola's consternation Mother Green, after putting away her spectacles, handed back the clipping to Viola without a word. Was the old woman beginning to fail, beginning not to take in things. No, not at all, Viola was sure. The truth about Bewie, the truth who he was had shocked her into this silence. After a long pause Mother Green smiled a kind of smile that meant, who knows, the dream was broken.

Doing her evening sewing, Viola stopped working for a moment and said, "Mother Green."

"Yes," the old woman answered.

"I come across upstairs in the little store room along beside the games of checkers that old German OUIJA board, planchette and all.

Mother Green's jaw dropped, and she reached in her side pocket for her handkerchief and wiped her eyes.

"You don't say," she spoke in a far-off voice. When Viola said no more, Mother Green, adjusting the lavaliere she wore about her throat said, "You mean you want to bring Ouija out then."

Viola nodded. After a silence she said, "I thought, Mother Green, Ouija might explain things to us, do you reckon?"

"You mean Bewie?"

"Yes, maybe."

"Explain him how."

"You said yourself the other evening as we lingered over tea that we can barely remember when or how he came to us."

Mother Green sighed in an odd off-hand way.

"And you think Ouija can tell us the why and how of him. And whether we'll ever see him again."

The next day Viola brought the Ouija board out and set it on the card table.

"I declare," Mother Green said.

When they had arranged the board both ladies admitted they hardly dared begin.

"Do you ask Ouija somethin', Viola, now."

They put both their hands on the planchette. It did not move.

"You got to ask it, Mother Green, dear."

Their hands began moving slowly, sleepily after a while.

"No, no, Viola, you ask it."

The board moved jerkily, stopped and then began slowly to move to the letters.

It spelled KEWPIE.

The ladies giggled in spite of themselves.

The planchette moved wildly, then slowed down, then very pokily spelled

LUKY THE DAY HE COME TO YOU

& LUKIER THE EVENIN HE BE GONE

LUKY LUKY LADIES

"Mother Green, whether it's me or Ouija, but Ouija don't know how to spell now, do he?" Viola commented.

"But is he gone forever?" Mother Green asked Ouija. The planchette was still, perfectly still.

Viola began to see then that she should never have let Mother Green know that Bewie was a famous film actor. It was after Mother Green found out that fact that she began going down hill in no small measure. She complained too of what she called the weight of memory.

"After a while," Mother Green spoke in a low voice now to Viola almost as if she was praying, "there is too much to remember. And there is too much of past days to know *when* it happened, and sometimes there is the doubt maybe it did happen or I dreamt it. And the people! All the faces and the talk and the shoutin' from the beginning until now. Why all those years of mine in Alabama alone would take another fifty years to tell you about."

But Viola was sure it was Bewie's absence and his never coming back which pushed her down to what she called the shady side of life. "I'm going down the shady side now" she had once said before Bewie came, and now it had got worse than shady—it bespoke the deep night.

"Where is he?" she would often shout coming out of a dozing spell in her chair.

"Now, now Mother," Viola would respond.

"You don't tell me nothin', do you, Viola."

"Whatever you ask I will tell you if I know," Viola answered.

"I feel I am bein' kept in the dark," Mother Green would mumble.

And so they spent many evenings consulting Ouija, but sort of dispirit-edly now. If Ouija had had one fault, that of misspelling words, now he had a worse fault, he was tongue-tied most of the time. When not silent Ouija stammered.

Mother Green spoke more and more of Ouija in fact as if he was a person, a person sort of like Bewie Freeth who was visiting them but wouldn't be permanent, a kind of transient somebody, yes, like Bewie Freeth had been.

Sometimes Viola wondered if she and Mother Green had only dreamed there was a Bewie Freeth. And Viola often thought Mother Green might be having the same thought.

They were both waiting for something, and Bewie had intercepted the wait, but now that he was gone, as Ouija said, they would have no occupation but to wait together.

Viola had taken over the tasks that Bewie had performed, bathing Mother Green's feet and bunions in the medicated water, cleaning sometimes the wax out of her ears (though it didn't cure her deafness) and answering the endless query, "Do you think Bewie is ever comin' back?"

Then one day she up and told Mother Green Bewie had been gone for nearly a year, but she was glad for the first time Mother Green's deafness had prevented her from hearing her words.

Viola's sorrow grew as she often confided to herself when alone.

Mother Green seeing Viola's sorrow spoke up sharply, "Viola, Viola, what ails you you are so weepy. What is going on, dear child."

"I didn't know I was weepy, dear Mother," she said trying to smile.

"You miss Bewie, don't you."

But the mention of Bewie brought back to her how Mother Green's memory was playing tricks on her. For she always wondered where Bewie had gone, and she kept asking when he would return.

As many times as Viola told her that Bewie was gone, and would not come back, she saw that Mother Green either did not hear this explanation or having heard it erased it from her memory. For Mother Green, Bewie was a timeless part of their life, and so if he was gone, no matter, he would be back.

The heavens themselves seemed to give warning of what was happening, Viola Daniels would later tell people who visited.

Mother Green and Viola heard the sound that was like thunder, only probably closer and scarier. The sky seemed to blossom with many flaming colors which then fell like stars.

Difficult as it was now for both of the ladies to trudge up the long stair-well, they felt they had to find out what the commotion was.

It took Mother Green nearly a half hour to reach the top. How she sighed and groaned, and her bunions were killing her. She would rest on some of the steps before going further.

"I should have brought the smelling bottle, dear heart," Viola muttered, but Mother Green only gave her a reproachful look.

The top floor had great high huge windows. They no more got up there than she realized what it was.

"Fireworks," Mother Green exclaimed.

"It means something," Viola shook her head.

"If that's what you feel, we might consult Ouija."

This time Ouija was not evasive. The planchette began to move as soon as they touched it.

Mother Green came up with a start when Viola queried, "Where's Bewie?"

Ouija responded, "IN THE SWEET BY-AND-BY."

"And what do you mean by-and-by, Ouija?" Viola asked as Mother Green stared at the board.

Viola stirred uneasily for she knew Mother Green was alert tonight.

"HE GONE," Ouija responded.

At this, Mother Green sat up very straight in her chair but retained her hand on the planchette.

"Gone where?" Viola raised her voice.

Ouija moved at once.

"GONE TO CAMP GROUND."

"Where Camp Ground?"

Ouija did not move. Viola raised her voice, but the planchette was still, and then finally Ouija spelled again:

"CAMP GROUND."

Viola Daniel's own memory was getting almost as bad as Mother Green's, and it wasn't exactly due to her drinking the strong spirits she found in the cupboard. No, Viola's memory was not what it was, say, the day Bewie had arrived.

She tried to remember how she had learned for a proven fact that Bewie had passed over. Soon after their episode with the Ouija , one day while out shopping, Viola in one of her now common absent-minded spells, found

herself more than a few blocks away from Mother Green's, in a kind of prom-
enade where there were expensive shops, saloons, and motion picture theaters.
She saw that one of the movie houses was draped in black cloth, and there
were wreaths and flowers and signs all everywhere. Her eye caught sight of
the marquee. She stopped dead in her tracks. She kept reading over and again
the lettering:

**"YOU WILL ALWAYS BE WITH US BEWIE. FOREVER AND A
DAY"**

Viola braced herself and went up to a uniformed man who was in charge
of inspecting tickets as you went into the theater.

"Excuse me," she began. The uniformed man looked at her carefully and
blinked.

"Tell me if Bewie Freeth . . ."

He did not let Viola finish but pointed to a large oversize photo from a
newspaper. Without her glasses Viola was hardly able to read the print, but
finally at least one sentence came clear. Yes, Bewie Freeth was no more, had,
in the words of Ouija, gone to Camp Ground.

It was several nights later that the first of the gatherings outside Mother
Green's house began. They were mostly of young men, some of whom played
every so often on a horn, others on a sax, and still others blew on what looked
like a little cornet. When they quit playin' they shouted to passersby, "Bewie
lived here for your information!"

Viola crept out on the frail front porch.

A smothered shout went up from the musicians.

There was the strong smell of something smoky, and as if it were their
final number, each of the players took out big handkerchiefs and waved them
at her in token, one supposed in tribute, to their idol Bewie

Mother Green slept through it and other "live" performances that would
take place as a tribute to their hero.

Looking at Mother Green after one of these performances, Viola heard
her own voice say, "Lucky you, dear heart, you don't know what this is all about
on account of I wouldn't know how to tell you, and I don't understand it
maybe any better than you do or would."

"So, he in the sweet by-and-by," Viola said later that night to herself after she had had a shot of spirits in the kitchen.

Time got more and more mixed up. After the night of the fireworks there was a long vacant pause in everything.

Viola was the first to say she thought something was about to bring them news. And this time it was not Ouija who warned them, no it was a ticking sound Viola heard coming from Bewie's closet.

Viola trembled and even sobbed a little. Yet she had to investigate what on earth was making a ticking sound in the clothes closet.

It took her a long time to locate where the sound was coming from. She had no idea Bewie would carry an old-fashioned very heavy, yes, antique pocket watch. Why it seemed to weigh three pounds.

She removed it from his breast pocket. The sparkling gold watch was ticking! After all these—was it months or years?

Later Viola talked with a very venerable watchmaker, oh Mother Green said he must have gone back to the early days after emancipation. Watches and clocks, old Tyrrwhit assured her, like dead people, sometimes would come to life whether by means of a loud noise, or a building shaking, or often because of an earthquake or cyclone, a very old clock or watch, that had not ticked for ages, would all of a sudden begin ticking away. Clocks he assured Viola were imbued with a spirit all their own, and a watchmaker, a good watchmaker, knows the clock has a mind and knowledge superior to the watchmaker.

She took the ticking watch down to Mother Green who stared open mouthed at it and agreed, oh yes it was a sign.

Nehemiah Highstead accompanied by two lawyers arrived in weather even more stormy than the day when Bewick Freeth had entered the lives of the two ladies.

Nehemiah was an elderly black man who wore very thick colored glasses from which there extended a fluttering kind of frayed ribbon. His right hand trembled and he continually wiped his eyes with a large handkerchief from which there came a faint sweetish aroma.

"This is a very strange bequest, ladies," one of the attorneys finally began after looking about from ceiling to floor suspiciously.

"Mr. Freeth came to our offices only a few days before his sudden decease."

Viola Daniels' full attention now rested on Mother Green whose face was devoid of expression. Had she heard the word *deceased*. And having heard it did she understand it, understand, that is, what Viola had tried to tell her time and again that their Bewie was no more.

"You are the sole inheritors of what is more than a modest fortune. Much more!" the attorney continued.

He waited sleepily, peevishly for his statement to take hold of his auditors as a judge will wait before he gives the verdict.

"He also provided for Mr. Highstead to look in on you ladies and be of any assistance as you may wish. Reverend Highstead was an acquaintance of Mr. Freeth from the actor's first days in the city. He is the pastor of the Ebenezer Resurrection Church which is on the other side of town. It would be completely up to you as to how much and to what extent you would request his support."

Viola nudged Mother Green from time to time as the old woman kept closing her eyes and breathing heavily, but the three gentlemen appeared not to notice this.

Finally the second attorney drew out from a Moroccan satchel a sheaf of papers. "If you ladies then will sign here on these dotted lines," he pushed the stiff legal pages to Mother Green.

Grasping tightly the pen he gave her she was able to sign:

Elgiva Green

The attorney repeated the name she had put down, confirming that she was the Mother Green designated in the will. It was, strange to say, the first time Viola Daniels had heard Mother Green's Christian name spoken out loud.

When the ladies had signed, Nehemiah Highstead rose, bowed his head, and asked everyone to join him in prayer.

It went something like this, as Viola recalled it some time later, "We are gathered here today chosen to represent a young man who went under the name of Bewick Freeth, originally from Tallassee, Alabama, who gained brief but almost universal fame as a film actor. We applaud his devotion to Mother Green and Viola Daniels and his generosity in bequeathing these two respectable ladies with his entire fortune. May the Almighty grant us the wisdom that we can administer it with integrity and zeal. We ask thee, eternal Master, to bless us all as we stand here in prayer and supplication."

No one could have foreseen the result of the two ladies coming into what even to wealthy persons would have been a sizable fortune.

Their disbelief they had inherited so much money was followed by a kind distemper and unwillingness to accept their change of fortune.

Ladies from the Ebenezer Resurrection Church called frequently not merely to rejoice with Mother Green and Viola so much as to give them the courage to accept their unbelievable change of circumstance. They also discreetly suggested that some of the money could go to the Church.

Mother Green hardly heard anything anybody said to her. She began to live in many different divisions of time. There were her early years in Alabama, then there were her later years of toil and poverty, followed by her proprietorship of the ramshackle mansion, and then the time when Bewick Freeth came out of the friendless blue and the unknown to stay with her and minister to her needs; then there was the time when Bewick, having left her without a word of goodbye, showered her with wealth.

She sat in the front window of the old mansion she now owned and nodded to passersby. She was the Mother Green then people came to recognize. She would raise her hand in blessing to them in the manner of an old film star herself. Everyone thought she was Bewick's mother. And at certain times of the day she herself may have thought so, for hour by hour her impression of reality changed.

"We missed knowing he was a world-famous movie star," Viola would confide sleepily to the visitors who now dropped in as if Mother Green's house was a sort of gathering place. Mostly young ones came. Crazy about their idol. They wanted to see too where he hung his clothes. But their request to go upstairs was vetoed of course.

The past, the present, the future became all mixed up in Mother Green's mind. Sometimes she thought Bewie was her own flesh and blood. Again he was her hired man. Sometimes he seemed like her grandson. He was hardly ever the famed movie star the world knew him by.

Often out of complete bewilderment and confusion as to what to do, Viola would hold Mother Green's hand and even kiss its worn flesh.

Once after holding her hand in hers for an unusually long spell Viola heard Mother Green say, "He'll be back, don't you believe now otherwise. Bewie will be back here whatever any folk may say he won't."

Viola actually almost believed what Mother Green said. For how could so vital so fresh so overwhelmingly youthful a young man disappear, anymore than sunbeams would one day cease to visit this world of sorrow and loss.

In this resplendent light then they went on with their lives, allowing Nehemiah Highstead and the Ebenezer Resurrection Church to tend to whatever arrangements so immense a bequest had visited upon the two retired ladies.

"I think he was sent," Mother Green often confided to Nehemiah on one of his frequent visits. To Viola's relief she saw that Nehemiah acted as if he agreed with Mother Green. Yes, he was not playacting. She believed the old man too felt Bewie's kind of splendor was not extinguished, would in fact make its presence known again.

From then on Mother Green if not Viola always spoke about Bewie as "amongst the living" and not ever amongst the departed. "He was like her very own," Viola often told the ladies of the Ebenezer Resurrection Church and the steady stream of young visitors who were Bewie's followers.

If for no other reason Mother Green's and Viola's daily lives were made more cheerful, more enjoyable, and yes more sociable. Their long years of lonesomeness and solitary grief (save when Bewie had come to them) was set aside for hours of joyfulness and even quiet mirth.

The church ladies brought from their own kitchens sumptuous repasts for supper, and lighter but even perhaps more enjoyable victuals for lunch. They brought daily fresh flowers and made other arrangements for brightening the premises.. They hired at times limousines and entertained the two ladies with little excursions. They even undertook to restore the ruined mansion to its original splendor.

There was also singing, for all the ladies were members of the choir.

And like Viola Daniels they would often agree with nearly everything Mother Green remarked, such as, "Bewie ain't gone far," or "Bewie will be here amongst us again, mark my words."

And so, even had the two ladies not inherited great wealth, the presence of the many young visitors and of old Nehemiah and the church choir ladies made Mother Green's last days, if not quite as heavenly as the fortune teller had foretold, nonetheless a peaceable kind of half-light that suggests the growing presence of angels from beyond.

Backward the Drowned Went Dreaming

Carl Watson

*I*t was maybe 10:30 PM, early October, 1974, a time of profound spiritual dislocation and emotional collapse. Only scientists had computers. Television had not yet begun dictating public behavior. Some people even lived without phones. The level of dialogue on the street was less confined. There were three eggs frying in a pan along with some left-over Chinese rice. Half of a bottle of Jim Beam was on hold but waiting when Tanya McCoy climbed into a kitchen window on the southwest side of Portland Oregon. It was my window, but she was looking for somebody else.

The song on the radio was Janis Joplin's *Piece of My Heart*. I should have thought it meant something, but I wasn't thinking anything. I was singing along in a theatrical manner. I used such music as a purgative. Get drunk, go through my repertoire of gut wrenching facial expressions. Wring my heart like a rag of tears. Usually I felt better in the morning.

But if I looked stupid doing it, she looked ridiculous watching; dressed in a stocking hat, railroad overalls, strapped-and-buckled, square-toed Frye boots. She was packing a bottle of Gallo Tawny Port and a joint of Vietnamese bozo weed. She said "Alright," as if she could identify with my folly, then twisted the cap off the port for a toast. Within hours we had sewn the seeds of our middle-class discontents and would spend the next three years running away from our separate demons.

Think Heloise and Abelard, Dante and Beatrice, Hammett and Hellman, Humbert and Lolita Hayes. This wasn't one of the great love stories of the ages though. To tell the truth I'm not even sure it was a love story. I'm not sure love stories exist other than as models for emotional oppression. Concrete walls erected by tiny romantic sadists in our minds to batter our souls against like bags of broken toys. But if it wasn't the stuff of legend it *was* a story of passive obsession and two people who thought they could turn their ennui into a religion.

A few months earlier I had been living up on 56th and 9th in New York City, working for some stage queen named Joey Campbell. It was a friend of a friend kind of thing. He had a set-construction business farming out incompetent labor to theaters around the city. Then he got in trouble with some local organization, and suddenly I didn't have a job.

They were strange times. The previous heady decade had degenerated into some collective entertainment anxiety. Individualism was about to become a disease rather than a cure. People were dropping like flies to various vague illnesses. One guy I knew went crazy from 'The Fun,' a term he used to describe some ominous evil out there, manipulating him, turning him into a party animal against his will. This 'Fun' looked like a clown, or a punk from a nightclub, or a babe from a beer ad. Sometimes it looked like his own face in a hotel mirror. Another guy died from what was later called 'Denial.' Actually it was the same guy. Then there was the 'Fear,' but that's been around a long time, under different names, different sanctions. Some called it the 'Horror.'

So that's pretty much it — Kurtz and Bozo, walking hand-in-hand through the collective psyche in bell bottoms and running shoes. Of course these days those days seem like a veritable renaissance. But you can't go back. I tried. I remembered Oregon. Oregon was supposed to be clean. Clean was good. People in Oregon smiled without knives in their eyes. There wasn't supposed to be any crime, of the physical sort. I had been there once. I went back. Which brings me back to the beginning—the fried eggs and the whisky in the kitchen and Janis Joplin.

Her real name was Teresa. Teresa Fleishman. Irish mother. Jewish pop. Half hillbilly, half princess. Confused and put upon. She changed her name to Tanya because she liked the funky downhome sound. She took her mother's surname of McCoy because she thought her father was a thug. She wanted roots in the soulfull South, not the airheaded Pacific Northwest.

Ours was a marriage of convenience. I knew it. I chose to ignore it. So did she. Why disturb a good thing by attaching emotions? Life was about adventure, alcohol, sex. All the themes of country-western music. So I guess it was no coincidence that Tanya's dream was to be a country-western singer.

She could sing about the way we lived, which might give us an excuse for living that way. She drifted from band to band, but she lacked self-confidence, and often sang flat and without phrasing. And her stage presence was erratic to say the least.

Tanya was a portly girl. In another age—the Rococo, the Baroque, perhaps—she would have been in style. She was also an ex-junky with a loud mouth, a chip on her shoulder and freckles dancing around on her face like fry-pan grease. It was cute. A lot of people thought so. Sometimes it opened closed doors. When it did she ran right through. In truth Tanya was always running: from the impossible shadow of her heroic mother, from her overbearing two-timing drunken father, from the anal-retentive over-achieving brother, from her latest demon lover, whatever. She was the blue-print for the daughter in one of those dysfunctional television families—those shows that hadn't been invented yet—but in her world the end just fizzles out. No one gets back together. No epiphanies. No laughs.

She had no shortage of reasons for her mildly anti-social behavior, and sooner or later I was to become one of them. Until that time we drank and travelled with a certain amount of fury, criss-crossing the country fifteen or twenty times — New York, Chicago, Portland, New York, New Orleans, Los Angles, Portland, New York, Chicago, New Jersey, Eugene. We didn't just run the hitch-hiking life-style into the ground, we stomped on it, flayed it, scraped it with stones, hung it in the wind like a Buddhist prayer flag—an offering to unknown gods.

We grew overly familiar with certain small towns and intersections. We could recognize water towers and back alleys, railroad embankments and tiny grocery stores, locations that became little kernels, 3-D snapshots of experience smaller than a fist. We kept them in our pockets like stones picked up from the road shoulder.

"Ain't got a ride yet, eh?" the mom-and-pop proprietors of nowhereville America might ask, not realizing we had already been to the East Coast and back in between packages of baloney, white bread and six-packs.

If someone pinned us down we tried to give the lifestyle an esoteric twist. We'd say stuff like "'The great thing is to move.'" or "Get complacent and you die inside." or "Movement is the opiate of the disaffected." We could keep it going—tossing off the aphorisms, stringing the cliches out like hot cheese. We'd drop names: Fitzgerald, Kerouac, Steinbeck, Kipling. We quoted people we'd never even read.

Tanya wasn't dumb but she had a tragic willingness to believe people who were and her information was often second-hand. "Trust no thought not born in motion," she once said. Someone had told her Bob Dylan wrote that. I think it was Fred Nietzsche. He would know too, a sickly shut-in with delusions of grandeur. I saw a photo of the man once, pulling a woman around in a horse cart. Still, we took the kinetic call-to-arms to heart. Sitting over cheap local brews in roadside diners, we fantasized that people wondered who we were. We let them wonder and we wondered back. For all they knew we could be heirs to the Starkweather/Fulgate heritage—reborn in passive bodies, but still carrying the momentum, the past-life memories. For all we knew they could be the ones who'd gun us down in the outskirts of town.

Tanya had a soft spot for junkies. Her parents were middle class liberals. She wanted to be wild and tragic—an antidote to their failed idealism. I thought she had something against herself she turned on others. But I don't know. Billie Holiday was her favorite singer. Mine was Janis. Both died on the nod, too young and too bored, and this appreciation of martyrdom was part of our bond.

They say the road is all about memory, about finding the thing you used to know. Dope is too, but there's nothing there—no knowing. In Connecticut, Tanya met this guy named Fat Mike who did remind her of someone she used to know. Fat Mike had hair on his neck that should have been on top of his head. He was a user, dumb and unthreatening, and they clicked. Dope has bonds that defy social or emotional logic. Tanya used to say it took you back to Grandma's house. Mike liked being there too.

So Tanya moved in with this Mike character, who, oddly enough, did live with his grandmother. They got a band together and played a couple gigs at the local bar. I moved back to New York—into the apartment of an old girlfriend. The old girlfriend wasn't living there anymore—she was in a mental hospital. Apparently the neighbors found her wringing chicken blood out of a rag onto the sidewalk and singing in German. And she didn't know German. A good enough reason to put her away.

The apartment was way the hell out in Brooklyn. Flatbush or Midwood. Small time hoods, babushkas, kasha knishes. It took awhile to get there. There were dogs and petty thieves along the way to slow you down. Miss the subway stop, go back five spaces—as if that part of Brooklyn was a board game of some kind.

Prolonged existence on the road allows you to short circuit whole parts of normal life. One jumps elliptically from location to location, conveniently forgetting everything that happened in between. Hindu and Buddhist saints can do this without moving. But the talents of holy men have been replaced and improved upon by TV. I suppose that's why we watch it, for some illusion of transcendance. In fact today they actually want you to believe that time is space, that everything is happening everywhere, that there are so many possibilities you can shop forever and never exhaust your potential. The down side is you might go through the wrong door—end up in a show you don't like, as a character you disapprove of. It happened to me.

One afternoon after taking three 50 mg. thorazines I woke up on the floor in a rugby jersey I didn't own. I had no pants on. One sock. One of my hands was cemented to a magazine. Apparently I had torn all the curtains off the windows. There was an upturned bowl of Purple Dinosaur Fun Flakes decorating the hall. The mailbox had been broken into and someone was ringing the doorbell. It was two days later than I thought it was.

Eventually the knocking stopped. I lit a cigarette, packed my bags and went back to Chicago. I was sitting in someone's apartment, staring out the window, watching shadows darken the wall of St. Boniface cemetary. A bleak night, early winter—it was just starting to snow. I saw a man whose soul might have weighed a thousand pounds but you could drink it with a straw. The white tombstones behind him were like the rows of teeth in the mouth of a shark, shining in the intermittent moon—a shark called Fate, waiting for my next bad decision. I didn't make it wait long.

The Twilight Zone was on. It always was. It was an episode I'd seen too many times. I turned the sound down, played a tape. Janis Joplin, for no particular reason. I was singing into the microphone of my fist, trying to sweat out some accumulated poison. The similarity to a previous scene might have been intentional. I like repitition. It brings me comfort. The phone rang. Then I heard it. There had been a delay betwen the physical occurrence and the sensation, much like my relationship with Tanya, who incidentally was on the phone, as if I had called her forth through this ritual. I was slightly shocked. I never thought about it until years later—this unlikely bit of serendipity. I didn't realize how much my life was changing.

I drove 40 miles through a blizzard to pick her up at a gas station on Route 20 outside Gary. She said she couldn't get a ride. I said she probably wouldn't have wanted one. Gary lost most of its working citizens years ago when the mills collapsed. Those that were left had little better to do than drink cheap beer and cruise the local roads looking for soft spots in the space/time continuum to empty their guns.

A week later we were headed down to New Orleans to live the wild life. We got a ride in a school bus headed for Normal, Illinois. The driver, whose name was Doug, had a bag full of porn magazines, some righteous pot and what seemed to be a trained dog. We didn't want to know what the dog did. It was too early in the morning.

Outside Peoria we got another ride with a family of glass-eyed kids heading to some Tennessee commune. They had invisible TV sets of a better world glued to their eyes and they were watching them. Next some half-pint-in-the-pocket, crumpled-felt-hat drunk hillbilly with one eyebrow and a hidden agenda, gave us a tour of the local back roads. I mostly remember it as a black-and-white film of rapidly approaching tree trunks looming in front of the windshield. He dumped us at some god forsaken intersection in Mississippi, and we were happy to be there. There were other rides. Offers of companionship, lifestyle choices. But we avoided the possibilities these parallel universes might have provided.

There's always that part of your life you spend chasing cliches. We were in ours. New Orleans is a road-dog cliche. You have to pass through there if you want any credibility. So the road-dogs say. It's a town where the smell of alcohol and Spanish moss blends into a murky bouquet which soaks into your skin, lungs and liver until you feel like you're living in some soft-focus nostalgia version of your own life. Some say the city makes you mean and lazy. Some say it makes you think you know something that you don't. Either way it's dangerous.

Me and Tanya got a cheap 3-room joint in a mostly black part of town just upriver of the Quarter. We rented the back room hourly to horny couples in exchange for drugs. But we made the greater part of our money selling flowers on the street—dyed carnations, roses, and some sticky carnal orchid-style number that smelled like old sweat and soap. We ate crawfish and fried oysters. We drank all day and pretended we still had a thing. Tanya got involved with a band for awhile, but they never played anywhere. The practices were just excuses to drink.

We knew everybody on the street who drank and they knew us. There was Clyde, the Chicken Man, Sal the Money-Man Mazolowski, and Raul the

Candy Man. There was Charlie the Lucky Dog Man too, and a runaway adding-machine heiress who called herself Antoinette, or 'Andy' Beausoliel. It was a good life. It was as if we belonged somewhere. But that's always the lure of a transient town.

We had a few people living with us—and off us—on and off. An emancipated stripper named Sheyly, a waiter/hustler named Smiling Bob, a half-Cherokee pot dealer who called himself Steven White Claw and his pregnant Italian wife, Sophia deAngelo. There were two others I don't remember well, two thieves who snuck out one night with half our stuff. They were all fakes, but then we were too so we couldn't call them on it. We loved the fringe people, the freaks.

Unfortunately, these fringe people, these freaks didn't like each other as much as we thought they should. One day Steven White Claw hit Smiling Bob with a length of motorcycle chain. I can still see the way it snickered out of his pocket—an articulated steel-link snake with a voice like a purring cat that snapped back into a cry. Bob was suddenly bleeding from the link marks on his cheek. For a second it looked like red quarter notes dripping from a red music staff on his red cheek. He had two smiles. Both red.

As usual the fight was over the woman. Something she said, or more likely, showed. Sheyly the Stripper was always getting us in trouble, flaunting her white stuff up and down St. Bernard Ave—a genuine glow-in-the-dark blonde runaway marching her teenage sex around like it was a prize. Maybe it was. Her friends were mostly Harley riders. Heavyweight guys with bad posture and testosterone problems. Even Smiling Bob began juggling nunchucks in the front yard. Road-Kill Pete did Buck Knife tricks. It wasn't exactly a welcome-to-the-neighborhood sign from the white boys. And they were all doing dope all the time. I was glad to see them leave. I would have been gladder to be the one leaving.

Memory can be a tricky thing, even a tacky thing. It uses you. You might remember killing someone when you didn't do it. Many people do. They say the bedroom is the most dangerous room on earth. Police know it. Emergency room workers can tell you. I wish I could say such passion was mine to regret. But reconstruction is hard. They say it's in my head. My sin. Apparently this is true.

"There are already enough people who have as their mission in life the extinction of the fire." I read that once. It's a nice thought—that the soul is not immortal by nature—it can only become so, if fed. So I guess the road is more food than geometry—more consumption than myth. In fact the modern road story is the opposite of myth. There are no heroes. There are barely any actors. There are only observers. What might be called events, or non-events. No one feels they make anything happen, except maybe by bumping into things, moving through life as a means of merely making contact with the world

Running no place, and from no thing, there's no start you can name, no beginning. The harder you look, the further it recedes. Sure, maybe there's the fourteen-year-old girl you loved as a child, the stepfather who sent you into a psychological tailspin. But a car travelling down the road might think it's fighting fate when it's really only illustrating the second law of thermodynamics. The White Queen bandages her finger, then begins to bleed—then comes the act that wounds. Backwards is the direction of order. The mistake you made is the last thing you see.

There's a way to beat the system though, to trick god and chaos. Because without punctuation the sentence can't mean anything, so you punctuate your life—you tag emotions, connect them to senses, smells, sounds. In fact the whole of experience is a tractless web that begs to be labelled. I think there's a term for it: transsubstantiation, transfixation, transference neurosis, something like that—the intense association of particular sensations and events in memory whereby one can't exist without the other.

By example, take a song — *The Lion Sleeps Tonight*, by the Tokens. Because of the conditions under which I first heard it, it will always remind me of the sight of the neighbor girl, little Beatrice, a pre-Lolita-creature who lived in our neighborhood as if she inhabited a surrealist painting by deChirico or Magritte. I once saw her running down the alley behind our house late at night under a full moon. I never found out what she was carrying or why she was out at that hour. By the time I finished high school I heard she'd gone insane.

Then there's *Daniel*, by Elton John—the song he wrote about his blind brother. I always associate it with the unasked for sight of a dog getting hit by a car during shift change traffic on US 20 as I drove toward the Gary Steel Mills the dog writhing around on the pavement, the sulphurous air, the noise, the anticipation of the bone deadening job, certain people I knew at that time. I'm placed right there in the driver's seat every time.

California Dreaming by the Mamas and Papas will forever be associated with the fork in I-80 where it goes north or south. I had decided to leave the land of steel mill. Me and Eddy Coogan sat there in a 69 Opel cadet. I flipped a coin. We headed north to Portland, Oregon. That's how I got there. That was the song on the radio. We did the opposite.

The next thing I remember is Patsy Cline's *Walking after Midnight*, on the jukebox in a Boise, Idaho bar, while two women circled each other with bloody pool balls in their hands. A crowd of truck-driving rednecks cheering them on. That's how the system works. The image is pinned to the bulletin board of the brain by the song. Life can be owned.

Before all that, there was *Pusher Man* from Easy Rider. But I didn't associate it so much with the movie as with the smell of US 30 dragstrip. I went with my brother's friend, Roy Lemoyne. The motorcycle is the connection here. Roy had one. So did Denis Hopper.

Roy LeMoyne was a displaced Texas biker hippie with an eyepatch. He lived with my brother in a basement pad in Hammond, Indiana. He was from Beaumont, not far from Port Arthur where Janis Joplin was born.. He was the same age as Janis. He might even have known her. He might have drunk in the same bars, met her at a high school party, or even seen her sing in a cafe in Austin. Being outcasts, they would have been in the same milieu. I didn't connect any of this at the time. It's only through hindsight.

Roy was skinny as a stick. He had this 200 -lb girlfriend named Mary-Sue Somebody, a gal very much like Tanya, who was also an aspiring country-western singer, although she might have been a little better. I don't remember. She could have been worse. They used to come over to the burger joint where I worked over on Highway 41 and I'd fix them up with a sack of burgers for the price of a cold drink.

Roy was tuned in, he had traveled, and he always had something new laying around. The Chicago Seed. Acid Rock albums. Surrealistic Pillow by Jefferson Airplane especially, and Cheap Thrills by Big Brother and the Holding Company—its R. Crumb cover laid out like the 'eyeball of god' with a woman standing in the center of the eye, wearing the ball and chain. It didn't occur to me at the time that the woman was Janis. More I remember the grainy picture of Janis in the middle. I remember the exhaltation in her face.

Roy rode a Triumph Tiger 650. It was really a rat bike, but he tricked it out with leather and chrome and kept it running. I used to hang out at his garage while he worked on it. Since then I've always had a predilection for the British machines. It was Roy in fact who turned me on to my first bike— a BSA 440 Victor Special. I got it at Molnar's in Hammond. Someone had traded it in on a Sportster. It was fun and fast but hard to start. So I sold it to some rocker down the block. Later I heard his brain went off, that he was moving about the world in fits, lurching through stop lights, 40 mph at rush hour.

Then there was the Triumph Tiger 500. It didn't run very well. But it ran until I wrecked it. I jumped it into a ditch to avoid eating the grill of a Mack truck. Thereafter it never ran at all. It looked good sitting in my front yard though. Made me seem like a mystic. I sold that one to some guy called Berny who paid me by taking money out of his girlfriend's purse while she was passed out. I never saw him again.

What the machine is I couldn't say. An extension of the body? I suppose that's true. One thing's for sure—it opens the senses, if you want them opened. It makes you aware of every nuance—of flowers, dead animals, wind and humidity, the cold odor of tires, oil, road dust and gas. I liked the motion of the springs. The way the headlights cut a tunnel in the dark, the gutteral pipes. And how, if you were slightly drunk it could make the asphalt winding out ahead of you seem like your guts being rolled onto a spool somewhere in the future, as if you were being disemboweled by your dreams. You might sell them off in time thinking you're avoiding that "death wish thing" but you always get another.

Which brings me back to New Orleans, six years later, with Tanya. We were, wondering how not to be in New Orleans, when, one day, I was walking down Rampart past the Mr. Acropolis used car lot. The song *Pusher Man* was playing on someone's radio nearby. Then I saw it—a 1969 BSA Lightening. I went to empty my account. The bank cashier didn't ask what I was going to do with the money. She knew I was locked in a self-fulfilling prophecy and had no intention of straightening my life out to marry her. She probably didn't care either. And Mr. Acropolis didn't care as he counted out our cash on the metal desk. He knew the bike wouldn't make it to the edge of town.

In fact I had to walk it home because the brakes didn't work. It wouldn't start either and the kickstand was broke. But that's the great thing about machines—unlike people they can be fixed. Tanya wasn't one of those women

who stalk the outskirts of a broken-down scene bitching. She never gave a
thought to any physical, emotional, financial or chronological impossibili-
ties. To her it made no difference that the bike didn't work. We would make
it work. She didn't mind if we spent the better part of our lives making it work.
We were gonna ride the Beezer to LA.. and then up the coast on Highway 1.
We had a couple hundred dollars between us. Screw the odds.

Tanya quit the 'band'. We said goodbye to our 'friends'. We left New
Orleans around 11 PM, on May 3. I remember sleeping out near a bayou
access road that night. We caught some blue gills in a backwater and burned
them to the bottom of an aluminum pan. We chased the seared flesh with
cans of Dixie. The night was murky but there were some VanGogh-style stars
to be had. The rhythm of the insects, their intense call-and-response, was like
a million fiddle players hidden in the trees. There were soft breezes and clouds
of blood-sucking mosquitoes to keep me awake. But when I finally did fall
asleep I had a dream of having my head bitten off by a preying mantis.

The Rainbow Bridge over the Neches River between Louisiana and Texas
was some kind of Wagnerian passage to Valhalla, if Valhalla to you is Port
Arthur. And for some I suppose it is. Suddenly we realized we were in Janis
Joplin's home town. It was exactly as I pictured it—oil derricks, fields, great
pumping cranes, burnoff stacks. It was like a southern version of Whiting
Indiana, but more spread out, more humid. We stopped at the first liquor
store we found and bought a bottle of Southern Comfort, most of which we
drank in the parking lot of a laundromat.

"Get it while you can," I said, hoisting the bottle to the oil stained skies.

"Freedom's just another word for nothin' left to lose" said Tanya.

Then some guy came and chased us out of the parking lot. I guess Port
Arthur is not so much like Whiting after all. In Whiting, Indiana you could
drink in the parking lot. I think you were supposed to.

We lit out for the long crossing: Texas, Arizona, New Mexico, California. We drove over white mountains and red deserts, romantic wastelands
and ravaged pastorales. We crossed fields of sunflowers like the yellow eyes
of ancient men, reptilian and tired. Morbid one moment, elated the next,
we drove and we drove. But while we should have been experiencing some
incredible lightness of the road, that freedom from emotion and home, we
were actually more attuned to its opposite—a heaviness we didn't want to
admit to, a sluggishness like some cosmic humidity, that made everything

unbearable, like we were in the midst of an intolerable curse and we had to keep moving to stay free of it. And we felt this weight, this density, in states that should have been the most subtle—the trembling of water in a roadside ditch, the vibration of a flower petal.

There were times when the bike actually seemed out of control, racing along an asphalt swell, and the progression of images, the beauty that flashed along either side often seemed lost on us, as much as we enthused about the grandeur. Still with Tanya's hands upon my shoulders or in the pockets of my coat, one might say we were looking for trials amidst all this, tests of mettle. But we knew we were just drifting, bouyed up on a sea of Port Arthur oil products—road tar, rubber, gas—all churned out from the distilled energy of an ancient sun, a thick soup of flesh and circumstance, which we, as sacks of sentient chemicals were part of, and no amount of mechanical clairvoyance or intuition would save us. Life was always elsewhere. Further back. Farther ahead.

Janis Joplin wasn't going to save us either—that raw voice of hers like sandpaper and motor-oil—but we heard it anyway, in our heads as we drove. We pretty much drove straight to LA, stopping briefly for drinks in Houston, Tucson, San Diego, Nogales, Tijuana, El Paso. We passed through Salinas, the stinking artichoke capital of the world. Tanya loved artichokes. She was the only person I ever met that did.

We took the little roads when we could, the blue highways, the diner-lined routes, the 66s and the 77s. There were scorpions in our boots in the morning, skies salted with stars, trucks like giant glowing grasshoppers in the night, naked drunks in small town gas stations screaming in the void, no flat tires and only one running problem—the bike would cut out erratically. I thought it was the carburetor. She said vapor-lock. We were both wrong. Loose battery cables. But at least we weren't hitchhiking.

Tanya had friends in LA. She was going to visit them. Some were 'weekend warriors' and some were full time. Roger was full time. It took nearly half a day to find Roger. He changed addresses every couple months. Sometimes he changed names. We spent a lot of time running down false leads. LA is all stop lights and telephone wires. It's hard to know where you are in the first place—forget about finding anything. Nobody is sitting on their stoops to help you either, because of the carbon monoxide.

Santa Monica had some tacky sections. We found them. We came to Elaine's house first. Elaine Robinson was a friend of Connie who was living in Colorado with another biker dude named Bobby Jesse, or Jesse Bobby. He had two first names. Jesse or Bobby was a friend of Roger's from the old jail days. Connie was Tanya's friend from different old days, partly in jail, partly in the golden light of the free and righteous life.

Elaine's mother, Camille, answered the door. "Well....Tan, been a few years, you clean?" she asked. This was a woman having no fun in life and she wasn't trying to hide it. Her face had that LA pancake-colored-mud-slide-frozen-in-time look that's lets you know.

"Been clean for a while, living in Oregon now," Tanya said, as if that were proof, like you couldn't be dirty in Oregon, even though we hadn't been living in Oregon. She opened the door to let us in. Whatever coated the furniture and the windows in that house was soon coating our skin.

"How's Naomi?"

"She's cool, living in North Africa, Tunisia I think."

"Cool," said Camille. The word seemed odd coming out of her mouth, like she was too old to say "cool' but she had to say it in order to communicate with the kids. Then I realized she was mocking us. I felt appropriately embarrassed.

Everybody asked about Tanya's mom. Naomi was a legendary figure among Tanya's less than legendary crowd. They all called her Naomi—using her first name as a way of bringing themselves closer to her mythic status. If they were asked to describe her they said that Tanya's mom was "cool, man". She was simply a very cool person.

By all accounts Naomi O'Connell had had an eclectic career. She ran around the country collecting kicks with the beats. Supposedly she was one of the characters in *Howl* and *On the Road*. But no one knew which one. She had been in the SDS. She had been at Woodstock. People had seen her in the movie. I never did. She was an existentialist, an early hippy, a mystic, an anarchist and an intellectual. She knew Blavatsky and Ledbeater, Steinem and Mailer. She lived in a squat in Paris with Sartre and Beauvoir. She'd hung out with the abstract expressionists and with the Golden Dawn. She worked as an activist with organized labor and was a major anti-Vietnam protestor and a proto-feminist.

There were many stories of Tanya's mom. Too many. She'd have to be

150 years old and have an ability to travel in space without using machines. She'd simply done way too much in too short of a life. Still, her myth was out there, mutating, attracting inconsistencies. Nobody pushed it, because they needed the myth. Especially Tanya. It served her sense of inadequacy. By maintaining an image of Naomi that was more than Tanya could ever live up to she could justify her lifestyle as an underachiever and a drug addict. It also, ironically, made Tanya the agent of her own demise.

At first it seemed odd to me that Tanya hadn't changed her name to follow suit with her mother. Years ago Naomi had traded McCoy for O'Connell. Perhaps to avoid the hillbilly connotations of McCoy. It was back in the 50's when there was a TV show called "The Real McCoys". Understandably, she wanted to avoid any association. For even though she hung with a liberal crowd, no one liked hillbillys. They were the same as rednecks to most northerners—the cause of segregation and war. The name O'Connell preserved her Scotch/Irish identity without the negative traits. Tanya however sought to reclaim the adjective 'real' that clung to McCoy like an appendix. It suited her career aspirations and her personality. It also severed the nominal umbilical cord. Tanya needed to have control over the use of her mother's legend. Not being immediately identifiable as Naomi's daughter helped. It let her weigh her options.

People used the idea of Naomi, often to bolster their own obsessions. I think it was Roger who once told me Tanya's mom had been one of the first women to take birth control pills, before government approval. They'd been smuggled in from Europe and passed around like candy amongst the hippest people. Supposedly Naomi's crowd was all taking them and screwing all the time. According to Roger, Naomi was a party girl and she and her friends had virtually invented orgies.

At first I assumed he was only into the prurient aspects, but as time went on his agenda became clear. Apparently Roger believed that while Tanya *thought* Harry Fleishman was her real father, the fact was she didn't know. This subliminal doubt was one reason she was crazy or depressed or whatever, and in Roger's acute mind, that doubt was his trump card—a key to some Pandora's box of demons in Tanya's psyche. The fluidity of Naomi's myth gave him a leg up. It fed his sense of power. Like I said, it was in his mind. But for most people that makes it no different from what is real.

I pictured Naomi variously as sexpot and scholar—obviously something to do with my own Electra fixations. Truth be known, proximity to her legend gave my life a sort of roguish intellectual quality that it didn't have in those years. As if I was drifting for a 'reason' as opposed to simple laziness or cowardice. However, since I had never actually met Naomi I had no way of knowing what she was like or by what right I could lay claim to my fantasies.

There was also a dark side to the woman that no one talked about, something beyond the name dropping and history-making. There was Naomi the absent mother, Naomi the tyrannical control-freak, Naomi the reckless libertine, Naomi the unbalanced, and Naomi the alcoholic whose scrapes with the law often had little to do with leftist idealism. These traits were seldom elaborated, since they were of little use to anyone.

"Have a seat, Lainy's upstairs. She just got out of jail last week—big bust down in Venice, but I guess you heard."

We hadn't.

She shouted. "Hey Lainy your old friend Tanya's here." The words '*old friend*' were italicized, and not without a measure of sarcasm. Camille returned to her lounge chair, and her vodka and lemonade. There had been some music but apparently the tape had run out. Dreadful silence held sway.

"Roger around?" Tanya asked.

"Not much." She answered indifferently.

Elaine came downstairs. She looked dull and under a lot of strain. She and Tanya hugged each other lightly as if they had forgotten exactly why they were friends and had little interest in rekindling the memories. Distrust was like some horror-movie goo between them, sticking them together in the worst sort of way.

"You clean?" Elaine asked, glancing nervously toward the kitchen.

"Yeah," Tanya said, "I don't do that stuff anymore, livin' in Oregon now. Where's Roger?"

"Staying in Venice, in that old building Tom Parker was in. Got himself this white woman, Redondo Beach. They've even got a kid, someone says. He calls himself Rolando when he's with her."

We heard a door close out in the kitchen. Elaine seemed to relax a little.

"Rolando?" They laughed. A car started. A large cockroach crawled across the wall. I smacked it. A glass broke somewhere.

"What an ass." Tanya laughed.

Apparently it was Roland for awhile in some misguided attempt to appropriate French cachet. Then Rodrigo. He finally settled on Rolando as the credible alternative—given that it was California. Roger was one eighth Mexican, which by his way of thinking gave him a diluted version of Castillian blood. He had taken to wearing scarves tied around his neck, Spanish berets, and affecting a roguish swagger to pick up chicks. Rich chicks. Why bother otherwise. It was something you could only pull off in California, where people were so desperate for class that even fake Eurotrash got laid.

"The white woman, she likes the danger," injected Camille, sarcastically, with a put-on accent, swirling the ice cubes in her glass as a form of punctuation. Most people couldn't pull off such an obvious cliche. Camille could. You got the feeling she invented it. Then for a second I saw her face go completely slack as if she had just seen her own death walk through the door with a box of candy. It was hard to tell whether these distortions were due to thorazine side-effects, simple boredom or some other primal force working its geological will under her skin. It was fun to watch though—a pleasant distraction.

She took another drink and managed to rein her muscles back to their standard holding pattern—the perpetual smirk of the fallen debutante, the has-been actress with a pill problem, a woman with so much past that it all cancelled out and you could pretty much attribute anything to her you wanted. But I'm being too harsh. Maybe she *was* a cipher. But I was a cynic. And she didn't deserve my judgement.

Still, I couldn't imagine the woman ever being seductive. Someone must have. There was a daughter to prove it. Here was the daughter now—talking. Talking to Tanya. They were snickering at some inside joke. I reached out and tried to grab a piece. I wanted to laugh too. But I missed and turned my head away.

In those days, in that part of California, 'white woman' referred to that middle class, clean, secretarial type who were really looking for a wallet but went sucker for an outlaw. They got pregnant or gave away their money. Then they went home. This one was pregnant. 'Rolando' was milking her.

"More power to him," said Tanya. The way she figured it, anybody could do anything they wanted.

"Family's the most important thing," Camille added, scratching her thigh.

Camille knew she was no Naomi. She resented Tanya for that. As if the mere existence of Tanya's mother had turned Elaine against her. Apparently she couldn't see herself in the mirror of her daughter's eyes. But then how could Camille keep it together when she had this wild child making her life miserable, drugging and drinking and seducing her boyfriends. Camille couldn't compete. Elaine resented her mother for being a whore. The two of them were teaching each other a lesson. It was going to take years.

Tanya and Elaine seemed unable to speak above a whisper for awhile, I caught little fragments like "Yeah, me too." and "Yeah, right, okay." Then I took a seat and talked to Camille until she passed out. Possessed by some spirit of alcoholic fundamentalism, she gibbered on. Finally the crank ran down.

At some point we replaced beer and vodka with tomato juice and gin. I heard a train whistle far off somewhere. Far off in my head most likely. As a kid at night I used to love the sound of distant train whistles, imagining the gaunt skeletal men hanging off those boxcars, their hollowed eyes gone dead from the overload of speed and booze, playing their harmonicas and banjos and beckoning me like bad father figures to a life on the road.

And here I was. I was afraid—afraid I too might one day live in those gondolas. I would have been happy in a trailer home. But wait. I *was* in a trailer home. At least the emotional equivalent. The more things change, the more they become the same. TV was proving the point over and over again. I watched for the comfort. Train robbers. Prairie dust. Gunfire. I started to doze. But I woke myself up. Things seemed a little too well synced-up. Someone shouted "Fuck you" out in the kitchen. It sounded like Elaine. I heard a glass break. A cowboy on TV said "Try new Rodeo Deodorant Soap. You'll feel fresh as a Montana morning. R-O-D-E-O. Yahoo."

It was a minor relief when Ben showed up, Camille's boyfriend. He stepped in the door like an angry actor coming on stage after weeks of bad reviews, knowing the audience hates him, and it's going to be real hard to get another job. Attitude adjustment hours at taverns were designed for people like him. Except he went before work.

His buddies down at the betting parlor called him Ed Sullivan—a running joke based on some money he'd won on a horse once. His real name was Ben Pantone. Italian, Irish, Jewish—a nervous mix. He seemed to have a carburetor in his neck that jerked his head around in sudden small bursts of paranoia, augmenting his chosen role as the ideal antidote for whatever tranquilizer you were on—simply because you just couldn't help being irritated by the guy.

He was about fifteen years younger than Camille and proportionately louder and drunker. They started fighting as soon as she came to. It was about money. Ben was one of those guys who's always going to get a job the next day. He's got an interview or a deal lined up and he just needs a little more time, a couple more bucks. For the time being he was living off Elaine's mother's money. She was taking advantage of the audience to let him know what she thought.

"Get a job yet, Benny baby?"

"Going downtown tomorrow, Cam (he called her Cam), I got a line on a gig selling real estate in the valley."

"Okay baby," she said, "Now make me a drink."

Ben picked up the can off the tray table, poured some juice in a glass, threw in some ice, added the gin. "Here's your fucking drink."

"Turn that shit off. Put on some Patsy will you, Baby." Ben turned off the radio and put in a tape. He pressed play without saying anything.

"You like Patsy?" she asked.

"Everybody loves Patsy," I said.

Camille apparently had a gushing take on Miss Cline's life in which all the unsavory details are edited out. She wasn't going to give up.

"You talk about failed love. Patsy knew about failed love." She poured another drink. "Men treated her like shit. Walked all over her. Daddy always listened to Patsy. It makes me remember . . . "

There it was. I had been waiting for the father to show up. The decor demanded it. I also knew there was a photograph in a drawer somewhere that explained all this. Maybe it was the man she really loved, years ago, the one who let her down. Dad. The boyfriend who went to Nam. Maybe Dad was the boyfriend. I wasn't going to ask.

"It's just that her music makes me sad." I lifted my glass to commiserate.

"Life is sad," Cam said.

"Sad and crazy," I replied.

The song was "Crazy." Apropos or not, I laughed. It was an ugly loose laugh. It scared me — I was starting to fit in.

Suddenly out of nowhere Ben threw a beer can across the room and broke a candy dish full of cigarette butts. The girls came out from the kitchen. We started in on bourbon and Seven-Up. I was adventuring in the American night, or rather a thickening Santa Monica afternoon version of it.

"I need some smokes. Bring me my purse, Benny."

"I'm putting your purse by the door, Cam."

"No bring it in here." He didn't.

We heard the door slam. Ben was enjoying himself.

The room seemed to fill with heavy water as if it wanted to preserve as evidence to the world outside what it should avoid, and for that time we were no different than those mutants in formaldehyde-filled jars one sees at Wisconsin county fairs. I even thought I heard a barker outside the house, charging admission to clean folks who wanted to witness the frailty of the human condition.

It was time to go. They did the embracing thing, then Elaine looked at me and said "Nice meeting you, come back again some time, any time."

"I'm sure I will," I said, trying to get out before I drowned.

I ran into Ben on the front porch. "Looks like you need a refill." He pulled out a pint bottle of Wife Beater, and poured some in my empty glass. We stood there, silent, man to man. He took a dirty toothpick from his pocket and stuck it in his mouth. Then he snuck a sidelong glance at Elaine's ass and said "...if she's anything like her mother, she's a pistol...." He started rotating his hips in that vulgar gesture men use to indicate they're getting some, and by god' they know what to do with it.

"Hot today," I said.

"This is a hot town," he said, wiping the back of his hand on his forehead. It was, but it wasn't that hot. He was probably just worked up from his recent act of virtual intercourse.

"Well, we gotta get. . . ." But he wouldn't let it go.

"Nope. Best reason to love the mother is to get a foot in the daughter's house, if you know what I mean. The daughter *is* the mother only 20 years younger, and you can't go wrong —going back like that." He grabbed his crotch as if the volume and weight of his manhood was a bother to him. Maybe it was .

But I was already on the sidewalk. I started the bike, wobbling on the footpegs. The thick currents were pushing me one way, then another. I called Tanya. If we didn't move soon we would be stuck in this aquarium of angst and anger.

Okay, maybe I asked way too much of life. I wanted it to be easy and it only got harder I followed leads and amazing consequences came from them. I sang a song. I took a drink and Tanya climbed through the window. And Tanya walked through the door.

And there she was now, coming into focus, emerging from the house looking wilted. Tanya. My lost hippy girlfriend. She carried the baggage with a certain grace. She bore down the sidewalk under the weight of the liquor, mounted the bike, and we pulled away.

I'd ridden drunk before. I was about to do it again. Maybe I would live through the day. It was slow going at first. The air had gotten so heavy in the last few hours. I wondered if we would make it. My face in the rear view mirror had circles under my eyes. I needed a shave. Then I saw Ben, standing there, surveying the street in both directions, rotating his hips and drinking, pointing his finger at me in the mirror.

He was still like that when we turned at the end of the block, bound for Santa Monica Boulevard, shimmering like the grey tines of a two-lane forklift jammed in the mouth of Mother Earth and making her feel the pain.

Is This Barstool Taken?

Cara Prieskorn

> Blonde. 36. Well-educated, well-traveled. Well-read. Wicked sense of humor. Seeks same in white male 26-56. I do want clever conversation. No grumpy old men.

*T*hat is how this whole thing started. I had been mourning my short marriage long enough and on the advice of several girlfriends, I resorted to the personal ads. I was through meeting men on bar stools. Just last week I was in my favorite place, The Beechtree Saloon, sitting with a girlfriend at one end of the bar, watching a cluster of men at the other end. The loudest one had a ponytail down to the middle of his back. He was wearing Mickey Mouse earmuffs. I announced to Cathy that I was too old for this and it was time to try something new. The personals seemed like a reasonable way to meet someone who wanted the same things I did. Enough with men who pretended they were happy being alone. I needed to meet someone who admitted to wanting to meet someone too.

I had never been the popular dating type of person. I was invited to all the parties because I could be counted on to bring something good to eat and keep the conversation going. But men were never drawn to me for the purpose of dating. They could spend an hour laughing over my jokes and still go home with an aerobics instructor who claimed to be double jointed.

This has been happening to me since Junior High. I got used to it, though I never liked it. But personal ads? I am looking for a date. They are looking for a date. No pretense. I get to meet perspective dates over the phone, where I am at my verbal best. This is a made to order situation. I place an ad in the local paper, which lists a voicemail box and the would-be suitors call in. There is no exposure or risk to me and I get to select whom I want to call back. I was sure I would want to talk to all of them. I wait four days before I call to pick up my messages, because even in anonymous print I feel vulnerable. It's been six years since I met and married my ex-husband. Six years since I have had a date. What if no one called? What if I am unattractive, even on paper? Does the ad sound as interesting as I think? If I were a man, I would call my ad.

There were fifty-six responses. I could not believe my popularity. I forgot every dance where I had been a wallflower. Men wanted me now, fifty-six of them. I was hot! I called the voicemail box from work and got my total number of calls, but cleverly waited until I got home to take down all the messages. On my way from work I stopped and bought a notebook, so I could begin keeping track of my new beaux in style. I was going to need some sort of system. I debated file cards versus loose-leaf or spiral bound. I wanted to make sure not one number got lost amidst my new found popularity. I propped myself up with pillows, a glass of wine, two pens (just in case) and my new big black book and began.

Carefully listing the date and time of each message (who wants a guy who is phoning personal ads at 3 a.m.?) I kept track of all my callers. I took notes and phone numbers. At first, I wasn't really listening, just basking in the idea that someone wanted to meet me. I recorded everything — their age, height, sign, eye color (does anyone really care about that?) and whatever personal tidbits they chose to leave. Unfortunately, most didn't leave any.

"My name is Gary. I am 5'10" tall and have brown eyes. Give me a call. 635-8442."

If that is the best Gary can do, he is off the list. At least make some effort. This is the point at which you are trying to impress me. They had to make some attempt in their response. Give me something to work with. A job. A hobby. Something.

There is a science and a language to personal ads that some don't learn right away. It took me about ten calls. I needed to use the word "single" in my ad, probably in bold letters. After spending an hour on the phone, talking to Frank, he admitted that he was "engaged, but I don't think it is going to work out." Not if you keep calling personal ads, Frank. "Going through a divorce" can mean two things. He hasn't had sex for a while and that is his primary objective, or worse - he wants someone to listen while he talks about his wife. Never call a person who is "in the process" or just separated.

I eventually eliminated about half before I even called them. One guy wanted to pick me up in his van and just drive around for awhile. I've read the Daily News. I am not that lonely. Another guy wanted to meet me very much, but we would have to schedule it around his chemo treatments. I soon realized that every white man between the ages of twenty-six and fifty-six who is reading the personals thinks that he is well educated, well read and well-traveled. Most of them probably didn't finish trade school, can't tell you the name of the last book they bought and have never had a passport. I needed to hone my interrogation skills even further.

Also the age range I had selected posed a problem. I soon realized that I wanted nothing to do with a twenty-six year old, and the twenty-six year olds that wanted something to do with me had a Mrs. Robinson fantasy cooking. Let some other woman have the young men. There was also the issue of appearance. Most men think they are "very attractive." The more simian they are, the more concerned with your appearance they become. If a man wanted to discuss my looks over the phone in the first two minutes, that was a warning sign of rejection ahead. He would often try to be casual about it:

"So, what do you look like?"

I had this answer down to a science.

"Important."

"Important?"

"When I walk in the room you will know it is me. I look important."

If he wanted more, I would proceed with,

"I'm short, with shoulder-length blonde hair and I need to lose about twenty pounds, but I'm not going to do it."

If there were silence I would usually say good-bye. If they launched into their physical attributes, the subject was moot. If they began to question me, it got ugly.

"Well, why wouldn't you lose the weight?"

"Do you have a medical problem?"

"I don't understand twenty pounds. What do you mean? How big is that?"

Back to voicemail.

I Have A Ph.D.

A Ph.D. is always intriguing. I love smart. It's up there with funny.

Stephen sounded like he had potential, even if he didn't currently have a job. "But I am interviewing." I agreed to meet him for a drink, and he got points for arriving in a suit. He drank club soda, while I had white wine. I asked about his thesis and his studies in Germany.

"I did my thesis on pronouns?"

"Pardon?"

"Pronouns."

I had to think fast.

"English or German?"

"Both."

That didn't help, but he proceeded to spend the next thirty minutes lecturing me about it. I ordered more wine.

When he stopped for air I brought up the election. Politics has to be better than pronouns, even if we don't agree. We didn't. It wasn't. He was convinced that volunteer organizations were mere fronts for bored White Republican women who were guilty about their privileged position. So what? If they are doing good things for the community, does it matter why they do them?

"I have a Ph.D. and I am going to overrule you on this one."

That was the good part of the evening. The check came and he wanted to figure out how much my wine cost versus his club soda. I used my privileged position to overrule him and pay for all the drinks. He called me the next week to see if I wanted to go out again.

"Stephen, did you think we had a good time?"

I told him he needed to get out more. But with someone else.

Can I Kiss You?

I moved on to the Scotsman, who over the phone sounded like Sean Connery. His name was Victor and he was the head of the local foxhunt. He said he was 5'4". I said that was great because I was 5'3". He informed me that he was "very good looking."

"Very good looking? Cary Grant is very good looking."

He insisted that he was very good looking.

We agreed to meet at a local restaurant. It was during the winter and it had snowed heavily the week before. The roads were still icy and I debated the issue of heels versus boots, but it was a first date and I braved the heels. I was waiting in the lobby of the restaurant when an undistinguished little man approached me. I thought he might be in charge of the coatroom, only to discover that he was Victor. He wasn't 5'4" and his heels were higher than mine were.

We are shown to the table. We order. By the time the appetizers come I know I don't want to see him again. We have nothing in common. I have begun to ask him the names of his favorite horses. I struggle to make conversation all through the meal, bravely nodding and smiling as he talks of the finer aspects of the hunt and how much work it takes to keep the fields and the hounds in shape. Nod and smile. Nod and smile. I guess I did that too well. "Would you like to take in a movie?"

"I'd love to." Why did I say that?

I pick *Mrs. Doubtfire* as I am sure there will be no sex in it. Let's just get this over with. The movie doesn't start for forty-five minutes and Victor asks if we can stop at the grocery store as it is by the theatre. Sure. Why not? Give us something to talk about. We drop my car off in the parking lot and drive across the street to the grocery store in his truck. He wants his Kix. Kix cereal. Kix is the only kind he eats. They have no Kix. He is starting to pout and have a little fit.

"I can't believe they are out of Kix. They always have Kix. I'm not going to have anything to eat for breakfast."

I suggest another grocery store down the street. We still have plenty of time. Victor drives a big Suburban truck and someone has parked too close to his door. He can't get it open.

"Slide over and you drive. People are so rude. No Kix and now this. Who would park like that?"

I got behind the wheel of his truck, trying to remember how much wine I drank between nodding and smiling. I did manage to maneuver it down the street and into the next parking lot, squeezing into a spot marked by small frozen drifts of dirty snow. Park. Stop. Open the door. In one smooth move I slid off the seat, onto my heels and then fell on my butt. Rather the same sort of arc made by a ski jumper, but without the lift-off. Thankfully the truck blocked everything from Victor. By the time he came around to my side, I was back on my feet and pretending to daintily navigate my way to the sidewalk. He was none the wiser. The only problem was that my skirt was now hiked up under my suit jacket around my waist and exposing my backside underneath my coat. It was a knit suit. Knits stay put. I was walking down the aisles at the grocery store, shaking one leg hoping my shirt might fall loose.

I lagged behind in the produce section so I might put a hand up inside my coat and tug at my skirt. A mother with her toddler gave me a disgusted look. I rubbed up against a display of rock salt rock hoping this might be enough to shake something loose. No luck. At least they have Kix.

He drives back to the movie theatre and I buy the tickets while he parks. Now this is true guilt. I feel guilty that I am not going to see him again yet he paid for dinner. I spot the bathroom and excuse myself to rescue my dignity before he tries to help me off with my coat. I meet up with him in the near-empty theatre. He has picked seats behind a couple that are already necking. The only thing holding them back a little at this point is the lights. Victor looks at me dreamily, probably thinking about his new box of Kix, and asks if he can kiss me.

"No!" At least I had enough sense not to nod and smile.

"Why not?"

"I barely know you." As though that would have stopped me. I am frantically trying to summon up a prudish air, which is difficult when you have spent the last half-hour with your skirt tucked up around your waist. We both knew it was going to be a long movie. At least in the end he'd figured out that we didn't have a good time.

I Could Draw That

Jay was a landscaper, which I later learned meant that he mowed lawns for a living. We were both pretending he was more successful than he was. But he owned his own lawnmower, which was something. We started to do all those things couples do at the beginning of relationships that they think they'll do later, but never get to. Picnics. Drives. Botanical gardens. Jay had just built his own house and was anxious to show it off. I agreed to meet him there for lunch, and then go to the new exhibit of da Vinci drawings at the Vassar Art Gallery.

Jay showed me all through the house — a split-level with no furniture and all the cost cutting features available. No dishwasher. Only one bathroom. He saved money with the washer and dryer by putting them on a platform so he wouldn't have to run more pipes. You climbed up a stepladder to use the machines. He bragged about not having to pay for garbage pick-up. He would put it in little bags and use the trashcans in grocery store parking lots. He owned no place mats, so for lunch that day I used two sheets of paper towels.

"You're just wasting them!"

Lunch didn't end there. He wanted to show me a video. I thought it was a little early in our relationship for a dirty movie, but I kept my mouth shut. It was a music video. *Anthrax in Concert.* Heavy metal. I watched about twenty minutes of it, repeating "What are they saying?" about every two minutes, just to show that I was listening.

"Jay, what made you think that I would enjoy that?"

"There's some really deep stuff there."

Jay thought he might have struck out with Anthrax so he decided he would win me over by showing me his books. "I have a whole book shelf."

This I have to see. He showed me the repair guides for various cars and mowers he had owned. He particularly admired a picture of a motorcycle. He told me he would like to buy it one day. Next, he dragged out two books he stole from high school. He showed me his textbooks from diesel repair school as well as his perfect attendance award. He then got out his sketchpad.

I was desperate to find some reason why I had agreed to meet him. Artistic? Did he say artistic? Did he ever use the words 'landscape architect' or had I just imagined it? He had sketches of motorcycles, muscle cars, men with Fu Manchu mustaches and iron cross tattoos. He drew snakes crawling through skulls and some sort of wizard. Lunch was over.

He insisted that he wasn't too tired for the art gallery where there was a small traveling exhibition of da Vinci's drawings done in different mediums. There was one done with an oil crayon that was intricate beyond belief. I was amazed that a man could draw something so perfect. It was as precise as a high quality black and white photograph. This drawing was the centerpiece of the collection, and one I circled back to several times. Jay was stalking around the room in a bored fashion and finally met me in front of this drawing.

"Can you believe the work in this? The detail." I whisper.

He pulls his glasses to the end of his noise for a myopic close up.

"I could do that."

"What?" I am giving him a combination sneer and lip curl in disbelief.

"Yeah. I could draw that."

I am thinking he is too dumb to live. "Jay, I have seen your drawings."

"I know. Don't you think I could do that?"

I wonder if da Vinci paid for garbage pick-up.

I Am Really Into Near Death Experiences

I gave Big Ed a call because he implied he was a psychology professor. The name 'Big Ed' worried me a bit until he explained that he was 6'4". So far, so good. The bigger they are, the tinier I look. We talked several times on the phone and he told me some great stories about his work with the criminally insane. With blind dates, I learned to judge them for the ability to tell good stories. Chances are you will only see them once, so they should at least have the potential for interesting stories. I was the first ad Big Ed had ever called and he was excited. "I know this is going to work out. I can just tell." I didn't have the heart to tell him he was about the twentieth man I had talked to, and I wasn't holding my breath.

I met Big Ed at a restaurant in the mall. He was huge. 6'8" would be closer to the truth. He was wearing cargo pants - those denim things with too many pockets, originally designed for people on safari who needed their gear at hand. These are not attractive on big men. He wore a pilled acrylic sweater with a white T-shirt underneath it that would peek out every time he craned his neck. But all this was nothing compared to his shoes. He wore steel-toed work shoes, with black patent leather tips. Why would they even make steel-toed patent leather shoes? If this was his idea of dressing up for a first date to make a good impression, I didn't want to think about what he would look like once he got comfortable.

We went into the restaurant for a drink and proceeded to make small talk. He told me about his two young children (he had custody of them) that he somehow had failed to mention before. This led to his ex-wife who just had his best friend's baby. I switched the topic to that time honored female ploy, "so, tell me about your work." He was a prison guard. I hoped my eyes didn't roll too badly. "Oh.... I thought you taught psychology." He explained that he taught it to prison guards. Since he had been a guard so long, that qualified him as an expert.

"You know what I am really into?"

"Tell me."

"Near death experiences."

I am fingering my car keys as I picture him into kinky sex practices. It's not a pretty sight.

"Just what do you mean by that?"

"You know. People who have died and them come back. Stories from the other side."

"Oh." I'm not sure if I am relieved or disappointed.

Big Ed proceeds to tell me about the show Oprah did, and one with Sally Jesse Raphael and others.

"This is real."

"Gosh, look at the time."

"Can I give you a call? We can have dinner as soon as I get paid next week."

"That would be great." I could say that in all confidence. The brilliant expert on criminal psychology did not have my phone number.

Antiquing A Plus

My girlfriend Cathy asked why I never replied to the ads men put in the paper, instead of making them call mine.

"That's simple. I like to be in control."

"Maybe that is the problem."

"Ouch."

But I promised Cathy that I'd go through the 'men seeking women' ads and call two. They varied between sex ads, "free-spirited," "non-committal," "safe adult fun" to the usual "short, fat, bald man seeks Cindy Crawford type for Dutch treat dinners." "I enjoy dining out, dancing and quiet times," was also a popular theme. Quiet times. That was my whole marriage. If I want quiet times I wouldn't be looking for a date.

The first one I called was an artist and musician, which is risky, but after spending six years with an engineer, it seemed a risk worth taking. He talked and talked and talked about himself. I called him on my lunch hour and realized I was able to eat my whole lunch without having to excuse myself for chewing. He didn't ask me one thing about myself. I heard about his paintings and his music. He played in a band. He thought I might like to hear them some night.

"In all honesty, I am the best looking one in the band."

"Oh?"

"Its true. Not only that, I am very secure in my masculinity."

Where could this be going?

"In fact, I am so secure in that I sometimes wear Mickey Mouse ear muffs."

"I think I've seen you before. Do you go to The Beechtree Saloon?" So much for that lunch.

I find a second ad that is appealing:

> Journalist, age 50. Enjoys fine wine, rare books and foreign travel. Can adapt to either NYC or country living. Appreciate good conversation and a quick wit. Antiquing and opera a plus.

This is too good to be true. No sports. No TV. No fitness enthusiasts. A man who would willingly walk into an antique store? I checked again to make sure the ad ran in the 'men seeking women' section and not in the 'alternative' column. I called and left a message. I stressed my love of books, food and travel, admitted to knowing nothing about opera, but willing to learn, and wine was definitely a plus. He called back that night. We talked.

It was an actual conversation. I talked and he listened, even asking questions. What a treat. I asked about his work and he had been the Arts Editor on a daily paper in New Haven, but his wife had died and he wanted to leave the area, so he returned to his family estate in Millbrook. Estate. Did he say estate? I tried not to sound over-eager. This was getting better and better. He had been in the Foreign Service right after college and had lived in several countries in Europe and the Far East. When they had decided to have children they moved back to U.S., but the kids never happened and then his wife got sick.

I was sympathetic. I was compassionate. I respected his loss and his bravery carrying on with his life. I asked what he was doing now.

"I am thinking about writing a novel."

"Thinking?"

"Yes. I have a lot of ideas."

Did he have enough money so he didn't need to work? A country squire? I could do this. I had a vision of tweed jackets, leather bound books and lots of dogs.

"So you're living in Millbrook now?"

"Well.... not exactly. When I came back to Millbrook, my father was sick and I took care of him, assuming that I would inherit the house. I didn't know the bank owned it."

"That's disappointing."

"So my wife died, I left my job in New Haven, my father died and the bank took the house and all the furniture."

"But you're still in Millbrook?" I was persistent. Dreams don't die easy. I had been on the phone with this man for over an hour. I wasn't going to let things fall apart now.

"No, I am actually in Poughkeepsie. Have you heard of Riverhaven?"

I had. It wasn't an estate; it was a homeless shelter.

"You're living at Riverhaven?…I heard it's very nice there. Uh, how long have you been there?"

"Six months."

I am really hurting. My initial reaction is to just hang up, but I feel sorry for this man. Not sorry enough to date him, but sorry enough to offer a little positive reinforcement.

"So do you have some plan in mind for your future?"

"I told you, I am thinking of writing a novel."

Those were his plans. He was *thinking* of writing a novel. Perhaps a better grasp on reality was needed.

" Well, I wish you luck."

"Maybe we could get together for a movie. There is a bus schedule that goes directly to the mall and I could meet you there."

"That's an idea, but I have to go out of town for my job for a couple months. Maybe we can get together in the spring. There should be some new movies out by then."

HONEY OR JELLY?

I almost didn't call Mike back because he was tall and thin — a foot taller than me and still he weighed less than I did, but he had made a big effort in his message. He didn't care about the weight because everything was cool. I am cool. You are cool. Life is cool…as long as we have enough pot to smoke. None of this was immediately obvious, but I hadn't dated for a while. There hadn't been any New Age Movement back when I was single. He read tarot cards, did astrological charts, practiced tai chi, collected guns and dragons. Mike wouldn't eat onions. He had a degree in philosophy, and worked as a lineman for the phone company. I figured he would have an interesting perspective on life as well as a pension.

The guns were kept in storage, so they never became an issue. The tarot cards were a successful lure to get me to his apartment, where the dragons lived. Dozens of them. I pretended to be interested. "And this one came from Sedona?...oh, a model of a kaboda dragon. Pewter. How interesting. Yes, I can see how the crystal reflects the light."

We proceed to the bedroom, where I discover more dragons and a single bed. More like a camp cot. I like to snuggle, but this is might be physically impossible. What kind of grown man sleeps in a single bed? Did I really want to spend the night? Yes. It had been a long time. I don't think the bed can even hold the weight of two of us, much less withstand what I hoped would be some energetic acrobatics.

It did. We even found a position somewhat comfortable to doze in afterwards. It was then I noticed the robes. Black robes hanging on the wall. Black robes like you see in horror films. Black robes used in satanic rituals. Black robes as in blood sacrifice. I am going to die. I will be dragged from this single bed out to the woods where I will be gutted, along with goats and chickens. Sacrificed for some strange dragon cult of non-onion eaters. Resigned to my death, and betting my immortality on a movie-of-the-week deal and I fell asleep gazing at the velvet tapestry of dragons hung on the wall by my side of the bed.

I heard the sound of dishes and cooking in the morning and awoke to find myself staring at a tray with tea and toast.

"I am so glad you stayed last night. Do you want jelly or honey? There is a robe on the hook there if you want a shower."

I took one of the navy terry cloth bathrobes off the hook on the wall and laughed to myself all the way to the shower.

I soon realized I had no business being with a new-age sort of guy. I especially realized it when he decided to move to the mountains of Utah and didn't want me to go with him.

"But won't you miss me," I persisted.

"How will I know until I get there. I can't tell from here whether I will miss you or not."

Mike left two weeks later, without saying good-bye. I decided that after all this, it was time I said good-bye too. Good-bye to the personals.

That was the end of my personal ad experience. Every once in awhile I will scan them again, which just confirms my decision to stay away from them. Men are still looking for "very pretty, very fit women with long hair for discreet fun." My solution?

"Is this barstool taken?"

The Face of the Ocean

Mark Jay Mirsky

T *he still, cold, movement of the rain across the windows in an April storm* — the downpour is mixed with snow and biting hail. This Massachusetts coastal weather is like early spring on the bleak hilltops of Tuscany, a foretaste of hell.

A few minutes before, I walked up from the ocean to the front door of the house. It was impossible to stand on the sea wall at the bottom of the hill, rollers rising out of a green gray sea, the spray filling the ditch behind the blocks of rock. Flying ice scratches one's cheeks, stings in the eyes. The wind knocks about on the massive rocks, piled on the ocean side some fifteen feet above the waves, a dangerous place for unsteady footing. In summer and fall hurricanes it is possible to walk on top of the broad breakwater without fear of the wind but this end of the winter has a sharp freezing spite in its tail and whips one quickly off the wall.

The sea is gray, green, brown, like the muck of a clam bed turned up and churned into an ocean of whitecap. There is nothing pretty in such a sea. All its colors are malignant as the eye of a shark. This is a point of shipwreck. It was still, fifty years ago, a wrecker's spit, where ships foundered, went smashing apart. During summer and fall, it is easy to imagine swimming in, between the heavy swells coming towards the rocks taking a breath, finding a lucky wave to bring one almost all the way and then — quick — to one's feet. Today the long swell is unpredictable — there is no way to calculate its roll. Today, blinded by ice, salt, frozen by the cold sea, a body floated toward this shore would be tossed and bludgeoned.

This is a small town. The value of property has begun to rise. It is after all on the sea shore, and the views of the inner harbor are spectacular. But it is a stubborn, corrupt place. Most of its inhabitants as the fish grew scarce were on the edge of poverty through the long depression that began here before the turn of the last century. The town's wharves lost earlier when sails came down and boats went out into the ocean with engines. Freed from the freak of harbor winds, the advantages to a fleet anchoring on the calm bay side of its peninsula diminished. The number of ships foundering on the outer shore, the teeth of rocks and sand bars where it faces the open sea sank below the level of a dependable income for salvage. As a summer resort its lots were laid out in a dumpy way, the houses and cottages often jammed up against one another. Many of the wealthy people who had built for the view, sold, and the rest put up their wooden summer castles in more particular towns. For further down the coast the charm of old fishing villages remained. Along the town's great sand beach too many dingy bars clustered with a reputation for shady dealings; prostitutes, pimps, petty criminals. Poor people built here, recent immigrants — Irish, Jews, Italians, and an occasional Greek or Armenian. If their children made money, they went on to the fashionable communities of the Cape, or settled up at the North Shore. Only a few held on—keeping the old cottages, or deciding to blow insulation into the walls, put up an extra story or two, winter through and commute to a job in Boston.

In most of the empty beach houses through the fifties, sixties, seventies, people with no other place to go rented — managed a mortgage, fixed up a house with the claims from storm insurance; colluding with a local carpenter on the cost of replacing a smashed in front porch, or setting the value of old, falling apart furniture swamped in the basement, at the price of Colonial antiques.

Through the winter, the town gets down to bedrock. Its citizens meet in the three or four convenience groceries; stores where one buys milk, cans of coffee for a few dimes more than it will cost in the supermarket; dry cereals, boxes of tea, packaged white breads, flashlight batteries and the newspaper. A stranger can feel their anger. Not red necked, nothing so easy to see, point a finger at. It shows in a drawn in, reserved irritability. It only breaks out, becomes obvious when our plumber's wife goes wandering across the street in front of her house, shouting gibberish at trucks and passing cars, or I hear that the nice fellow, a few streets over, who worked with disturbed kids, last week put a shotgun in his mouth.

The neighbors across the street have stories to tell when I come by in March or April for a cup of coffee. I have driven out on the peninsula to look over our shutters, back lots, get the beach cottage ready for the summer. I am a stranger though my family has been here longer than any of the people living on either side of me. I know the town, have inherited quarrels with policemen, assessors, that run back fifty, sixty years. I have no reason to be here out of season. It's cold, and the house, a wooden castle without insulation, can barely be heated by the fireplace and the portable electric unit I plug into your bedroom.

Coming up from the gray granite, salmon blocks of the breakwater, flecked with mica, shivering, I feel with satisfaction the icy spray under the collar of the rubber jacket, seeping down my back, a storm that gets into the bones. It occurs to me, shivering, that this town is a landscape for a murder.

In the ditch behind the sea wall the spikes of the old railroad that ran along the Atlantic lie rusting. The ties long ago were carried away for firewood, although the ribs of boats and broken up wharves litter the beach, caught in the crannies and gaps of the breakwater like dinosaur bones where its wall juts out into the ocean. Opposite the lighthouse just at that point there is a graveyard of salt white timbers. They have piled up behind the wall where high tides have flung them. The Victorian turrets of houses along the cliff above, the wreckage on the rocks, the angry dead end town, and now the storm lashing the beach and the wide empty porches, suggest in this winter desert, to put hand to a bloody deed out of season, to answer the weather shaking the canvas of the backdrop.

It's not murder I have come up here for. It is another crime, one felt like a spirit moving across the wide green lawn behind the house that is so much trouble to keep cut through June, July and August. A wind whips the bare trunks of the wild cherries, the belt of naked woods, and then the heavy cover of the pines between the house below mine on the hill, to the other cottage where the trouble lies.

The State Senator, my father, bought enough land to make the other residents of the cliff, and the houses beside and below our own, angrier still. It was all worthless scrub lot, filled with sumac, poison ivy, blackberry vines, crab apple — gone back to the town for non-payment of taxes. The town was happy to sell it to the Senator and get a few hundred dollars a year in revenue. Now it is worth far more than the house. This is one of the things that has made our neighbor, Lowford, angry at us. The land belonged to fourth and fifth cousins of his. It was pear orchard once, and hay meadow. Land wasn't worth having in the town until five years ago when the building began and lots valued at a four hundred dollars shot up to four thousand on the assessor's books and sold for twenty, thirty, forty thousand.

The trouble started though long ago, over small things, I was told. A hand saw was never returned, empty beer bottles flung into the bushes, noise in the backyard, a path that stamped the constant trespassing as a claim. Then there was a fight over where Lowford's property line was and my father's. Lowford had four sons and one daughter. My father was getting old, testy, and there were several run-ins on the back lots. My father harbored a grudge, so did Lowford and it was passed on to the children on both sides, except for one, Lowford's daughter.

It's strange to watch a child I first saw as a baby, hanging on to the slats of a white picket fence, grow up to be a little girl stealing over our lot lines to pick raspberries, then a teenager bundled into the wrecks the local kids drive, coming up a road late at night, seeing her wrestling in the back seat, her blonde hair flashing under the lamplight. I watch discretely from our elevation, in the belt of cherries, as she comes out into her backyard in a white wedding dress, a woman, getting married. And I am there the week she comes home, driving her husband's Buick, with a dent in the front fender and a black eye. I have been watching her for almost twenty one years now and she has looked up at me, quickly, since she was three, hanging on the white pickets, smiling out of the corner of her eyes, inviting me to say more than hello, how are you? We both share the secret of that smile in the moment when I lift my eyebrows and look back into her sharp blue eyes.

In my childhood and when I was a young man, there were many places in the town one could be alone, unobserved, private. The old inn, half burned, at the tip of the peninsula, had back rooms still intact, their floors littered with empty bottles and collapsed rubber condoms. The same evidence could be found in the crumbling cement bunkers of the Fort, its abandoned under- ground rooms. This privacy was half public. More romantic and remote however, was the cliff face itself, for the grounds of the fort rolled out to the brow and then fell steeply down to the sea wall. Coming up the hill from the sand spit at the end of the peninsula there were fourteen or fifteen houses. Ours was one of the last before the rusted cyclone and barbed wire fence of the fort. From our lawn, a path, barely to be discerned among the bayberry and blue- berry bushes, ran along the top of the cliff just beyond the fencing of the Fort. Since the cliff had tumbled away in several places it was easy to climb under the fence into the Fort. It was difficult to get up, however, to the path. You had to either pass through our grounds and the watchdogs, or climb to it further on from the beach below. The sea wall here was high and only an agile body could go from toe hold to toe hold up to the top. Once on the wall, the hillside above was covered with stinging nettles, blackberry vines, thick groves of sumacs and spreading fields of poison ivy. It took some experience to get up the hill safely, especially in summer when the grass was thick with thorns and the cover of bushes and low trees, in places, impenetrable. Climbing from the top of the wall, to the hill's brow or just below it, sitting in a grove of sumacs, their heavy red crowns smelling of lemons and raspberries, tropical foliage, between bamboo and Japanese dwarf oaks, a boy, a girl, whoever lay beside them, were invisible. Not even the boats, far out on the blue sea, by the rocks white with sea gull droppings, or the erect tower of the lighthouse, could be seen through the veil of the sumac leaves; though from this eagle's nest I could pick out figures, bending to fishing lines or lobster traps with binoculars. If I wanted to flaunt myself at the boats, I could lie in the long grass outside the sumacs, grass. Its blades long enough to make a skirt, the beard of a hill which had never been scythed or mowed within the family's memory tickled; the long strands under my buttocks, or my partner's, turning, under the tense nipples of her breasts.

The Lowford's are a very old family in this town. One of them came in the boat that was drummed out of Plymouth Colony in the first few years of the Pilgrims existence in America. He put up a shack next to the minister whose dissolute nature had become obvious at the Plymouth colony. There is no trace of the minister's name any more in our town, or those of the other eleven men in the long boat that was cast off from the shore of Plymouth with oars, food and a few muskets, to fend for themselves in another place. They rowed north until they found the peninsula and the island which is now part of it. From where I sit, by the window, watching the rain scratch, was separated at that time by the sea at high tide from the rest of the town. The long spit to this final point in the ocean where Lowford alone, stuck, still isolates it from the noise, the honky tonk bars, the tourists on the sand beach, the mass of cottages dumped into each others' back yards.

It is an old name, Lowford, but no distinction attaches to it in particular. There are neither Congressman or Senators from Massachusetts by that name, no judges, magistrates, writers, merchant magnates. Occasionally its two syllables can be read on the side of a bait shop, or a gas station in other towns down the shore, where a mixture of Indian blood or French Canadian has given pluck to the family. The real Lowfords have those blue eyes, sandy hair, a slightly cross eyed look.

My father admired the Yankees but not the Lowfords. He was proud of his own name, the first name among the Jews, the priestly name, Cohen. He liked getting up in the synagogue to claim his right to climb the stairs to the platform where the scroll of the law lay unrolled, the first one, the Cohen, to whom the opening of the week's portion is reserved. He carried himself that way, like a priest, among his constituents, taking their vote, not asking for it. And they admired his pride. The proprietors of the pickle stands, the little groceries, the notions shops, the bookies in the cigarette and candy stores valued it. He advanced their own standing in the world. His Harvard education, his perfect diction, seemed more Yankee than Eastern European Jew, although he had been born in Grodno, and fluently scolded the petty criminals of the ward in Yiddish. Lowford was trash to my father. When he saw the trouble brewing, he tried to buy the Lowford place. It was too late. He was out of the State Senate and not powerful enough to get rid of Lowford, only to wound him. My father losing his grip on the rational, hurt his neighbor just badly enough to make the latter an angry beast, prowling the edge of the property looking for ways to gore us.

Lowford — I couldn't look in his eyes.

But there were many reasons for that.

In the back of our yard there is a hardy patch of azalea bushes, red and white. My father took the two small pots that came to the house as gifts of condolence when my mother died and planted them in the lawn. Wild blackberry vines have come up in the midst of the bushes, some fifteen feet thick now, a wide circle of blood and bridal white blossom at the end of May, and later in July, the blackberries, fat and juicy as if feeding off a rich rotting body in the roots of the azaleas. There is something sweet, prickling, extravagant, awful, in the flowering and fruiting.

The struggle between our families has been going on for forty years now. It seems as if it has become rooted in the clay subsoil, where roots, sumacs, blackberries, have a deep, stubborn life, and come up unexpectedly when we thought we had dug them out, and civilized the lawn.

A white mist shadows the landscape. Thirty, forty feet in front of my face, figures trail off. From the sea, cold April fog rolls over the peninsula, the islands, like a cloud of jealousy. My neighbors observations disappear in a fabric of suggestion. This weather lends however, a shroud of privacy to the comings and goings in town. People meet in places which are normally open to everyone's view. I can walk up the beach, below my house, and not be seen. Nothing can be seen distinctly either from windows in the houses along the cliff. Even homes below our hill that sit just across from the the flat spit of stones rolled by the tide, have their unobstructed sea view wrapped in obscurity. One can make out walking through the fog, at best, a form.

I am looking from the cliff at such a figure. Hidden from the beach I can see some thirty feet behind the first ghost, a second, standing behind a tall hedge then walking a few steps further along and crouching in bayberry bushes. The second is just keeping in sight of the first's back.

And I know that it's not safe to keep an appointment in the baby blanket of cold April mist despite a childish excitement, taking off my stiff wet blue dungarees, tight cotton briefs, feeling the cold saw edge of the long grass under the sumacs, not able to spy on the ocean, only hearing the long moaning of the horns, the sharp repeated peals of the harbor bells, all coming together with the volleys of the sea like a wild symphony as I touch her small erect breasts and listen to the horn, a ship or buoy's, shuddering, shuddering, as if a fragile bottom was about to go up on the rocks.

The first figure turns. Is it aware of the second? It ducks into a bank of white mist so dense it is lost, both to me, looking from the bayberry bushes and the figure following it. The latter runs forward, stops, turns to the right, then the left, coming up against what must be the wall, and wanders back and forth in circles until it too is lost. Has the fog swallowed it up? It seems as if the mist is darker, deeper, more impenetrable. Whatever outline of the rocks just beyond the figures was visible from time to time, as they threaded the footpath down on the beach, is now lost. Sea, hillside, wall, are all hidden in the fog. I think I hear the cry, but it could be the sea, or the bells, or the horns.

Who is following her?

I thought it was her father. But as I lose both in the white mist, it occurs to me that her brother might be walking behind her.

A fresh wave of revulsion comes up in my throat, thinking of that bluff, smiling young man, in the midst of his front yard full of torn apart sports cars and trucks, down the street some dozen houses or so from his father and sister.

It could have been her husband. How much did he know about the family, about her, or me?

In the fog everything is forlorn. Shadows of shapes become as real as the solid objects we seem to make out. Even touch is arbitrary in the wet dank air. Have I imagined it?

A hand against my cheek, the long, strong fingers, and then the lips up against mine — I put my thumbs in her belt and grasp that small waist, grip her buttocks, fall back with her, greedy for a mouth which seeks mine, into the bushes. Not saying anything. Creeping down to a second, then a third clump of sumacs, from the top of the cliff, where it is almost impossible that anyone, even following closely can follow or see anything. Finding the buttons of her shirt, to feel that her small, hard breasts are still there, shivering for me.

What am I doing here early in April — this shore's raw month? The peninsula's tree branches end in black fists unwrapping the first few leaves burnt by the winter cold to the sun, brown covers, before they burst into green? Even though its three sides are warmed by the ocean, everything in the ground is fragile, tentative, a few white and blue blossoms poking up with the onion grass, the tulips still rolled like umbrellas around their stalks, the wheels of color just showing in the furled leaves, more red than green in the branches against the sky. Without the mist, everything would be nude, public.

She is reaching for my pants, to unbutton me. She wants me inside her. But I am afraid. I can't help listening, trying to hear in the sounds of the harbor and the sea, footsteps, above us, below us. The sumacs are bare and if the fog lifts it will be easy to see us.

"Why come back?" I asked.

She couldn't answer.

"They are crazier than they used to be." The words come out of her with a sigh, after the silence between us has gone on for over a minute.

Her father pulled lobster pots for awhile, then went out with an old fishing boat, dragging the bay for flounder, the black back and yellow tail that lie on the sand banks out in the harbor or Quincy Bay, fish smelling faintly of motor oil when you fry them up in the pan or bake them in a light sauce. At the Boston restaurants they call the white stomachs filet of sole. But my wife won't take the flounder when I bring up half a dozen from the pier in the summer. There are unhealthy patches on the skin, tumors, and the taste isn't quite right even when the yellow or black back looks okay. The water it's been feeding in—what sifts down to the bottom when not swimming through sewage, gasoline, worries her. The Fish & Chips restaurants bubble them in deep fry vats so that the customers can only taste the grease and the breadcrumbs. But flounder disappeared in big numbers anyway several years ago. Other things come in on the boats under the noses of the coast guard. The visitors who pull up in the driveway of Lowford's yard, men in slinky suits and narrow ties, drive Mercedes Benzs, not wholesale fish buyers, not with their carefully trimmed fingernails. The latter with manicured hands take out bills from a leather wallet of lacquered crocodile at the counter of the local restaurant when I recognize the Mercedes with the same license plates parked in front of its bay window.

On the peninsula, strangers, out of season, are always noted. But Lowford has two or three cousins on the police force and the town assessor is an uncle by marriage. The police here like to grab a kid and make him, her, cry; or pull up to a young woman at a stop sign and harass her under the pretext of a noisy muffler. Lowford is a man who always goes to town meetings and the select-man are wary of him. He's dangerous. My father warned me long ago not to get involved with the family, but. . . .

Her brother, James, is the youngest, next to her. He still seeks my eyes out deliberately when our paths cross, once, twice a summer, at a grocery or liquor store. You won't see him at the beach or on the dock, despite the three or four boats with rusting engines at the back of his yard. He drives down to Plymouth every morning during the week where he works at the nuclear plant on its computers. He's gone to college and he has an engineering degree but almost every afternoon and late into evening in torn dungarees he is still fiddling with a few of the town's juvenile delinquents over a truck motor, a sports car of twenty, thirty years ago that someone bought for a song, his beard stubble showing through the grease specks on his cheeks. The front rooms of the Cape Cod on Main Street he bought from a disgruntled summer resident for next to nothing five or six years ago look like a fraternity house on the skids, after an all night bash. There are armchairs rescued from the dump on the front porch, the stuffing spilling out and the springs exposed. I imagine the living room rugs spotted with oil and alcohol and the paint is flaking off the walls. Automobiles cram every inch of the tiny front yard, torn apart, the salt water eating into transmissions, crankcases, chassis, while he patches in them. His specialty is the paint job. One of the local mechanics told me James had a genius for lacquering over all the problems when they are ready to move out to some hapless customer responding to the advertisements in the local newspapers. The car for sale looks like a taffy apple, sparkling, new. It purrs, a newborn — the loose bolts and missing steel swaddled in plastic and glue.

There is something so cute about him, his affable smile, that it's hard not to return it. But his look at you implies something else. He doesn't talk about his father's feud over the boundary line. It's not his property. It might never be. He has other stakes in the family.

He wants me to know that he knows.

He wonders if I know.

And I want to know why she has come back to this too.

She can't answer that.

Not now, she insists when we finally meet. *And it starts like that too, in the call to your office in Philadelphia,* "Can you come up?"

"Where are you?"

"At the beach?"

"The beach?"

"I left him."

Why, I want to ask, but that is too bold, direct and it—the answer—may involve me in something I don't want to know but I can't admit *that*. Even if I could, would I want to— to ask why—and hear yourself as a part, at least, of the response.

I ask after a pause — a big one, in which I can hear traffic behind her, on the other end of the line, so I imagine she is calling from a safe place, the middle of the parking lot, with a pay phone where she can see for several yards around her and it's impossible for someone to eavesdrop (I have called her, long distance, twice, three times, from a parking lot like that, so that she could hear cars and trucks starting up at a liquor store or grocery behind you)— "Can I call you?"

My secretary is discreet but the office is a poor place to ask questions and have this girl break into tears over the phone while clients are buzzing, trying to get through. "No," she answers shortly.

She understands where I am and so I have no choice. *You have to respond.* "What happened?"

"I don't want to talk about it now."

"What *do* you want?" It comes out much too quick, almost cruel, because one of the younger brokers in the doorless entrance to the office is trying to get my attention and I know that in thirty seconds or so my secretary will break in and ask if my present party can hold while someone else speaks to me for a minute.

"I want you to come up."

"I'll come up tomorrow." I say it, not quite believing what the words make explicit. I have appointments tomorrow, and dinner at home, but it's too late to try to qualify my offer or even make arrangements as to where to meet, or how, because she hangs up just as I finish the sentence and it's not clear whether she is being considerate or angry.

My desk is a mess and the phone calls, letters, to be returned are already a week in arrears. The dinner I will have to miss is important, among the guests, one of my best accounts, his wife, a leading politician in the city and a talented painter whose reputation has reached London, Paris, whom both my wife and I have been cultivating for some time. It takes an hour of frantic phone calls to straighten out the mess, assemble the players with different people in the succeeding weeks. Clearing the desk so that the next day, mercifully Friday, will not be a disaster in the office requires the rest of the afternoon. My firm is a small, independent one and I am already a senior partner. I can come and go as I want but that is rarely the case. Friday has been a dangerous day in the Stock Market lately and I leave precise directions if something should go haywire during trading session on the exchanges.

Explaining why I am suddenly going up to the beach house to my wife is the next stage of difficulty. Either I will be met by suspicion or pity—it is a long, interminable drive to Massachusetts, between seven and ten hours, depending on the number of stops to rest you make. To get a head start, it's best to push yourself out of bed at four in the morning. Otherwise I have to fly.

I would rather drive this time. There are some cases of books I can bring up, take back, tools, a chair to be jammed in the back seat. Those are my excuses. I want the drive, to think. I can't think the way I would like to in an airport terminal. I want the assurance of my own automobile, its thick leather upholstery, the comfortable back seats where I can curl up and nap, if I get too sleepy, the cassette deck. I am already too far off the earth, wondering what happened, what is going to happen.

"It's your fault," she had flung in your teeth during one of our final painful meetings before she got married. I had forgotten that moment. Abruptly, slamming the car door behind her, she jumped out and ran off leaving me alone by the car.

The first part of the trip is the easiest. I am half comatose, anyway, and the pavement of the New Jersey turnpike, the meadows of farmland, the oil cracking and chemical plants, drift by in a half sleep. Even swinging across the Tappan Zee bridge, and into upstate Connecticut, is easy and the traffic is all going the other way, to work. In Connecticut I know a good breakfast place and around eight o'clock is perfect. The eggs are fresh, better than what one gets in Philadelphia and they know how to brown the home fries crisply. I have eaten here with her, several times, driving down from Massachusetts or back up. Some time after nine in the morning, she will call my house, hang up after a signal of two rings on the chance, that her father is out in the harbor and she can answer.

It's in the south of Connecticut that I will start to get depressed. Off one of the exits there is a river that meanders through a forest down the slope of a long hill.

I went crashing through the underbrush with her one afternoon when she joined me at the bus station in Hartford. There were beaver ponds along the river. The two of us saw one of the short, squat animals swimming, a wriggling body in the water, for a moment, diving into the underground burrow they had smacked together of mud, sticks, logs. There were fat brown trout in that stream too. And I stripped off all my clothes and swam where the water was waist deep. Laughing at the oozing mud between my toes, trying to get back into socks and shoes without too many telltale scrapes of leaves and dirt. She stood watching, not wanting to swim, but the nakedness under her blouse, jeans, the magic I needed to disrobe and dive in the cold water melted off the ice in the hills.

Later, I tried to find the spot but it had disappeared, though half a dozen times I led my wife and children in charges through deep forest, off roads that looked the same only to end in a bog or a flat field.

I call her at ten in the morning, from a delicatessen, in Vernon, Connecticut, just past Hartford. It's a place where I can get kosher corned beef, pastrami, tongue. In the past few years I have begun returning to rules I knew as a little boy — part of the ordered world — as against the chaos, the upside down universe, when I take her hand and want to pull her close, go tumbling. She has sat at tables here, humored me, the same tables my wife and children have eaten at. I tense, wondering if a waitress might recognize that I come in as two different people, or the woman behind the counter say something in front of my two boys. Yet I want the girl I can not name, now, her ghost, to reassure me, even if I have made the whole idea of clean — meat made fit — unfit — unclean, by mixing our two lives in the same restaurant.

There is no one in her house when I call at ten o'clock to Massachusetts. I sit down to order a couple of eggs, sunny side up, coffee, home fries, rye toast. I haven't had time to pray, to put on the phylacteries, I carry in the back of the car.

Is she going to be there? Is this a trick or has she panicked? How am I going to get together, just sit in my house and wait for her to sneak into the trees, across the lawn, at night, seeing the light in my windows? The phone isn't connected yet and there's nothing I can do about it on the weekend.

She has called many times, asked me to meet her, in the past. I have driven to New York City, waited at the Greyhound Terminal, in a crowd of teenagers, sailors, harassed black families with crying babies, waiting for the first, the second, the third bus from Boston, waiting until two in the morning when the last one came in without her on it, and I finally gave up and went back to my hotel room alone.

She has come down, though. More than once, jumped off the middle steps of a bus recklessly, into my arms, as I sweep her up and safely off, in a taxi. A single duffel slung under her arm, taking off a weekend from the junior college she was going to, at seventeen, eighteen — the two of us have walked New York City, the cheap glare of Times Square, hustle of the Village. Drunk in the painters' bars, listened to jazz, perfunctorily, then going back to the hotel room, we held each other as if all the sweetness one could imagine was pressed between our two bodies. "The treader of grapes — overtaking the sower of seeds, and the mountains shall drip sweet wine, and all the hills shall melt." It didn't seem possible to want a woman, a child in a woman' body, so, but it made me dizzy. When I saw her on the bus steps with her cross eyed smile, and neat, tense body, I trembled and was ready to throw everything away, just to be with her. Later on, in the room, when the love making was over, I sobered. She was too young. I was too old. I had responsibilities and beside that I loved my wife. This girl was a marvelous gift, but I couldn't afford it. The exchange would ruin me. She never asked for anything though. She wouldn't talk about what the two us, she and I, were doing then and stopped me with a cold stubbornness when I tried to.

It had been that way since she was fourteen. The only way I could gauge what she was feeling was when she wasn't on the bus, despite the telephone calls, the insistence that she wanted, *had*, to see me. She just had to *talk,* walk along beside me. But she wasn't there and I guessed that she was angry or had found someone her own age. I would sit there alone, after pretending to my family I was going away on a business deal, swearing to break off, never to see her again. Later in the week, the month, once six months after the appointment, she would call, "Are you mad?"

"No."

"Do you want to see me?"

I couldn't help the excitement. But I said what I was supposed to say, "No."

"You *are* mad."

"I just don't see the point of not showing up."

"I have to explain it."

"Now. Tell me. . . ."

"I have to *see* you."

"Why?"

"I can't say it over a telephone." Something in a phrase like that would hook me. "You have to *see* me." And the plaintive tone, the dry sense of guilt, the spark of excitement I couldn't deny suddenly in a succession of stolid, finally disappointing days, made me agree, as I had yesterday, try to arrange a time, a place, a phone she could reach me at before, impulsively, assuming it was all arranged, she hung up.

I have driven toward her, how many times? In a bus, my own car, the taxi from a train to New York City, Boston — for the past twelve years it seems — although for the last five years I haven't seen her except across the line of pines, at the window of her car, once in the shopping market, late at night, between the aisles, both of us flustered, looking at each other, trying to exchange a few tags of easy conversation, furtive glances like the first few I shared with her when she was at the verge of infancy.

The road that crosses into Massachusetts coming up from Hartford — depending on whether one's car is flying out of the hills of Connecticut or nodding behind a line of trucks droning along as if they were still climbing the winding grade from the old tobacco country, instead of speeding across the flat plateau before Sturbridge — is some fifteen or twenty minutes to the gates of the Turnpike. The weather has a say in acceleration. A car here is caught up in the currents of an inland sea and has to sail accordingly. At night a heavy mist comes down between the hills and rolls almost to the steel bars in the Turnpike booths. When it is sunless and damp, the short link between the Pike and the wide lanes of the Connecticut highway, can turn into a torturous three quarters of an hour, groping from taillight to taillight with flares marking where a truck has gone off the road or one car crashed into another's rear. Even in June, high in these hills and on stormy days through the summer, the fog is cold enough to require a car's defroster and its heater switch.

The Turnpike is a dead road.

It is fenced. No place to get off it, except at the exits, where the ticket booths force payment. There are no real rest stops, no way to wander to the sides for a picnic or a swim, cheap gas, a shopping spree, a restaurant which looks interesting from the road. There are two mediocre points to eat at — the first just beyond Sturbridge, a town full of good restaurants but that requires a detour from a forward trajectory. The second point comes just before exits in Wellesley or Newton leading toward the Cape. The meals are just fast food, though keeping a haphazard kosher, one eats only tuna fish, French fries. The parking lots of the Turnpike's eating places are full of diesels, engines grinding, rumbling like an upset stomach, vibrating night and day. The road's symbol used to be a cocked green Puritan hat, with an arrow through it.

My father hated the Pike. He was for freeways, jaywalking, egress and ingress without payment. He wouldn't fence our property, no matter how angry Lowford and his incursions made him. About the corpulent Irishman who built the Turnpike with the political brawn of a steel driver, my father had only bitter words. There *was* something Puritanical, priggish, priestly, about the Massachusetts Turnpike, the high prices at the gas pumps, its bad food, the constant patrolling of the State Police, all swimming in a sea of green paint. The most likely adventure on it was a speeding ticket.

To call from the Turnpike is an ill omen. It's better to ring from a small town off Route 128, or 3, when the grueling three quarters of an hour on the road — which runs like the straight arrow in the cocked hat, but knocks one out, making the driver sleepy, unpredictable, liable to side swipes and rear end collisions — is over.

Why call? It makes me angry since she may not be there. Stopping for the fourth cup of coffee that morning, or is it afternoon, now? In the back of a rest stop somewhere. I went to sleep—my watch reads three p.m. I've lost time. It's impossible to call anyway and my head is in a shambles. I didn't get enough sleep and don't trust myself to be quick enough to get off the phone if her father answers. Or if she proves difficult. The icebox at the summer house is empty, electricity off. There is nothing to eat but I don't have the strength to stop for something. Tomorrow is Saturday and I can't cook until dark. I won't drive the car, if possible, or pay for anything. It's the day of rest.

It's too late now in fact to turn around. I am trapped between my notion of the law — my will to break it.

That is when the weather makes itself part of the day. On the road it has been sunny all morning. The tight red buds are beginning to unfurl, a first raw blossoming spreading a pink mist through the woods of the valleys and troughs the highway runs down into and up from. I pull up to the side of the road at one spot where the woods are dense and walk into the trees. The branches swollen with life urge one to put lips to the rosy, opening tree buds as if they were nipples. I want her so hard I touch the trunk of a flowering shrub as if it were her arm, waist. If she were here I would tear her blouse open to feel her breasts. But I go back to the car, start it up, try to keep awake in the pink haze, broken at times by the yellow flame of forsythia and light green veil of willow branches, the uncut, reviving grass. Spring, the smell of it, is in the melting hollows, even up on the hills where the trees are still black, a forest of wires, and it makes my foot snap on the accelerator pedal, laughing, as if summer and its full heat was rolling toward me from the sky.

This is the moment — I barely miss side swiping the car overtaking me on the right. In the wake of its horn, blaring, shocking me from dazed driving, weaving back and forth across the lane, an angry sound that dies away as the other automobile shoots ahead, it becomes obvious that I have to stop. But I drive on and on, until a familiar sign signals and pulling violently to the right, I slump against the wheel, fall back and under it.

A dry ache in my head, a sour stomach, I wake up on the Turnpike, behind the last cafeteria to the sound of diesel engines turning like cement mixers. I get up in rumpled clothes to urinate. Rain drops wet my hair and shirt crossing the parking lot — no one could imagine that a few hours before the sun was out. It is gray and the white clouds puffing out through the sky, warn not of a storm but an oppression, a low wet blanket of mist. The sky has drawn the warmth, the color, from the landscape. It is cold even in the rest rooms. When I return to start up the engine, it seems as if I am moving through sludge, road, land and sky, ill defined. Getting off the Turnpike, the main artery, driving toward the road which skirts the sea, fog banks muffle the car. I have to crawl through the streets of the neighboring towns.

At a forlorn grocery — its sign looming in the dense, wet air, I pull up to buy a carton of juice, milk, some cans of tuna fish, bread, a withered tomato. A few hundred yards on is a liquor store where I buy a quart of black rum, a fifth of Irish whiskey, two six packs of beer, three bottles of the best Bordeaux they have on the shelf and a familiar glass rectangle filled with medium sweet Kosher Concord. I might as well be in my pajamas and the customer behind me warns that the change from the twenty dollar bills I paid with is falling out of my pocket. The fog is like a narcotic pulling me down.

How I got to the front door, parked the car, climbed into bed is part of the silent movement of intention through the damp medium of sea, earth, road. The bells in the harbor — when I hear a ring at first, I mistake it. The phone has been disconnected.

The Hirsute Woman

Yvonne Murphy

A love story, really,
which my lover refused
to see, taking the control,

he changed the channel past her
to a game, but I pleaded,
grabbed the remote,

turned back to the woman.
I didn't catch her name—
her face, an ape's, nuzzled

in the neck of a man. Her man,
who said she was his joy,
met her at a carnival

one night and knew.
My man found her
detestable, screwed-up

his face—wouldn't look,
then looked, then could only
look away. He snatched

the control and switched her
safely off. The furry-
cheeked lover, living

in Florida, or somewhere.
I imagined them always
together, naked in bed,

his arms twined around
hers, both heads finding comfort
in a sensuous carpet of hair.

Combs and brushes danced
on their table—leftover revelers
from the giddiness of flirting.

When my protest grew
unbearable, my lover finally
left the room. I turned her

back on, decades had passed.
Her husband dead now, the woman
sat somber, clean-shaven, shorn.

Monk Parrot

Yvonne Murphy

In a tree over the carport where my window looks out
in this section of Houston there is fabled to be a bird,

a white tropical cockatiel, hooded, albino last of its kind.
Monk parrot, parody on words, rhythm-a-ning

in the wings of my parking spot, seldom seen
by regular neighbors. I call to him: *Dabadeep da ba dabap.*

My songs get lost when nobody hears them, plotted
pre-planned patterns of taking-off . . .

I seem I must be of the not-seen, invisible
to the naked eye like the cockatiel, we might

rival tunes of the immortals if only, that is,
he'd show—goofy mute pacing to my own flow

of rhythm, complicated inner scores few would
care to understand. Solitude is a glass of Pepsi

sitting half-finished on the writing desk, or is it half-
started? A parrot call: *Well You Needn't,* over and over again.

A chorus of Benedictine brothers, birds all, join in.
Outside my window they dovetail chants among magpies,

grackles, magnificent plumage tucked inside their robes.
I wonder: why *not* be known?

Express this weird beauty to others
who'll be kind?

The parrot pops up in the window where I watch.
Eyeing him, I think: *I believe I exist, isn't that enough?*

Tales of the Blue Mazda

Stewart Andrew Engesser

*T*onight my car wants to go to Canada. Last week it was the White Mountains, only this morning it was Portland, Maine. Right now, from where I'm sitting at my desk, I can see her out there in the driveway, a few yellow leaves stuck to the windshield, the right front tire slightly flat, a dent in the side showing dark from where she was struck by a Winnebago somewhere late at night in South Dakota. I can hear her yelling at me.

"Canada!" she yells. "Stop writing and let's GO! We can be in Montreal by tomorrow, Yellowknife, Yukon sometime next week. Are you going to write all night? You're only sort of young once, you know."

Mine is a Blue Mazda with spirit.

When I bought the Blue Mazda I had no idea what I was getting into. I bought her nearly brand new from a Salerno dealership in Massachusetts. I was twenty. I still have the "For Sale" sign. I didn't know how to operate a manual transmission at the time, and so spent the better part of the ride back to New Jersey learning an impressive number of ways how it should not be done. I sometimes think that any trouble we have had between us stems directly from this one ride we took.

My inability to drive her smoothly insulted her. At one point, as I was grinding the gears, trying desperately to merge back into traffic outside a McDonald's in Rockville, parts fell off. One of them was pan-shaped, the other what appeared to be some sort of largish bolt. Mesmerized, I stared into the rear-view mirror and watched these things bounce and roll away into traffic, when suddenly the Blue Mazda surged forward, as if enraged, and I was forced to slam on the brakes in order to avoid running into a meat truck. I never did find out what those parts were. Apparently the Blue Mazda did not really need them; she kept running and still does. They were sort of like appendixes in that way, I have concluded. But she was trying to tell me something.

Occasionally the Blue Mazda sees fit to remind me of the indignities she suffered on that long six-hour cruise. When I try to take her certain places, she leaves me stranded. I have found that generally she dislikes going anywhere in or even near the state of Delaware. Atlantic City is also a place she is more comfortable avoiding, and in fact I find that when riding on complicated, dirty, high-trafficked roads, such as the Van Wyck Expressway or the Major Deegan, she is almost guaranteed to require what I have come to term "periodic rest stops." It's as if the strain of driving these congested, mean-spirited roads saddens her to such an extent, when there are so many roads out there that are BETTER, and go to BETTER PLACES, that she feels the need to stop and give me time to really experience where we are and how much better things would be if we had never, ever, gone there. Some people call this breaking down. I think the Blue Mazda would be more comfortable with the term "instructive pause."

The Blue Mazda likes open spaces. She likes driving on unpaved one-lane roads with no names. She likes the entire state of Maine. She likes driving in places where there is a good chance of seeing bear. And yet, sometimes, when she's in a certain mood, she also likes screaming down Broadway at three in the morning, ignoring lights. At these times, when I can feel her smiling, I am perfectly at ease behind the wheel. When she is smiling, I would drive her on back roads all the way to Costa Rica.

It is that time, though, in the life of the Blue Mazda, when certain things in her are no longer functioning as they once did, when she was in the prime of her youth and blazing her way across the country with me at the wheel and a good tape in the deck. She sputters and emits a thick, hazy cloud of blue smoke when I start her. She needs time in the morning to warm up. She has begun slightly disliking hills. And I know this embarrasses her.

Last year, for her birthday, I gave her a new clutch and a brake job, and this helped some, but there are other, darker problems afoot. Her radiator leaks fluid, her struts are gone, she burns oil. There are strange clunking sounds coming from the rear wheel wells that may or may not be the shocks.

A few weeks ago, I offered to drive a girl I'd dated a couple times (I'll call her Lisa) to her "power yoga" session. I have no idea what power yoga is but there's a tiny, smoke-stained Irish bar across the street, and it was my intention to wait out whatever hell Lisa was paying good money to put herself through by drinking a few stouts, reading the paper, and listening to the Pogues on the jukebox.

When I picked her up outside her building, Lisa made a point of standing on the curb for a few moments, hand on cocked hip, regarding the Blue Mazda with what can only be called an expression of disgust. It was the first time she'd seen my car.

"Climb in," I said. "You can just throw those empty quarts of oil into the backseat."

As she lowered herself carefully into her seat, after first taking care to wipe it down with a towel she'd produced from her gym bag (she was only wearing sweats, for God's sake, what was she worried about?), I could feel the Blue Mazda begin to tense up.

"How long have you had this...thing?"

I told her that it was going on seven years, and she sniffed. "I'm surprised it even runs," she said.

"She's actually even older, because I bought her used."

Lisa emitted a groan that reminded me of the sound sometimes made by dogs when they are puzzled by something, or just about to temporarily set aside their domestic passivity and go for your throat. A kind of whoofing moan, with a slight sigh at the end for good measure. I did not tell Lisa what the sound she'd made reminded me of.

"Have you ever thought of getting a real car?" Lisa asked.

This time it was the Blue Mazda's turn to groan. I began to feel ominous vibrations through the floor, and when I gave her a little gas to make it through a green light she raised her voice in a thick, guttural growl. I casually reached for the radio knob. "How about some music?" I asked.

"Whatever," Lisa said. "Sure."

I popped in a tape of Scottish bag pipe music, thinking the shriek and moan of it would drown out whatever sounds were beginning to wrench themselves out of the Blue Mazda. I was wrong. The roar was growing in intensity, and now the unmistakable odor of exhaust was beginning to fill the car. I turned up the music and rolled down my window.

"Beautiful day," I shouted. "Really warm for October."

Lisa hunched over in an attempt to avoid the frigid wind now whipping through the car.

When I was in high school I worked for a while in the cafeteria of a nursing home. One of my co-workers had been deaf all her life, and had taught me how to read lips. It was a skill that, in the years since, I honestly hadn't had much use for, until then. Lisa was yelling something at me, but with the roar of the whiskey-maddened pipers and the growl and bark of the Blue Mazda, only a man with my special skills could have understood her. I watched her pretty lips as they reddened with the effort of screaming. "Does the music have to be so loud? I'm getting a headache." And then, "What's that smell?"

I could have told her that the reason for her headache might be that right this second the car was filling up with invisible and deadly carbon monoxide fumes, which explained the smell, too, but I didn't know Lisa very well, and frankly I was leery of getting into that kind of conversation. We would be at her Yoga studio soon. It was already clear to me that Lisa and I wouldn't be seeing each other again; maybe I could drop her off and then plead sickness: a flare-up of malaria, perhaps, or sudden acute appendicitis. I was trying to figure out where I was going to come up with the four hundred dollars or so a new exhaust system costs when a new sound made itself known: the horrible, grating, shriek of dragging metal. It was as if I'd suddenly run over Yoko Ono.

I checked the rear view mirror and was treated to the festive sight of a "spark shower" pouring from beneath the car as I drove. The entire exhaust system had dropped. The spark shower reminded me of fireworks displays I'd seen in a segment on the Travel Network focusing on Caribbean Carnivals. I began to crave rum.

The Blue Mazda was now roaring at a pitch entirely new to me. Pedestrians on the sidewalk stopped walking to watch us pass by. A dog tied to a tree began barking ferociously and, as if in answer, the Blue Mazda roared even louder and then backfired a few times. The dog stopped barking and I saw a middle-aged man throw himself to the pavement, thinking a drive-by shooting was in progress. I motioned to him awkwardly as I drove by, hoping that he would be quick in getting to his feet so as to avoid being burned by the streams of red-hot sparks trailing crazily behind us. Lisa was clawing madly at her door handle. It was clear that she was upset. There was a pause in the tape before the pipers lurched into their version of "Tom Billy's Jig," and in that pause I heard Lisa's cracked and horrified voice begging to be released. I coasted the Blue Mazda up to the curb a block shy of our destination.

"That door kind of sticks," I told her. "You've got to push."

Tonight my car wants to go to Canada. But I get the feeling that she wants to go, not out of excitement, but out of fear. The Blue Mazda is afraid she might spend her last days putzing around Westchester County, New York, being insulted by strangers, going on short junkets to the supermarket, the library, the movie theater, and never again taste what it's like to drive up Cadillac Mountain at dawn.

The Blue Mazda and I have been through a lot together. She's carried me from Key West to the Kenai Peninsula of Alaska; across the U.S. three times, and down into Mexico. Most of the important people in my life have ridden in her. I've leaned on her hood to watch too many sunsets to count. I've slept in her, I've been arrested in her, I've had sex in her. My map collection is in the glove compartment, right on top of the photograph Jay Speiden took of me next to her, upside down, a few minutes after I'd rolled her by accident into a ditch on the way to the ski basin above Santa Fe. There are seven years of my life in that car. Sure, a lot of people would have gotten rid of her years ago, but the Blue Mazda carried me safely through my youth, and I owe her for that.

I can hear her right now. "Still typing?" she's yelling. "Bring the damn typewriter if it means that much to you." When I'm done here I'll open a beer, go outside, and get in. I'll sit behind the wheel, the cold night washing over us both, and after a while we will tell each other stories about where we've been and where we want to go. "I won't let you die in Tuckahoe, New York," I'll tell her.

"You'd better not," she'll say.

The View
from New York

The Fame Lunches

Daphne Merkin

*T*his is a story about sadness, writing, the promise of fame, my mother, and, oh yes. Woody Allen. Marilyn Monroe figures in it, too — as someone I've thought about enough to try and rescue from her own sadness, after the fact, in the form of writing about her — and somewhere over in the comer is Richard Burton, with his blazing light eyes and thrown-away gifts, who I've also written about in a redemptive fashion. Elvis never spoke much to me — too Southern, too baroque — but if he had, you can be sure I'd have tried to save him, too. What this really is, then, is a story about trying to save myself through saving maimed icons. Famous people, in other words, but famous people who required my intervention on their behalf because only I saw through to the desolation that drove them.

It begins, I guess, with my mother, because it begins with my sense of not having been loved — or responded to in a way that felt like love "as a child." It's a deeply subjective feeling, this sense of emotional deprivation, of not having gotten what you needed when you should have. It's hard to prove, in any event, which is why it gets its share of eyes-heavenwards impatience on the part of people who believe, briskly and perhaps correctly, that this kind of self-interpretation is an overly indulgent, uniquely contemporary phenomenon. Still, it seems to me to be a feeling a lot of people share, and I think it has to be given its due, even if only as a negative trope — a context of origins that explains all later failures or shortfalls. It can lead to radically different, outcomes; you can become a serial killer, or you can become an artist. Jeffrey Dahmer or Kurt Cobain. (Interesting, though, how both of them ended up dead.) Most people, of course, end up somewhere in the middle: they try to arrange themselves around this perceived loss and go on from there, hoping they'll do it better with their own kids or that they'll find what they need with a lover or spouse, the dream of grown-up romance bandaging over the wounds of childhood.

What it led to in my case was an imaginary life as a serial killer and an ongoing real life as someone who was afraid of — not to mention furious at "her parents" but who sought refuge in writing, who kept trying to establish herself, firmly and concretely in her own mind, as a writer. (It's hard to think of yourself as a professional writer: I still think of it as something I do on the side, even though by now I make my living at it. I think this has a lot to do with the fact that there's nowhere to go in the morning when you're a writer, even if you have an office, except inside your own head.) As for the serial killer thing, what I mean by this is not that I was furtively luring people into my home and chopping them up and then sprinkling their remains with Chanel No. 5 so no one would suspect anything because of the unspeakably foul odor emanating from my apartment. It was a far more mediated kind of thing, in which for a rather sustained period during my twenties, I continually aired the possibility of killing my parents on my then-therapist, a gifted guy with a red beard. He tried to defuse my very evident distress by giving me every anti-depressant known to man — this was before the Age of Prozac — and he also used to suggest, only half-humorously, that I walk up and down in front of my parents' apartment building with a placard saying "Merkins unfair to children," as though I were an underpaid worker on strike against an oppressive feudal regime. I read a lot of books about serial murderers, to help fuel my wavering but quite genuine parricidal impulse: one, called *The Shoemaker*, about a father-son homicidal duo, stuck out in my head, because of the atrocity of the details, which included the use of a hammer to keep the family in line. But I also wanted to figure out whether any good could possibly come out of this course of action, beyond an extended prison sentence. Perhaps I'd grow strong and well in my little cell, away from the impositions of everyone I had known in my past life. . . It was in this light that I envisioned myself becoming a sort of Birdwoman of Alcatraz, an expert on the mating patterns of the humming-bird. What I really wanted to know, though, was whether my shrink would appear in court in my defense, explain to the stony-faced jurors that I had been mistreated from birth and hence was simply exacting my due,

The shrink in question died on me, of a recurrent illness — but to cut to the chase, which is a phrase a friend of mind always uses whenever I go on in my loop-the-loop way, in which one dangling thought leads to another with no clear narrative pattern in sight — what I think I'm saying is that I was a desperate character from way back. Even when I was younger and thinner than

I am now, I was desperate, although it's hard for me to imagine from my present vantage-point how I could have been desperate then, when I was so young and thin. But I was, and one of the ways I tried to rescue myself from my own sense of desperation, aside from musing about murdering my mother and father, was to imagine that other people — not just any other people, but people who took up space in the public imagination — were as desperate for validation as I seemed to be. I was a nobody, but even "somebodies who hadn't been loved enough in the cradle" — felt themselves to be misunderstood nobodies. I knew this in my bones, just as I knew that I had never liked that famous poem by Emily Dickinson, the one where she trills in her mysterious hide-and-seek voice: "I'm nobody. Are you nobody, too? Then there's two of us." The woman had it all wrong, but what would she know, stuck in those New England snowdrifts all by herself? The trick was to get out of being a nobody by harnessing yourself to a somebody who was, deep down inside, a nobody, too. *The trick was to give status to your own woundedness.*

So I went and wrote a letter to Woody Allen. The early, achingly funny, pre-scandalous Woody Allen. After watching "Take the Money & Run" and "Bananas," and reading "Getting Even," I had fixed on him as my alter-ego, somebody who dared to take up space even as he pretended he wasn't taking up any. He was the perfect non-celebrity for a non-groupie like me. It wasn't a letter, really; it was a poem, one that I had written in a college writing class. It was, I suppose, a fairly interesting poem as far as such things go, but what I remember about it are the last two lines: "You are my funny man," I wrote, "You know you can be sad with me." There it was: I was a nobody who understood the hidden torment of a great comic mind. What can I say? The hook took. He wrote me back, complimenting me on my poem, and pointing out that if you X-rayed his heart, it would come out black. I had been right all along, it seemed. Desolation Row. I rushed in to show the letter to my mother. I shared everything with her, even my plans to kill her. Now, finally, she would realize who I was, hiding my light under a bushel all these years, this savant who she mistook for an ordinary girl, one of three daughters. Now she'd see: I was me, which was to say I was more than me. I was the wounded icon-by-proxy.

Time passed. I went on from publishing movie-reviews in the Barnard newspaper to publishing book-reviews in various places, such as *Commentary*' and *The New Republic,* the sort of magazines where you had to disguise your heart under your brain, where the price of entry was that you sounded like you had always thought in polished sentences and never ever sounded like you were the kind of person who stood in your kitchen staring at the knife in your hand, wondering if you should use it on yourself. I was living near Columbia, on 106th Street and West End Avenue, no less desperate than I had been when I was living at home, on Park Avenue, when I got a fan letter in the mail. It was the late seventies, the period of elaborately plebian stationery. Woody Allen, his name printed in bold red type at the top of a brown sheet of paper that looked as if it were meant to wrap an egg-salad sandwich, had written to tell me that he liked a book-piece of mine in *The New Republic,* about another maimed creature, the writer Jane Bowles. He added that he wondered why I was wasting my talent on book-reviews, and I answered, rather primly, that I considered book-reviewing to be an art form and well worth my while. I did, and I still do, but I knew what he meant. *Dare to take up space.* He wrote me back and I wrote him again, assuming a correspondence was now in swing, and he replied, not unpromptly. There were promises of getting together for drinks that were always put off, and he continued to send encouraging messages about my writing, but I suppose he never knew what I really wanted from him. I mean I couldn't come right out and say: *save me.* I must have come close enough, though, because once there was a phone-call from his secretary, offering me the name of a psychiatrist. His psychiatrist, I think it was. But what use was that to me? I had seen every psychiatrist of any repute in New York City, almost as many as he had. They always threw you back on yourself, when what I wanted was for someone to come and knock on my door and say: "You, Daphne Merkin, are hereby invited to lean your head on my shoulder forever and ever. You are small and wounded and I am large and wounded and together we will create an invulnerable universe." Or something like that. Needless to say, it never happened.

I did finally get to have a drink with Woody Allen. It came years later, after I had written a novel, gotten married, become a mother, gotten divorced, done many of the things that are supposed to make you realize life is not particularly amenable to the wishes of the unhappy child you once were but substitute gratifications can be found. The two of us had never completely lost touch, although there was a long barren period after he had returned one of my more inchoately miserable letters, filled — in those Smith-Corona days, before we switched to computers — with xxx-ed out typos and splashes of White-Out. He had gone and scrawled across it: *I don't understand what you're asking me to do. . . If there's any way I can help you, please let me know.* I guess we were able to meet on slightly more equal footing after I had become a movie-critic for *The New Yorker.* We had one drink and then another and then lunches every so often. I can't say it's changed my life, or even that it's changed my habit of coming late to everything, although I wish it had, I'm still a desperate character; I'm probably destined to be one until a ripe old age. In fact, it wasn't so long ago — four or five months ago, to be exact — that I leaned over the table in the fancy Upper East Side restaurant where we were having lunch and told Woody that, under my sprightly patter and carefully applied makeup, I was feeling depressed. How depressed, he immediately wanted to know. Quite depressed, I said. Did I have trouble getting up in the morning? Lots, I answered. Did I ever stay in bed all day? No, I said. but it was often noon before I got out of my nightgown. But of course I continued to write, he said. I answered that I hadn't written a word in weeks. He looked quite serious and then gently asked me if I had ever thought about trying shock therapy. *Shock therapy?* Yes, he said, he knew a friend — a famous friend — for whom it had been quite helpful. Maybe I should try it.

Sure, I said. Thanks. I don't know what I had been hoping for — some version *of come with me and I will cuddle you until your sadness goes away,* not, *go get yourself hooked up to electrodes, baby* — but I was slightly stunned. More than slightly. We shook hands on Madison Avenue and then gave each other a polite peck, as we always did. It was sunny and cool as I made my way home, looking in at the windows full of bright cotton summer dresses. *Shock therapy?* Who on earth did he think he was talking to? A chronic mental patient, someone who was meant to sit on a thin hospital mattress and stare grayly into space? Didn't he know I was a writer with a future, a person given to creative descriptions of her own moods, not all that different from him? Shock therapy, indeed; I'd sooner try a spa. It suddenly occurred to me, as I walked up Madison Avenue, that it might pay to be resilient, if this was all being vulnerable and skinless got you. No one stopped and clucked over the damage done, unless you made it worth their while. Indeed, maybe it was time to rethink this whole salvation business. Or maybe I was less desperate, less teetering on the edge, than I cared to admit. Now, *that* was a refreshing possiblity.

Services After Dark

Lionel Abel

"You are Mr. Smith?" the delivery boy asked him, and assuming the question affirmatively answered, handed him a large manuscript envelope. Was it meant for him? Then could his name be Smith? He didn't think it was that or Jones either for that matter. While the delivery boy waited for his reply, he wondered whether his name might be Brown and then recalled the line in Auden's poem to the effect that there could not be, and had never been, any person actually named Brown. From which thought he went crashing into a fact of real significance: he did not know his name. Had he forgotten it? How was that possible? If he had hidden it in his mind, he could now order his mind to deliver it up. His very sinking feeling was, though, that such an order might not be obeyed. He then gave the order, and as he had anticipated, it was without result. Evidently his mind was following a different agenda from his. Couldn't he find his name now by simply reading off those under the house's letterboxes? But what if he failed to recognize his name? Would his name recognize him and sing out, "I belong to you?" He decided not to make the test, being more interested for the moment (so he thought), in finding out why he had forgotten his name, than in finding out what it actually was.

He looked at his watch. It was half past five. He did know where he was going and he was resolved not to arrive late. He thought, "By the time I get to First Avenue, I'll know," but he was still trying to remember his name without success as he prepared to cross First Avenue at 79th Street. It was then that he saw her. She loomed up between him and the curb, all six feet five inches (or there about) of her, massive, muscular, and very confrontational.

Yes, this was the woman who regularly haunted the blocks on First Avenue between 79th and 82nd Street. She was tall and not unhandsome but her features were too large, he thought for someone of his height to take in comfortably, he being only about five feet nine. He was also thinking of avoiding her. This he often did, when such a maneuver wasn't easily noticed, but on this occasion she came straight towards him. Was she going to insult him, as she often did those she stopped to talk at — never to — on the street? And what was her insult to him going to be? He had heard her ask a pretty blond young woman as she went by, "And how are your six bastards?" She was almost abreast of him now, still favoring that peculiar rolling gait others, swinging her arms at her sides in a mechanical rhythm that made him think of a soldier goose-stepping. And she is a soldier, he thought, the soldier of her ego, in whose behalf she is marching, and at whose order she will probably insult me. Studying her face now he saw that she had been crying. Fortunately, he thought, she can't see that I am crying too. And then he thought this: she is letting me see my own tears. So in a way we're connected. And then she said to him — not insultingly or demandingly, but rather pitiably — as tears rolled down her cheeks, "Could you spare me a buck?" He answered, "Perhaps," and reaching into his pocket came up with a five dollar bill. "Oh shit," she exclaimed, reading his intention to give her no more than the dollar she had asked for. "Look," he reassured her, "I do have a dollar in change," reached into his pocket again and this time came up with four quarters. "God bless you," she said sweetly, as she accepted the coins, thus lapsing into the language of the most ordinary beggar, which he knew she was certainly not. Her need had reduced her savagery which — from a distance, of course, he had sometimes marveled at and once or twice had even admired.

Certainly he had more in common with this woman, however mad, than with the hostess of the literary party to which he was going. Even in fancy he could not imagine his hostess's tears — assuming she had any — as his own. And then he thought that his notion about someone else shedding his own tears brought him back to the dilemma he was in: he could not name the person the tears were for.

He knew that in asphasia one forgets what one had most recently learned while retaining memory of what one had learned earlier - in which case how could he have forgotten a name as early known to him as his own? He tried to call to mind his father's first name and found it at once, and then his mother's first name, and without any effort he had that too. But their first names did not point in any way to his own. He then tried out the name of the hostess of the party to which he had been invited and even called to mind the names of several of the guests he expected to be there. He did remember some names, but for all that was still as nameless as before coming on them.

Reading off the names of others did not lead to the one name he was apparently denying himself knowledge of— and why was he doing that? To answer this question was quite as important as finding out how he was called.

As he went on to the literary affair which still beckoned to him, he was well aware that nobody was likely to call out his name as he stepped over his hostess's threshold. He began to regret that he had not inspected the letterboxes where his apartment was located. But it was still possible to find his name; he had only to take his social security card out of his wallet. Could he do that? Why was he so disgusted with the idea of doing that? But surely there was some better way of finding out who he was?

He did know some things about himself. That he was a writer of some kind and that he was middle-aged. What he looked like too, for he had seen himself in a store window. But he could not recall the title of anything he had written. Were they novels, plays, literary articles? He could not provide himself with answers to these questions. At one point he began to wonder: (supposing I were famous — would I have forgotten my name?) He thought not, but would he have remembered it simply because others knew it? The fact could hardly be consequential in the grave circumstance — whatever it was — that had caused his forgetfulness. Had he pursued his line of inquiry, it is possible he would have found out what he was searching for. But instead this question came into his mind: was he really looking for his name? But if he really didn't want to find it, why was he turning over the piles of first impressions xeroxed in his memory? Here he came on this thought: there were no real first impressions remaining there; the firstness of his impressions was gone for good, and Proust — that name did not hide itself from him — was quite mistaken, if he had really meant to assert that the firstness of one's impressions lasted almost with their contents. Perhaps the emotions stirred by them could come back by reading off their xeroxes, yes, that was possible, but a second appearance of firstness was not.

Going on towards Park Avenue he relieved his feelings by thinking of Mrs. Giles who was hosting this affair. So in a way he did know what he was. Since he knew the party to which he had been invited and also that he had been invited because he was known. The party was one of those to which the guests come not so much for the enjoyment of being there as to be numbered among those who have been asked to come. Names would be important in the apartment to which he was going and he had no doubt he would hear his own name mentioned. But first of all he might have to spell it out to the Park Avenue doorman merely to be admitted. As it turned out, though, the doormen —

there were two of them — had been instructed to send up anyone who came by and asked for Mrs. Giles. So he went up without informing or being informed further about himself. Upstairs he held out his hand to someone who had introduced himself saying, "I've quite forgotten my rank and serial number," which brought an understanding chuckle. Many greeted him, and he could not help wondering what would they say if he asked them, "Could you tell me who I am?" The question was on his lips; better think of something else, he thought, and then proceeded to think about his hostess, Mrs. Giles.

She was a very handsome woman with classic Greek features including of course what the Greek poet, Demetrius Karpentarckus had called, "The Grecian aimed nose." How is it, he wondered, that I can remember that poet's name — never cited nowadays, by anyone — and not recall my own? Silent about his name, his memory told him about Mrs. Giles. Her money, a certain bitterness at having had to abandon her philosophy courses — advised to do this by someone she respected — her good looks and success as a lecturer in psychology — and something else too, a hard-line feminist turn of thought she had imbibed at the university, had turned her into a kind of female Don Juan trying to strike sparks of sex from every man she felt to be of true metal. It was said that she carried on with five different men at once, expertly playing them off against each other, and that she had only to think that a man had refused to yield to her charm to set out at once to entrap him. Paradoxically, such were her successes that the one story people repeated about her was her single case of failure. She had set out to seduce a happily married middle-aged man, the dean of performing arts at one of the city's colleges. People had observed her attempts to get him and nobody thought she could succeed. When he left his town-house and moved into her Park Avenue apartment, their mutual friends were more astounded than scandalized and people began to think that after such a triumph Mrs. Giles could not be denied any man she desired. She received fewer invitations to dinner, but at the parties she was absent from her name was tossed back and forth with increased respect. And respect, she knew, gets back to the one respected, even if one is not present when the desired opinion is voiced. So the Dean had moved into Mrs. Giles' apartment but shortly afterwards had expressed discontent and a wish to separate. Mrs. Giles was enraged. Was her most heralded triumph to turn into a miserable failure? She suggested that they go to see a marriage counsellor — but they were not married, he objected. He was a public man, he told her, and could not put himself in this ridiculous position — which the press would certainly not ignore — of not knowing the difference between a mistress and a wife. Besides, he said, marriage counsellors aren't there to keep adulterers together. Is that what we are, adulterers? she asked. To calm her down he agreed to see a marriage councillor just once. But he was already planning his exit from her apartment and this took place the first time she left it on a lecture tour. When she got back to her place hoping to tell him of the compliments she had received, he was not there and his books, clothes and papers were gone too. There was a note to her but it was not a nice one. "I am going back to Lenore" (his wife) "and happiness." Somehow the contents of that note got out— travelling like the respect for her seductiveness, in both waves and bursts.

He looked over the guests around him and experimented with pronouncing the names of those he knew. So who was to his left? He answered himself: Lincoln Host, the villainous photographer; to his right was Cynthia Freemont, a spy for some Arab action group; and facing him across the table of GLORIOUS FOODS, was August Klemperer, the literary agent, famed for his lack of interest in any writer not on his list; to the right of him was the crafty art-dealer, Simiosa; and after him, Gordon Foot, the brother of a good friend whom he did not see — the talented satirist, Amelia Foot. Should he go on naming? But no one else's name was bringing his own within his mental reach.

He helped himself to a mousse of sole inside a brioche and then looked around again. He wanted to see someone he did not know to whom he might be introduced by someone he did know. Now there was no lack of persons who had gestured their acquaintance. Wasn't there somebody there he had not yet met? Finally he asked his hostess directly, "Is there anyone here I don't know?"

She replied, " Nobody important."

"Please introduce me," he responded, "to someone of little importance whom I happen not to know."

Mrs. Giles looked at him suspiciously. Was he ridiculing her interest in having only people of note at her parties?

"I don't know what you're up to," she said, "but looking over this group; I can't see anyone who meets your specifications." With which she left him, and as he looked over the group once more, he saw no one to whom he could ask to be presented.

Probably the most important guest — that is the one with the best literary reputation — was Lily Potsdan, a novelist with a fine prose style but something of a conversational problem, for she either told you outright lies or just held her tongue. She would keep silent no matter what was being talked about until a moment came, when she saw an opening for some pure fiction, which told as fact might be damaging to somebody. Then she would intervene to the delight of some and the dismay of others. But at the moment he was too concerned with his own problem to find anything she was saying interesting. So instead of giving her an occasion to lie to him, he defined her character to himself as accurately as he could, preferring to talk about her to himself than to hear her talk about someone else. It was not always thus. There had been many parties at which he would have made straight for Lily to hear her lying gossip about the many writers he knew she disliked.

Turning away from her he took note of Sadie Zucker, who had written a book in which every single therapist in the country was mentioned at least once. He considered her a person who thought sex was about psychoanalysis rather than the other way round. She had just said, "It is wrong for a shrink to play the part of someone who doesn't deserve to be that. I mean a shrink should never commit suicide, even in a film. And that is what happens in Woody Allen's *Crimes and Misdemeanors,* which I just saw on TV. Someone replied, "The shrink did what the script called for." But Sadie would have none of that; "He could have objected and if Woody Allen insisted, resigned from the cast. Don't forget that the man who played that part is a real therapist with real patients. And he has hurt them; they will regard him as a possible suicide. How will they be able to make a transference to a man they watched taking his life?" She was told: "They'll know he didn't really commit suicide." Said Sadie Zucker, "They'll know it consciously but in their subconscious they will think he killed himself. And isn't a shrink supposed to think of the subconscious?"

He turned back towards Lily Potsdan. And then it happened: the party event. Lily Potsdan had confided to some friend that she had bought tickets for all the local lotteries hoping to come up with a winning number. "I'd love to win millions," she said. And when she was asked why, she had given this answer, "I'd like to have enough money to help anyone like Bernard Goetz who shot those four black muggers and needed money for his defense." She added, "I want to be able to defend anyone with the clarity of mind to shoot a black mugger who has threatened him."

A silence settled over the whole apartment. Finally Mrs. Giles emerged from the group she had been with and said," Lily, I want you to say that you didn't say that." Lily responded, "What I said? But everyone heard me." "They heard wrong," said Mrs. Giles. "Tell them they heard wrong." "I think they heard right," Lily replied. Said Mrs. Giles, "If you insist on that I will have to ask you to leave. You can only stay if you deny having said..." "What everyone heard me say?" "That's right," said Mrs. Giles. "Just tell them you didn't say what they may think you said."

At this point Lily yielded. "OK," she said. "You made a mistake." "About what?" one of the guests who continued the struggle had asked. "Tell them," advised Mrs. Giles. "I never said what you may have thought I said," said Lily. "You never did," Mrs. Giles remarked approvingly. And then someone was moved to approve of her. Milton Shawnstein, the expressionist photographer, said, "You are a great hostess."

Mrs. Giles addressed her guests: "Let's go on enjoying ourselves."

He thought then that it was time to go but one thing held him. He heard a dark, quite pretty and heavily rouged girl, whom someone had described as one of the joyous blood suckers on the body of literature, say that being worried about her health and dissatisfied with her physician, who was on the list of the hundred best doctors in the city, she would like to find a different judge other condition. From whom, her companion wanted to know, "I think," she said, "what I need is a quack."

This gave him an idea. He said his goodbyes to Mrs. Giles and went down to the street. Only a block away on 81st Street just before Lexington Avenue was a sign he had often noted: *Psychic Tarot Readings.* Once before he had his future read by a Tarot specialist, an Italian sculptor, and everything the man had predicted had come to pass.

There was the place, on 81st Street. He went in and was greeted by the card-reader, a middle-aged woman in jeans.

"Yes?" she asked, giving him the opportunity to state his needs. With a sudden inspiration he said, "I'd like to write out a name, and for you to identify, if you can, to whom that name belongs. Do you agree?"

"It's an unusual request," she said, "but I'll do my best," and she produced a sheet of paper and a pencil. He wrote on it the name: Brice Gighot. The woman looked at the name and said, "I believe that's your name, sir."

Next morning, alone in his flat, Brice was much less sanguine. He asked himself: why had he forgotten his name? And it was strange, the way in which he had finally recalled it, not exactly as his, rather like a name in the wallet of a dead man, found lying in the street, which comparison told Brice something else of importance, immediate and long-time, which he had not until then realized: he had been thinking of taking his life. The first step to this end had been to get rid of his name.

Looking in a mirror he recalled that someone he had seen at the party the evening before had said of him, "It's hard for you to be; or even appear to be, somber," and he had wondered whether he had appeared somber to anyone else during the hour or so when he was there.

Forgetting his own name, he decided finally, was somehow connected with his remembering someone else, the Portugese poet Pessoa, who had written and published poems under three different names: it was then that he recalled something very much to the point: a particular poem of Pessoa's, written in English, not in Portugese, a poem he had found in a 1992 issue of the French literary review *Quinzaine*. He looked up the poem and reread it with pleasure. Even its awkwardness helped it poetically. What was awkward he thought was a kind of release from glibness. And it was good for a real poet not to feel altogether sure of his words. But what mattered to him now was not the form but the content of Pessoa's poem, which was about still another poem, one not yet written, still secret, but which Pessoa, or as he signed himself, Search, was planning to write. What had he himself kept secret in his own mind but planned to write after he had read Search's poem? It seemed to him then that it might have been an accusation against himself, and then his mind had intervened and made him forget his name. Why? Had he secretly formed the notion of committing suicide as if it were a poem he wanted others to read but which he was not yet altogether ready to write? If the poem were to be a death warrant then it would have to have his signature. By forgetting his name then, he had been keeping himself in life, even as he remembered the phrase of the Portugese poet, who had asked "what is between me and myself?" This was Brice's problem too. But whatever he had tried to hide from himself in forgetting his name, he should now be ready to look squarely at. It was then that Brice began to realize that the thought of taking leave — French leave — of his own life — was a kind of suffering, like what would probably be felt if one were told in no uncertain terms that one had been sentenced to death in the near future, let's say soon. He suddenly felt death — death soon — to be an ever present pain. Just where was the pain located? He could not say. It seemed in every part of his being, in his hair? In his eyelashes? Probably not, but certainly in his center, in the him of him, whatever that was, there the pain was, and had been all along, though he had only now become cognizant of it. And it was at the center of him that he would have to strike if he was going to be rid of it.

How had the thought of embracing his end come into his mind? What had prepared for it, led to it? How did he happen to have invited such a thought? For Brice realized that this thought would not have visited him unbidden. But when had he asked it in? And had he asked it merely to drop by, or to come and stay? And until when? Until he, Brice, had left for good?

He was sure of this: the thought of dying had entered his life as the result of an adverse judgement of it, its attainments and remaining capabilities, a negative judgement then, whose truth he had in some sense accepted. But how had that judgement been expressed? Brice here began to fill out the onset of his new thinking with collaborating details.

At a literary party only a few days before, he had volunteered an opinion which he had expected to be asked to elaborate on. The talk had been about Solzhenitsyn and how it was that this writer's novels were so much less interesting than his description and analysis of the gulag archipelago. Brice had expressed the view — of which he was by no means certain — that a writer might be better off from the standpoint of literary value if his own life lacked interest. He gave as an example Balzac who apparently had sacrificed any real existence for himself in order to animate the existence of his various characters. For instance, when having the heart attack from which he died, he had asked to be examined by the doctor he had invented for *The Human Comedy,* in preference to the real doctor, called in by his friends. One could not imagine Solzhenitsyn, threatened again by cancer, asking to be examined by a doctor he had described in his novel *Cancer Ward* (besides Solzhenitsyn's fictional doctor was a real person, not a character wholly created by him). Balzac had never thought of refurnishing his own lodgings but French families living in Italy or Germany often refurnished their apartments to meet the taste requirements set forth in his novels.

He had expected his view to be resisted, and he had been looking forward to defending it, but after he had said his piece it was as if he had not spoken at all. The others present dropped the subject of Solzhenitsyn and went on to discuss quite different topics. He had not even been asked to clarify what he had said.

It struck Brice then that the view he had expressed, such as it was, had not really been rejected by those who heard him out. It was he who had been rejected, and it occurred to him then that if someone else had expressed the very same idea in an identical language (he tended to become eloquent when stimulated by thought) others might very well have responded, argued perhaps, but in any case shown themselves challenged by what had been said. The only thing wrong with what he had said, then, was that he was the one who had said it.

With this thought came a rush of pain, unbearable and quite unlocateable. This was surely not an ordinary kind of pain: physical pain may be terrible, but it is by no means incomprehensible and in that sense can, and not improperly, be called "ordinary." The pain he felt, but could not comprehend, was the pain of being wrongly thought about, perhaps also of not having been sufficiently written about . . . After such pangs death could be thought of as somewhat less injurious . . . Maybe it could even spell a certain aspect of victory, like the poetic suicide of the sun, hurling itself into a basic blackness, propelled there in Mallarmé's sublime rhetoric.

He had felt something of the pain he now called "literary" at the beginning of his career, before he had become known for his novels.

Brice thought of the biblical injunction never to throw pearls before swine. But in fact he did not think of the group before whom he had held forth on Solzhenitsyn as swine, or as his notions about the writer as pearls, but there was some connection between the biblical injunction and the way in which his view had been received. He knew that the others present there thought of him as able to come up with a different look at any kind of literary event which they themselves were condemned to see in the very same way; and to know this about him — he had proved this on many occasions — to anticipate yet another idea from him, and then to have to listen to it as he argued for it, was — Brice could see this — wearying in the extreme. It was like meeting a man known for his witticisms, who you can see is preparing to tell you one of his jokes — which may even turn out to be genuinely funny — and to which you might be quite unable to respond, simply because you could see the joke from its very commencement all along its way to being funny: when you got there you might find you could not laugh. In which case, were you the swine the Bible had warned against, before whom it was unwise to throw pearls? Weren't you the one with the pearl of understanding, rather than the presumed wit who could not see that he was preventing you from laughing?

He once again recalled the not comparably intense but still "literary" pain he had felt when his writings were neglected at the outset of his career. But that pain had disappeared with the publication and success of his second novel, which had won a national award. From then on people had taken his frequent expressions of opinion seriously, sometimes more seriously than he did himself.

Had he perhaps exaggerated the coldness with which his remarks about Solzhenitzyn had been received? Perhaps. But there were other signs of lack of interest in him and enough of them to make him want to probe the matter further. He had a sudden urge to inform himself more thoroughly about what was thought and said even casually about him. Suddenly he wanted to be at every gathering where an opinion about him might be expressed. He felt he no longer had advance knowledge of what the opinion might be, the kind of advance knowledge he only now could fully appreciate. So, he thought, he had been going from the singular condition, of being present at occasions from which he was in fact absent, to the very opposite condition of being absent from the thought of others on those occasions when he was in fact there. And was this not the first stage in a process at the end of which he might not be anywhere at all?

He began to think of the relationship between two thoughts — the thought of death and the thought of anonymity — so serious for an artist who had known fame. In his case it was the slippage from well-knownness to less well-knownness and not into anonymity; that, at least, he did not have to confront Yet all the same, there never was and never could be enough well-knownness. There would always be someone who had never heard of you or if he had, disliked what he had heard. Visiting a friend in Vermont who did industrial designs he had to listen to a jeremiad against Picasso's draftsmanship, yes, against an artist called the greatest draftsman since da Vinci, but the arguments of artists, critics and art historians were of no help against the industrial designer whom nobody was able to convince that Picasso could draw at all. At best the very greatest talent had to hope for luck in the understanding of his or her work, and there was no hope at all of being praised if a moment came when the thing to do was not to praise at all. Had he reached that point? The next point would most likely be further down the slope when to praise their own taste people would begin condemning him. From that point on all was certain to be lost; the descent of his reputation would become precipitous. He could hear people saying, "Poor Brice, no one says a good word about him now." Reputations do have to go even as we all have to die, so why should the praise of any one of us be lasting? It did for some, though, there were those who having once been praised and after that dispraised, who managed to get praised again. Could he count himself among those winners in the fame-for-a-long-time-game? In any case his own thought of suicide had come after it had been born in on him that his reputation was in danger. He fully realized that nobody now believed that there was the remotest chance that a novel by Brice Gighot could turn out to be a masterpiece. It was as if he had forfeited the right to suggest to anyone with a firm literary mind that such a thing was even possible. Were his already published novels so poor that there was no hope of bringing out an even better one? Nobody had said this in so many words, but this was what the words they used suggested: he was not to hope to add even one to the number of great books.

He was still questioning what brought into his mind the idea of ending his life when he recalled the event of the past week: the announcement of a particular death-plan, even a death threat by an acquaintance. The death threatener was a sculptor, Mitchell Bardo, known, but insufficiently, by the public, certainly not enough to satisfy his wealthy wife, who had married him despite his advanced years simply to have a husband famous in the art world. Bardo had turned out not to be the valuable property she had expected and her wealth had not helped him improve his reputation. Brice had dined with them at the Carlyle the week before, and had noted that both of them had reminded him of sculptures. Mitchell, who was lean and rickety, reminded him of Giacometti's "Man Walking," and Evelyn, who was burly, of the stout-legged girls of Maillol. They also differed in their speech patterns. Evelyn spoke softly, caressing every syllable, while Mitchell blurted out his words in a rush as if in a hurry to be rid of them. Had he made a speech syndrome of the typical American painter's distrust of words? He was going to show some new work, he said, but he spoke so hurriedly that Brice did not catch the name of the gallery that was to show his pieces. About the event Evelyn did not want Brice to have any illusions. She said, "He would not be shown at Knoedler or even at Emmerich's. The gallery is uptown but it is just as lacking in cachet as Mitchell's sculptures."

Then she went on talking directly to Mitchell: "The last time you had a show it was in some obscure gallery; *The New York Times* reviewers never even came to the opening. It may be the same this time." "Perhaps," said Bardo, "but are you suggesting that I shouldn't show my work at all since *The Times* didn't review me last time? I have to hope that they will this time." The words were dignified, but barely intelligible. However, Evelyn knew what her husband was saying. "You are always hoping," she said, "but I've given up hoping for you. I don't believe you'll be famous even when you're dead." As Brice looked across the table he saw Bardo's cheeks go from pink to white. Bardo slowly got up from the table. "This is it," he said, and for once he got the words out carefully, almost one by one. It was as if his antipathy was no longer directed at words, being concentrated now on his wife. "I'll go out to our place in Hampton Bay," he said, "and I'll walk out into the ocean which will be no kinder to me than you have been. You haven't seen me famous, maybe you'll see me dead." Brice had prevailed on Bardo to sit down and Evelyn Bardo had apologized for her remark but the effect of the event on Brice was to make him think of dying or, to put it more exactly, to think of deserting his life — which is more or less what Bardo wanted to do — and go over to the side of its main adversary.

Brice had not been satisfied with his most recently published novel, *Mistress Flesh,* nor with what his friends had said about it either. He took down a copy of it from the shelf where he had arranged to keep fully in view all the books he had published to date. Their color covers cheered him as did the college pennants of a football crowd, an encouragement necessary to him as he sat at his desk trying to produce yet another book which might bring him greater renown and even, this possibly was not to be overlooked, stimulate some new interest in what he had already published.

He opened *Mistress Flesh* and soon found himself incapable of reading it. Which is not to say that he couldn't now make out the words clearly imprinted on the page. He had read his novel of course some four or five times before it had gone to his editor. He was asking himself now to read it once again. He could indeed follow the words in their proper sequence taking note of what they said. But he could not read with the pleasure he had intended them to give to others and it was to feel that pleasure that he had looked into his book. He would have to talk to someone else about it. Whom could he ask about it? To protect his pride he thought he would ask a woman he knew was interested in literature, and that meant Molly Zorn.

She had been married to a left wing unionist who had tried to interest her in the political problems which he had found hard to deal with. But she had felt little interest in trade union politics, and had never given up the hope of being directly involved with writers. But all this had seemed a dream to Molly — the only writer she knew was Brice himself, until interest in the

Holocaust had caused the major universities to open courses in Yiddish literature. And Molly did know Yiddish, though she did not know and could not read German, or Latin, or any Romance language. But she was offered and got a tenured professorship at CUNY. Molly Zorn was one of the very few persons whose wildest dream had been realized and the dreaminess of her status still clung to her and gave an added zip to her real — but not too evident - good looks. He remembered how once having described her as very attractive and only after that had noticed how attractive she in fact was, with fine features and a head whose shapeliness was made clearer by an elegant close cut of dark brown hair. How was it he wondered that he had not thought of her as pretty right away? Maybe her beauty was like the virtues of a book you only know to be a masterpiece after having read a preface to it by a critic you respect.

Molly had never been able to meet any literary people; she had no chance of meeting such folk at the union's public affairs and she had regularly invited Brice for dinner hoping he would introduce her to his literary friends. Once, when Brice was leaving his apartment after dinner (she was with her unionist husband) — the latter had made this suggestion to Brice, "Why don't you give our telephone number to some of your literary friends?"

"Which ones?" Brice asked.

"Anyone you think would enjoy our company," was the response.

Brice did not comply with the request and until Molly — via the Holocaust — got her tenured appointment to teach Yiddish literature, he remained her sole literary acquaintance. But all this was now changed. She was now in the very center of academic discussions of writings on the Holocaust survivors; and had even been invited to give a talk on this topic at Harvard. And now, here was Brice, a notable author, humbling himself before her to get an opinion of his latest novel.

Brice had indeed found Molly attractive, and as long as she was able to stay married to her leftist husband, he had refrained from making a pass at her. But once she had broken off with Bill and had introduced Brice to a male friend, an Oxford Yiddishist (a gentile to boot), Brice felt he could show his very real respect for her attractiveness and made a show of his interest. Molly then told him this: she invariably responded to passes made to her when in a moving conveyance, a cab, a train or a plane "That's very bizarre," Brice commented and then added, "but Baudelaire has said there's something bizarre about anything that strikes us as beautiful." However he had left the matter there and had never suggested going on a trip, even just uptown or the other way with Molly, so as to satisfy her bizarre and perhaps beautiful penchant for being sought after in a moving conveyance.

Brice set up a date with her at a Starbucks in his neighborhood. They met and talked of various things but at a certain point Brice asked if she had read his latest novel.

"No," she replied, explaining, "You see I've lost all interest in works of fiction — unless they are in Yiddish."

Brice replied, "You can't expect me to believe that"

"I'm telling you the truth," she said.

"I don't believe you," he came back at her. "I can't see why a work of fiction has to to be in Yiddish to be interesting or even...."

"Readable," she said, completing his sentence.

This was the way she explained herself. "The value of fiction is of course not in question. Obviously a French or an English novel could be interesting even if...

"Only to someone else..." He interrupted, completing her sentence, as she had his just before. It seemed right for him to retaliate. He, who had once been recognized as superior, was now fighting just to come on as an equal.

"Look here," she said, "the only language I know besides English is Yiddish and it is only as a teacher of Yiddish literature that I am in any demand. I realize that I'm only interesting to the university and to literary people in general because I'm a Yiddishist."

"But why not admit that my novel, though not in Yiddish, might interest you."

"It probably would," she granted him.

"But are you going to read it?"

"Of course," she replied, "since you want me to."

"You see to what I'm reduced," Brice said. "I have to beg an old friend like you to read a book of mine. What's the word for beggar in Yiddish? I bet it's more interesting than its English equivalent."

"It certainly is and more interesting than the German word for beggar which happens to be *bettler.* The Yiddish word is *schnoror.*"

"That's the word I wanted. I like it. I'm schnororing for a reader, one who can appreciate me. I hope you understand what that means for someone like me. The fact is I have actually been thinking of suicide..."

"Seriously?"

"Seriously."

"But you would like to be talked out of it?" "Yes. But I might even like to be talked into it."

"You know," she said, "you may have come to the right person. I really may be able to help you..." She went on, but Brice wasn't for the moment listening. He noticed she had developed a new speech style. She talked with great care, punctuated her speech with very considered gestures, as if she were correcting a manuscript; every gesture emphasized some point, and in whatever she said there were points to be emphasized. She certainly had changed.

"You must want someone else to decide for you," she was saying.

He corrected her. "Not exactly. But I would listen to the opinion of someone I respected."

"To be sure," she said, "and maybe that's why I am right in thinking you came to the right person."

Here was her explanation. Her apartment uptown was in a co-op known as Morningside Gardens. Now there was something special and interesting about it. Thurgood Marshall had lived there and Weinreich, the great linguist. Molly's building at 90 LaSalle Street had a theatrical company (recruited from the tenants), a dance group, which put on shows, and a philosophy professor from Columbia University who gave lectures free of charge to the tenants interested in modern ideas.

"Are you suggesting," Brice wanted to know, "that I should ask this professor of philosophy if I should live or die? The prospect does not interest me."

"No," she said. "I did not have that in mind. I just wanted to give you a sense of what is going on in Morningside Gardens. Among many other skilled individuals there are two very well known poets, one of whom calls himself the poet of life, the other the poet of death... Maybe you should go up there and talk to both of them about life and about death."

"So the first one can talk me into living and the other into dying?" Brice asked. "Now what good would that do?"

"I don't know that it would do any good," Molly answered. "But something might come of it."

"Maybe I will go to see them," Brice said. And then she supplied him with their names. The poet of death who lived in the basement of Morningside Gardens was named Viera Ocassio and the poet of life who lived in the penthouse of the same building was Amos Bodley. Brice had not read anything of either of these poets but had seen something about them in the press.

"You don't know them. But these poets know you. They know your books, and have often quoted you...."

"Have either of them read *Mistress Flesh?*" Brice could not keep himself from asking.

Here Molly had to disappoint him. "I don't know if they've read *Mistress Flesh,*" she said, " but I am sure they would read it if you asked them to. What I do know is that they value you, and most especially for an essay you wrote at the outset of your career, an essay which I don't have to tell you is famous now. You suggested in it that with the widespread disbelief in religion, marriage and funeral services might well be organized by poets, who might also officiate at such services, replacing priests, ministers and rabbis."

"I don't know whether I hold that view any longer," said Brice. "You know of course that my daughter was a suicide. Yes, she did know. "At the funeral service I did not ask a poet to officiate. I fell back on tradition and had a rabbi say the prayers What I should explain to you is that even when I wrote the essay you've referred to, I was thinking most of all what poets could perhaps contribute to divorce proceedings which are always emotionally arid. I thought that maybe poets who specialize in satire could equip the husband and wife wanting divorce with savage verses, each ridiculing the other, so that as a result neither one would ever want to see the other again. I was less interested in replacing religious figures with poets though I did suggest this, and it was this which caught the fancy of the public."

"You were even compared to Nietzsche," Molly reminded him. "And you created with that essay the views of both the poets I'm suggesting you see. They both admire you. After talking to them you may stop thinking about suicide. And you may find them a turning point in your view of yourself." With that admonishment she got up and left.

My Mother's False Eyelashes, My Aunt's Coral Shoes

Maria Solomon

When I was a student at Sarah Lawrence College in the mid '70's the women's movement was at its height. There was much talk of our independence and insistence on our equality with men. Most of my friends switched to seeing a female gynecologist so that they could feel more "understood." We talked endlessly about the passage from "girls" to "strong women" — whatever that meant. But what it definitely meant was wearing blue jeans, reading Virginia Woolf and staying clear of lipstick. I didn't think of independence as a remote goal to be achieved as it was present in our family almost by default. My father died when I was eleven and my sister Carla was twelve. My mother was a working writer — and combining a profession with the raising of children was the normal way of life. My maternal grandmother was a gifted artist, and my Aunt Mitzi (my father's sister) was an accomplished sculptor. The central women in my life had intense passions that they pursued for both professional and personal reasons. And yet, what really mesmerized me about them — and what I saw as a tremendous source of their power — was precisely their female allure. As a little girl living in the midst of these women I was enticed by their perfume, their mystery, their wickedly high-heeled shoes. Alas, my true memories lack ideology!

Aunt Ree, my favorite aunt, used to tell us about her Cherokee Indian blood. She said her grandmother in Minnesota had Cherokee ancestry, and that is how she came to have straight, shiny hair and an upright walk. She lived eight blocks away from us on Central Park West and ninety-fourth street.

My cousin Lizzie and I would have dates in the afternoon and we spent a lot of time looking through Aunt Ree's closets. I particularly liked the tall and narrow shelves on the side of the closet. They were filled with rows of shoes. I fell in love with the coral-colored high heeled ones that had a little "v" shape just where the toes began.

My aunt's closet smelled of the Miss Dior perfume she wore. If I put my face against one of the dresses hanging in the closet, it felt like she was standing there. As long as I could remember, she had gray, silvery hair. Aunt Ree talked about going gray "early" and laughed as she threw her head back so that her "early" silvery hair fell back in one chunk. She made it sound like an accomplishment, as if her hair grew faster than other people's. She must have liked the silver because she never colored it. I guessed she felt proud of it and liked to show it off. I admired everything about Aunt Ree. In the afternoon, after I returned from school, I would telephone her. She was at home most of the time but I wasn't sure what she did all day. So I asked her. But before she gave me that information, I insisted on knowing exactly what she was wearing. It helped to fix her in my mind — the next best thing to being near her.

My favorite of her outfits was a purple knit dress. She put a silk scarf around her neck that had the same shade of purple in it. She never threw just anything on, but thought about how she wanted to look even if she wasn't going out. How she looked seemed to have as much to do with pleasing herself as it did with pleasing other people. I was impressed with her confidence in herself. It seemed to give her a sturdy strength without making her seem superior. After she told me what she was wearing we talked about our day. What she did was less interesting to me than the way she talked about it. She was very matter-of-fact; occasionally there was a pause as she took a puff of her cigarette. Though I would tell her what I did in school that morning, my life didn't seem nearly as fascinating and complicated as hers.

I liked to imagine myself wearing her coral-colored high heels, spraying some of her Miss Dior on my clothes and walking around the apartment holding a cigarette between my fingers. I could then forget that I was small. Instead, I would be a woman with very long legs, wearing a dress made out of thin, silky material that would show the outline of my long legs when I walked.

I also adored exploring my mother's bathroom. She kept some of her make-up in the medicine cabinet above the sink. The rest of it was on the white marble shelf above the sink and on a small dressing table that was made entirely of mirrors. On the white marble shelf there were three bottles of Revlon Touch 'N Glow foundation make-up in different shades depending on how dark or pale her complexion was. Her standard shade was "Ivory" but she also used "Beige Bisque" and "Light Rose." At the edge of the shelf was a blue glass container that was shaped like a miniature vase. In it was a thin brush and a thick, gold case that had red lipliner pencil in it. When the red pencil wore down, she turned the bottom and more red pencil came out. She outlined her lips with the liner and then filled in her mouth with a deep rose lipstick. The lipstick color was paler than the liner, so that you could see the deep red outline of her mouth.

The dressing table had two little drawers where she kept bobby pins and lots of brown, wiry curlers that she put in her hair to make it fluffy. There was one mirror in the middle and two smaller ones on either side. When she fixed her hair, she could turn the mirrors and see how her hair looked from all the different angles.

But the sink area was my favorite. Another mirror was attached to the wall above the sink. This mirror had two sides. One side was just a regular mirror and the other side magnified everything to twice its size. When I looked at my own face in the mirror I could see the tiny specks in the center of my eyes and each separate hair of my eyebrows. My mother used the mirror when she was doing the trickier things like putting on false eyelashes or liquid eye liner so that she could see every detail. She also used it when she had to turn around to see how her hair looked from the back.

Watching my mother fix herself up before a dinner party fascinated me. Before she got dressed she prepared the food in the kitchen — we had a huge avocado green refrigerator. She would arrange a platter of cheeses and then make odd appetizers out of salami. She would place thin slices of salami on a tray and sprinkled them with parmesan cheese and olives. Then she put them into the oven until they were slightly scorched. When she took them out the sides of the salami had curled up so they looked like little brown tubes. My father's role was to make sure that there were clean glasses and enough ice in the ice bucket.

I remember in particular one party. I was four years old. I was already in bed in my flannel pajamas when I heard music playing in the living room. I got out of bed and walked in. I saw my mother and father dancing in front of the sofa to fast, jazzy music. The recording was of Eartha Kitt singing "I Want to Be Evil".

> —And in the theater I want to change my place
> Just so I can step on everybody's face.

Even when she wore high heels my mother was much shorter than my father. He twirled her around and made playful gestures like putting one finger on the top of his head as he swung her in circles.

After my mother had prepared the food she started to fix herself up in the bathroom. She needed the double mirror to arrange her hair into a French chignon. She gathered her hair together in the back and then, very slowly, folded it over a few times. She held the hair with one hand while she put bobby pins in with the other hand so that her hair wouldn't fall down.

I loved to watch her put on false eyelashes. It's hard to describe because no one wears them anymore. At least I don't wear them, and my mother stopped wearing them a long time ago. They came in plastic boxes with a clear covering. The pair of eyelashes sat in the box. They looked like closed, sleeping eyes. In order for my mother to put them on she had to take each one out of the box and put glue along the edge so that they would stick to her eyelids. She held them very carefully. Then she opened her eyes wide and glued on the false eyelashes.

Her next step was to plunge a thin brush into a jar of jet black liquid eye liner. She then drew a firm black line above the false eyelashes. She did this so that if the glue oozed out it would be covered and invisible. This gave her a "natural" look, as if she just happened to be born with dark, black, curly eyelashes. Even if it didn't look like they were hers, it didn't really matter. They made her eyes look deep and shiny like freshly washed hair.

Even now, I think of make-up as something that older women do in mysterious bathrooms with secret bottles and brushes. At the dark end of a day, after leaving work at a Manhattan hospital, where I am a psychiatric social worker, I pass Zitomer's Pharmacy on Madison Avenue. Before going home to my son and husband I pause at the window. I am drawn to the display of cosmetics. The Chanel lipsticks in their art deco black and gold holders are arranged in rows of deep burgundy and plum shades. It has a familiar feel. I go in to Zitomer's so often that Ariella who works at the counter recognizes me. I stand in front of the glass case of perfumes and ask to try a splash of

Miss Dior *eau de toilette.* I ask her which color foundation might be right for my complexion.

Ariella takes some cotton balls and samples different colors to see which one is the best. She dabs a little on my face and I spread it around evenly. To give a smooth look she takes a big brush, dips it in loose powder, and brushes it across my face with the flourish of a pro. Sitting there, I feel reassured. Connected. We look for a deep red pencil to line my lips and then I apply a wine-colored lipstick. I search the collection of Chanel blush for a particular shade of rose. I pause. I linger at the counter. I buy the lipstick and lipliner that I don't really need. For a short time I have returned to the magical marble shelf in my mother's bathroom.

In mulling over then and now I realize why, during my Sarah Lawrence years, I felt so ill at ease with the popular '70s pitch to abandon femininity. It went against my gut feeling that the paraphernalia of female embellishment — the lipsticks, the perfumes, the stuff of personal adornment — was a signficant part of my sense of self. Ironically, these artifices, assumed then to be needed solely in order to gain the attention and admiration of men, were for me more of a "woman thing". It's what girls do. It's what girls see their mothers do. It's a female coming of age. An act almost independent of men. As for the art of male/female sexual seduction, well, that's another story.

Living Pictures

Linsey Abrams

We were sitting in a restaurant on Broadway not far from Carlotta's apartment, and it occurred to me that I hadn't spent this much time uptown since I'd moved to New York. Or certainly since I'd stayed with Dale for a month right after Ronnie left, an attempt to pull myself out of a hole into which everything I'd thought of as my life had tumbled. Most of it was still down there.

"You don't mind if I drink, do you?" Carlotta asked.

"No," I said, but she'd already flagged the waitress and when she arrived, ordered a double vodka.

Tonight was the first time since we met that we'd actually gotten out of bed and left her apartment voluntarily. It seemed odd to be around so many people, conversations surrounding and interrupting ours...snatches of which reminded me how little Carlotta and I had talked about anything other than ourselves. Up above was a tier of tables, most of them full, and where we sat in several rows of couples running along the window and back toward the bar there was hardly any room to walk. The truth was, though it hadn't occurred to me before, we hadn't been around anyone together...not my friends, not hers, and not so many strangers...since the night we'd met in November.

Outside now the snow, which as a Californian Carlotta barely tolerated, had been shoveled to the curb. It was just after New Year's and we'd been apart since the middle of December when she'd left town for the holidays. Though we'd talked almost daily in the last two months — I had her cell phone number since she was never at home in either city — we'd been together on a dozen occasions, if that. It was as if time with Carlotta operated on an entirely different set of principles from in normal life, putting everything to do with her on a separate continuum and calendar. In my lighter moments I thought of us as living in something like dog years.

The waitress came back with Carlotta's drink, placing it on the table. I watched the glass travel to her lips, where she tipped it then drank till the liquid was drained. Her body language, as she settled back against the chair, seemed neither female nor male, the way definitions in Carlotta's case seemed elusive. Even her hair, too short to curl which it nevertheless did, had this indeterminate swirl at the back, almost but not quite a cowlick.

"What a shitty day," she said, expelling a sigh. In the artificial light, her eyes had shifted from brown to that translucent gold like a cat's eyes. Her pupils contracted as she lifted the small barrel-shaped candle between us to a menu. "This print is too small," she complained, angling the page away from her.

"Welcome to getting old," I said the first thing that came to mind, a bad habit. Carlotta glanced up over the stiff white paper, her lips closing from their usual sensual expression, before she dropped it to her plate. She was pissed off, suddenly, and I had no idea why.

"I'm a hell of a lot younger than you are," she answered with surprising vehemence.

I reached for her hand on the table cloth, the thick silver of the bracelet she'd given me for Christmas jangling against a ring she always wore, two bloodstones sunk in a platinum band. Staring beyond me, Carlotta didn't respond but she didn't pull away either.

"That's true. You are a lot younger," I said, reassessing the seven-year difference in our ages. "But what's wrong?"

Carlotta dangled the salt shaker, like ringing a soundless bell, then looked at me. "Oh, I don't know," she replied, thoughtful in a way I hadn't expected. Infrequently, she'd open up like this, sometimes after sex but also when by chance we slipped into that kind of time where everything slows down and because of that so much seems possible . . . in yourself and the other person. She went on, "It's commuting, work, winter —"

Though she was seldom forthcoming unless it suited her purposes...a bewildering change after Ronnie's absolute directness where half the time she'd say more than you wanted to hear about yourself or anything...Carlotta had been almost relentlessly upbeat since I'd known her. Before tonight, she'd rarely expressed a doubt, a longing, a hope that might not be met. I was relieved to find she had feelings like other people.

She stretched in her usual languorous way, then started, as if coming back to herself. I had this image of a body vacated by a soul suddenly receiving it again...though soul wasn't the first word you'd think of in Carlotta's case. She lifted her knuckles to my cheek, drawing a line from ear to jaw. This was her way of apologizing.

Just then the waitress interrupted us and Carlotta turned her attention, flirting a little the way she liked to with everyone who crossed her path, female or male, young or old. She was liberal with her sexuality. On the street, in stores and taxis. The way some people laugh wherever they go. While we ordered, I thought about how I'd known a million women who wanted to come across like that, only they always seemed to be trying too hard. But Carlotta didn't appear to know any other way to communicate. She might have been one of those children raised by wolves who later have no clue as to human customs.

"It's been an insane asylum around the auction of that one book," she commented, as if I knew the one in question, which I didn't. "But I'm going to get it, whatever anyone else might think." As she cocked her chin, no doubt picturing the desired outcome, I wondered who could imagine Carlotta being dissuaded from the things she wanted...whatever they were.

It had turned out that what Carlotta did for Warner Brothers was buy options on literary properties, which is why she spent so much of her time in New York, meeting with editors or the subsidiary rights people. Though a lot of what she did was to keep on top of upcoming lists, when there was something the studio wanted Carlotta would negotiate it with the help of a lawyer. One of the first times I'd been at her apartment, I'd opened the linen closet looking for a towel only to find galleys floor to ceiling. But for some reason, it was hard to picture Carlotta reading.

Carlotta looked tired as she sat across from me now, behind her the traffic on the short staircase to the second level of tables, waiters with their aluminum discs of plates and glasses, customers on their way up or down. She'd flown in on the red eye the day before, but we hadn't gotten together because by the time she made it home from some party for work it was already midnight, and though when I was younger I would have hopped in a cab, now it was hard enough getting up for work. Besides, I was pissed off that she'd called at ten to cancel dinner when we'd planned to meet at eight. Watching the familiar white scar like some hieroglyph across the bridge of Carlotta's nose, I was thinking how it was a good thing after all that she lived most of the month in California. Because I didn't intend to land myself in one of those situations where you sit waiting for the phone to ring or cancel all your plans in case some woman might show up, which in those circumstances she never does.

"Listen," I said. "I want to talk to you about something."

Carlotta broke from a reverie, leveling her shoulders across the table. Those high cheek bones and forehead, the full slightly parted lips, made her face nearly beautiful. But as it was, the effect was undercut by the way her eyes looked too far apart because of the scar. It was this wide stare that made her looks. At least for me.

"Did I do something wrong?" she asked, responding to my tone of voice.

"If you put it that way, no," I told her.

"That's what I was hoping," Carlotta said. Not that she was concerned in any way.

"I just didn't like being stood up last night."

"I wouldn't call what happened being stood up, exactly." She pronounced this sentence as if the spaces between words were as significant as the words themselves. For the second time that evening, Carlotta's expression set, losing the fluidity of her usual amusement. "I would call it having work commitments later than expected."

"I don't care about that. I have work commitments, too," I told her. "I'm talking about calling to tell me."

"You're overreacting," Carlotta said. To my horror we sounded like characters from a soap opera, and I had inadvertently become the girl.

In spite of myself, I couldn't stop. "Well, how would you like it if I left *you* sitting at home?" I asked.

"I'd figure something came up and just order in." Carlotta seemed pleased with this answer, the way it fit her roll-with-the-punches, the-world-is-my-playground sense of herself. Not that this wasn't mostly accurate. Still, the same as with reading, I couldn't quite picture her staying home.

"But the point is, I wouldn't do it to you," I said. She looked at me and smiled, as if that were precisely the point. I considered socking her in the jaw but knew she would sock me back.

"Well maybe you better reconsider your options," Carlotta finished the conversation, at least as far as she was concerned.

"Maybe I better," I said.

Carlotta raised her hand, and I thought she was going to order another drink. But she didn't. Instead, she called over the maître d' to impress on him how long we'd been waiting for our order. There was a mercurial quality to her behavior, which the waitress understood quite clearly when, without comment, she delivered the food a minute later. We ate in relative silence after that, intermittently discussing a movie we'd seen, but apart on the two coasts. In my mind I pictured us as living on opposites sides of the world, antipodes not only in the sense of geography but also in our concepts of reality.

Not long after that, as we were waiting for the check, I was tempted to say something funny about what it had been like to turn forty, Carlotta's next birthday. But I decided the joke might backfire and get her ticked off all over again. So instead I said, "That was our first fight, you know." I didn't know how that would go over either.

But a familiar amused smile crossed Carlotta's face. "So I guess we get to make up later," she said.

"I guess we do," I answered, wondering what that whole thing had been about.

Since we were out for once, we decided to go to a club Carlotta knew, downtown below Canal Street. A block off the West Side Highway, the cab pulled up to an old brick factory building remarkable only for its pitted facade and because of the circle of girls, all of them underdressed for the cold, talking with the bouncer outside. Standing in the charmed circle of a floodlight, she looked to have a very specific appeal...that she could deck any interloper, female or male, without much effort.

The bunch of them looked at us as we got out of the cab. At the door, Carlotta pulled a twenty from her pocket for the door woman, who looked briefly as if her politics had been offended before tucking it in her jeans then waving us in. By now I saw this dispersal of ready cash as a typical Carlotta maneuver...the way she overspent and overtipped and generally got rid of money as if it were something you'd be penalized for holding at the end of a day. The people I knew, myself included, didn't have anywhere near that kind of money. Or if they did, certainly didn't dispose of it to prove a point. I wondered, and not for the first time, just how I'd explain Carlotta to my friends.

At the bottom of a flight of stairs, we entered a long concrete corridor marked with a cardboard sign that read COAT CHECK. It was wide enough for us to walk shoulder to shoulder as if in some ancient viaduct. The echo made our voices sound hollow and removed from us.

"Do you come here often?" I asked Carlotta.

"Every now and then," she said.

"For any particular reason?" I was wondering if she'd come here to pick up women, though that seemed unlikely since it was a strategy with diminishing returns as you got older. On the other hand, our own meeting had been spontaneous, not to say erratic. Or maybe that was just from my perspective.

Carlotta wore a pensive expression, as if preparing to answer me, but that was the end of it when we arrived at the makeshift coat check. It was a testament to just how peculiar our relationship, if that's what it was, had been — that we'd never discussed going to bed with other women. Particularly since we lived half of each month, and more usually, in different cities. I guess I'd assumed that for her, like myself, the sex between us was enough. Sometimes more than enough. Not that fidelity or monogamy were terms I intended to apply to any relationship I might have now or would want to have. All that had come to an end with Ronnie.

Fashioned from heavy olive drapes hung from hooks in the ceiling, the coat check demonstrated a brilliant solution to a lack of walls that would turn out to prevail throughout the club. Sitting on a chair inside it, a crewcut girl in a t-shirt that said *She Devils*, was dancing with her upper body to music that had grown louder as we'd made our way along the corridor. She made no move to get up or even to look in our direction, these days a popular solution to working with the public.

After I unbuttoned my coat, Carlotta helped me slip it off, pulling slowly away to free both my hands. I lifted them to her face then kissed her for a long moment...aware as you always are in a lesbian space how much you restrict your body and activities elsewhere, whether you intend to or not. She seemed surprised though pleased before shrugging out of her own coat, which was lined with fur against the cold.

"I hope no one sees that. We'll never get out of here alive," I said.

Carlotta considered this, as we continued following the corridor, which by now seemed endless as some catacombs. "Everyone in New York is so uptight," she said finally. "People in L.A. could care less what anybody else does...what they wear, who they vote for, how much gasoline their cars guzzle."

"But that's politics...even if you disagree," I pointed out.

"Politics?" she repeated. I don't know why I ever dreamt this would mean anything to Carlotta. In our time together she had paid attention simply to her own circumscribed world and, if I had to pinpoint it more exactly, to the necessity of getting her way there...with me and everyone else. She was good at it, too.

Up ahead the corridor opened into what looked like a fairly large open space. Just inside it, I glimpsed a bar where a few dozen women sat or stood, some with their backs to us and others half in profile to talk or look at someone else. All of them backlit by the familiar raked panel of bottles. But before we got there Carlotta ducked into a gap in the fabric wall of what now had become the ubiquitous olive drapes, which, in this instance, formed the fourth wall of a smoking room furnished with couches and stuffed chairs. Inside, there was a skylight...unexpected, to say the least, in a basement. A few of the glass panels, fixed in lead, had been opened so that the smoke could rise up and outside somewhere. It must have been in a cul-de-sac at the rear of the building.

"Look," Carlotta said, gesturing at the elaborate interior, which included a Persian rug, several lamps and some paintings suspended by guy wires against the concrete walls. I had the strangest feeling of having left three-dimensional space for the more expansive world of the mind. "One thing I'll say for New York over L.A.," Carlotta added, "is that people here are more original. Ingenious even," and with that she lifted one of the heavy flaps through which we'd entered in order to slip back into the corridor.

In the club's main room, the music, which had grown progressively louder, was blaring from speakers hung at its four corners. A DJ's booth, empty on a week night, was perched on a sturdy-looking catwalk ahead. On either side of it, women were dancing, and not with each other. A cultural note, which together with the coat check girl, wasn't exactly an endorsement of the social contract.

The seats at the far end of the bar had a particularly good view of these dancers, which people were taking advantage of — with the music, it seemed impossible to talk anyway. On the dance floor, which took up the entire rest of the space except for a small area of populated tables, there were about the same number of women as at the bar. Girls, actually...the same as the circle around the bouncer outside.

And if Carlotta still retained some fantasy that she, at least, was young, I begged to differ. Leather, pierced noses and eyebrows, entire outfits bought at the boys' department or conversely seventies miniskirts, the consistent lack of hair except among a whole new incarnation of *femme* girls — Carlotta and I looked less like women from a different generation than visitors from another planet. As she left me to weave through the tables, where women sat in each other's laps or with their legs and arms entwined, it seemed strange to be in a club of all places and with Carlotta of all people. Though perhaps it was perfectly plausible...the way dreams proceed with a logic that sometimes doesn't appear to be your own but always is.

As she turned to walk back from the bar, I tried to picture how Carlotta would strike me if I didn't know her. If I'd seen her from afar first rather than begun from a physical position in which I literally couldn't get perspective. That face that could have been beautiful, and thankfully wasn't. Her hair, sleek as a sea otter's while cropped into dense curls. Moving, she expended what seemed to be the smallest amount of energy, giving the impression of enough in reserve to knock you over, which I supposed was what had happened to me.

"It's too noisy in here. Let's go to the smoking room," she spoke into my ear a moment later.

As we retraced our steps, I looped my arm around Carlotta's waist and after trouble with the drapes, found the opening. The room looked just the way we'd left it, like an idea someone had had. "Really, this place is like a cross between some cell block" — I was searching for the right image — "and a seraglio," I said.

"You wish." Carlotta ran a hand down my side as we stood there, deciding where to sit. "If I had a harem," she went on, "I'd give you your own apartment...and fabulous costumes."

"Like what kind of costumes?"

"Oh, I don't know . . . feathers, fur, satin . . . that kind of thing. Fezes, jumpsuits . . . whatever's traditional —"

"Dream on," I said. "But thanks for the apartment."

"I would, you know," she added, as an afterthought. "And whenever I came to visit we'd have a holiday from life."

We sat on the nearest couch that was empty. Thrusting out her legs, Carlotta set her drink on an end table then stretched her arms, too. She was in her element. Never mind that everyone was half our age — it didn't matter. Or perhaps it did, the way for me those girls with their just developed bodies were like something detected in the air, a presence in your bloodstream immediately after. Intoxicating, in my present mood.

Our clothes set us apart, too. I was wearing black pants and a black-and-white striped sweater I'd had on since work that morning, while as usual Carlotta was wearing a suit. Change the locale and we could have been two women in a meeting. This made me think of the double life we all lived, and by that I didn't mean anything clandestine but simply the project of moving from our spaces into theirs then back again. How the meaning of everything changed, the valences...like the furnishings in the odd room where we sat.

I looked at Carlotta. "We're overdressed," I told her.

"I know," she said, as if I'd told her particularly good news.

That night, Carlotta was more approachable than I'd ever found her...leaning her head against my shoulder, elongating the thigh I was stroking with my hand. More approachable than when we'd been out in the world, more than when we'd been alone. It was as if she'd taken a drug. Or I had.

"I could stay here forever," Carlotta said, then laughed. "At least temporarily."

I watched the wide horizon of her eyes. "You know yourself pretty well, don't you?"

"In some ways," Carlotta answered. Her drink was still on the table, where she picked it up to carry to her lips. Then she held the glass in her lap but returned to looking at me.

"*I* wouldn't mind knowing who you are," I said.

And really, I knew nothing about Carlotta outside the little I'd gleaned from being with her...the same she knew about me. Maybe it was the time in each of our lives or the whirlwind quality of our affair, but we'd never exchanged those heartfelt autobiographies that couples, in beginning, do. Beside me, Carlotta was staring off into the distance and didn't seem about to start now.

"I'll tell you something about me if you tell me something about you," I suggested. Put like that, it seemed a ridiculous request.

"OK then, I murdered my last girlfriend," Carlotta said, and though I knew she was joking, for a split second it seemed possible in her case. She must have read this reaction in my face, because she shifted her hips against the couch to sit taller, then drummed the fingers of the hand behind my head on the couch back. "I could tell you anything," Carlotta said, finding the whole thing funny. "But I won't...only the truth. Now it's your turn," she added. It wasn't, but I decided I could live with going first.

"Well, one thing is that both my parents are dead," I told her. "Each lived a fairly long life...it's just that they were old when I was born, at least by the standards then."

"How old?" Carlotta asked.

"Early forties," I said. "The age that half of our friends are adopting or having children."

"Not in my circle," she commented, seemingly unaware of the current baby boom. Carlotta returned to our earlier topic, "And by the way, my parents are dead, too...but for a long time. They went down in a plane when I was in my twenties."

"A plane crash?" I said.

"In the Amazon. They were biologists," Carlotta informed me.

I smiled. It sounded like a tale told many times, without embroidery or analysis. In fact, it was a classic orphan story, the protagonist's character forged by fate and tragedy...as farfetched as Carlotta's having murdered someone. But when I looked over to see that blank expression I'd noticed very rarely on her face, I realized she hadn't been kidding. She'd meant it. And from another angle, maybe it wasn't so surprising that Carlotta would have such a past — I'd already pegged her as a kind of picaro character, alone and roaming the countryside. Either that or she was one hell of a good liar.

"Well, I'm sorry," I said. I lifted a hand to her shoulder, which she shrugged off.

"I wasn't close to them." Her delivery was abrupt. "And it was a long time ago. Not that I wanted them dead or anything." Her feelings seemed as electric as they had at dinner, and working on a current that Carlotta herself didn't control.

Silent, she reached to the nape of her neck to pull at what hair there was, a habit, before finishing off her drink. These gestures were like a little dance, reminding me of the symmetry of all her bodily movements. Not an *absolute* balance — you could see that in her face — but a kind of perfection according to her own stylized physicality. I could have sat there and just watched her. For a moment, I wondered if she thought of me the same way I thought about her...as someone whole, with an existence that continued when I wasn't there.

That's when our exchange took on a structure, the way I imagined other women to talk. There was a flow to our conversation, I suppose because Carlotta and I were at last interested in its content rather than simply the dynamic between us.

"Siblings?" I asked her.

"No," she replied. "You?"

"No," I said, mulling over the similarity in our bios.

Carlotta reached to drag over a coffee table from the couch just beside us, which was vacant. There were fewer women in the room now, and the smoke and also the charged atmosphere had dissipated some. We both kicked our heels up onto the table, where I crossed my ankles. She was wearing a pair of glossy short boots that she balanced at the edge.

"Spouses? Lovers?" Carlotta asked, which was something of a loaded question since she was really asking about Ronnie.

"You know the gory details of my before-Ronnie life." Carlotta nodded, because sex was the one thing we *had* talked about. "But Ronnie...my most indelible memories of her, at least toward the end, are about how little control either of us had. How something much bigger than our individual thoughts or desires had started to drive our relationship...so that you had no idea how to start anything or stop anything." Carlotta didn't comment before I added, "Or at least I didn't. I don't know what Ronnie thought she was doing."

"Do you ever see her?" Carlotta asked.

"No," I told her. "Mutual decision."

"Where does Ronnie live now?" she asked.

"San Diego," I said, "and that's it on this topic." Once again, I'd let Carlotta in on things I hadn't wanted to.

"I'm sick of it myself," Carlotta said, "except for one thing. What was that something bigger that started to take over your relationship?"

"I have no idea," I told her, which was true. In fact, this not knowing seemed the hardest part to get over in regard to Ronnie. "Your turn again, Carlotta," I said.

"Let's see," she began, enjoying herself now. "I've been involved with a lot of women, and before that I was involved with a lot of men. Surprised?" I shook my head. Since Ronnie I was post-surprise. "Most recently I had a long relationship with my boss that ended when I got promoted and stopped reporting to her." Carlotta seemed admirably philosophical about this as well as unusually candid. "We used to live together," she said, "in Pacific Palisades."

This last comment seemed to obscure the point. "Wasn't that problematic at the office . . . sleeping with your boss?" I asked.

"Don't be so naive, Kate. It goes on all the time," Carlotta answered.

"Well then, it does," I said. "Fine. Congratulations on your promotion."

But suddenly Carlotta didn't want to fight anymore. She lifted a hand to run her fingers through my hair, lifting the curls that had fallen across my forehead. "Other lovers?" she asked.

"I've just about run out...I don't know about you."

"Lovers *between* Ronnie and me," Carlotta made herself clear.

In fact, that was the first time I'd thought of her really as my lover and not just someone I slept with...that night when she mentioned herself and Ronnie together, as bookends to a period of time that I hadn't even realized was over. It would change everything, that thought, but not for a while.

"That's easy," I said. "I went to bed with one girl, and I *mean* girl, that I met at an opening."

"Was she that bad," Carlotta wanted to know, "that you gave up sex entirely?"

"She wasn't the slightest bit interesting," I said. "That was all."

"Then I'm interesting?" Carlotta's voice carried the same restrained force of her body. In itself, it was like an invitation, one you'd be ill-advised to turn down. Or maybe accept.

"Oh, you're interesting," I told her. "But I don't know what else you are."

Carlotta laughed. "Well, you will," she said, as if we'd spend the foreseeable future getting to know each other.

Meanwhile, a few slow songs had been playing in the other room. It must have been late. And since the only barrier to the music was a double curtain, you could hear it perfectly from where we sat...muted but distinct. A few couples had given up smoking, or whatever they'd been doing, moving together to lock arms around each other's waists, hands lifted to a partner's luxurious hair. Carlotta's eyes travelled around and over these women's bodies, the same as mine did, and it seemed obvious now why she'd intended to stay there forever.

"You want to dance?" I asked her.

"We've never danced with each other," she said as if this fact were the craziest thing imaginable.

We both stood, getting used to each other's bodies within the music. It seemed to me that holding her was less like dancing than beginning some descent in a single parachute, destination unknown. Or alternately, like being in one of the paintings I'd seen at a show, the previous fall. Their subjects, pairs of women...in a formal garden, a Victorian living room, on a whitewash porch swing, within an opera box...all improbable settings to my mind. Each couple wore the same unsettled expressions, giving the impression that at any moment they'd be lifted without their consent but together.

It had been quite a night.

Spicy Ease

Donald L. Maggin

As an orange setting sun
paints New York purple,
so can lovers triumph.

We conjugate love
As we link
In spicy ease,
And the soft sighing breast
Carries us,
Twined like fingers,
To a blazing, smelly, tight night jewel,
A ruby isle,
Where we ride air
And blanket wool,
And hope,
Young,
Bounces from
Eyes, teeth,
Shining shoulder.

We stand and invincible light
Cleanses us
To a pale yellow whiteness,
Color of sullied lovers.

What else is there to praise?

Stomping the Blues Away

Donald L. Maggin

The Columbus Avenue El
Banged and shook the air
A block away,
And I aged 12,
Filled with a despair
I felt but
Could not know,
Quickly felt it leave me
As I danced to a 78,
Ella's Tisket-A-Tasket,
The beat in my blood
Lifting me to joy
In the mote-filled sunlight
Of the living room.

In 1976
An erudite black man
Told me that
What I was doing
Back there in 1939
Was stomping the blues away.

When They All Went To Maxwell's

J. Schwartzman

*F*lorence is a real New Yorker, the kind they stopped making in the early fifties. In her wallet are the green and red plastic charge cards of Saks Fifth Avenue and Lord & Taylors, the pack of Pall Malls, the lighter, the compact and red lipstick. She's the real thing, you can tell by her accent—a hoarse, cigarette scraped voice, elegant nonetheless, like Lauren Bacall telling Bogey to just whistle. Another New Yorker.

A real New Yorker has a way of speaking; a sharp tongue and utter confidence in humor as the appropriate tool for unraveling any event. When humor doesn't do it, there is always foul language to fall back on, although that approach is usually reserved for traffic related matters like taxi accidents and Jersey drivers. A real New Yorker has an approach to fate tempered by a languid paranoia, knowing the worst might happen and when it doesn't— commentary, New York style.

Florence has it, the sharp tongue of every girl-reporter in every forties' movie, the elegance of a woman who knows what a peignoir is, who knows where to find the best shoes, luggage, bedding, dishes, or deli, the wit of a woman in a town where a certain amount of toughness has always been a valued quality that set you apart from other Americans. From her shoes— always perfect, and styled with just the right heel for the current fashion—to the top of her head, complete with hairdo and hat ideal for the year in question, all purchased with the red and green charge cards, my mother was created by New York.

People are not generally like this today, not created by a city. They don't refer back to any place in particular, only back to themselves, a crowed loop of reflections in mirrors that direct you deeper and deeper into nothing. Style today is not regional. What does a pierced body part or a baseball cap tell you when it's worn the same way coast to coast? It tells you nothing. There was a time when to look like a New Yorker, you had to *be* a New Yorker.

A New Yorker had a way of talking and it was not just the muddy accent you hear today from the fat detective by the coffee machine on every TV cop show. No, there was a kind of chewy, muscular talk that varied depending on your borough, a recipe of Dutch, Italian, Irish, Yiddish, and a slew of other ingredients. For New York men it was a way of speaking that says "I can handle it." For ladies, a New York accent showed a grasp on the realities of life and an ability to transcend them, for instance, a way of saying "bitch" and "whore" that are downright exquisite; "bitch," pronounced crisply, like a tiny dart hitting a balloon, and "whore" pronounced "who-er", with a lightness that is almost refreshing, offsetting any vulgarity inherent in the word's meaning.

She has the kind of Jewish looks that can pass for Mediterranean or South American—brown hair, an exotic nose with a fine hook that was later surgically reinvented, dark skin, dark eyes, beautiful clean-lined lips, pretty teeth. She likes to tell people she is Spanish, Egyptian, or American Indian, depending on her mood. She always passes.

Florence loves language, she loves to joke, and has a passion for colloquialisms and colorful talk. Phrases, patter, banter, odd expressions, repartee, all this she loves. I never figured out whether it was growing up in a household where English was the second language, or whether she just had an extraordinary knack for words; Florence sure could talk.

Losing her hearing did not change this. She still talked. Only the talk was less funny and much louder.

Break out the martinis, gang.

We have to go to radiation now, mom.

I have a better idea. Take me to the Plaza. Pick me up at 5.

What I remember about Florence has been fixed in a handful of symbolic items; a leopard skin bedspread, a white brassiere, a wall phone. These objects have been made so lean by time, so stripped of other meanings that they exist almost at the level of electronic data. Files in my mind named leopard.doc and brassiere.doc. Lean as they are, each of these things expands when I close my eyes to recreate a time and place, even though thirty years have passed between then and now. It's a trick of the mind you just can't digitize yet.

I walk through the kitchen to her bedroom where she is stretched out on a fake-fur leopard skin bedspread. She is crying over a man named Stan Lindbloom, a man who likes fishing, a man who owns a van and in autumn likes to drive upstate to Bear Mountain to walk in the woods, then throw a few dogs on the beat-up iron barbecues that belong to the park.

Stan dated my mother enough so that she cried when he didn't call. She usually cried while lying on a cotton, leopard skin bedspread in her small room with the dandelion-yellow shag carpet and wall of bookshelves. Her bedroom, originally designed to be a dining room, was just off the kitchen, the 'junior' in a junior four apartment.

Her bed stretched next to a window of our Bronx apartment with a tenth floor view that looked south over an acre of trees to red brick apartment buildings and Manhattan beyond. The profile of the city, hazy and blue-gray in the day, sparkled at night with the jewelry of three twinkling bridges. If you looked to the West, the Hudson River spread out with the Palisades cliffs beyond. So serene and timeless is the scene, you almost expect to see Indians paddle quietly by in a canoe, traveling along the Hudson's shores. In the late afternoon, the sun poured in from the west through the metal venetian blinds, making gold stripes on the wall like prison bars. It was a beautiful view, there was lots of sky and when my mother didn't cry she could look out the window.

I sat on the bed while she wept, studying the leopard skin bedspread, pushing the brown synthetic fur in different directions to see what would happen to the pattern of tawny rings and pale yellow spots. The other side of the bedspread was a crusty flat weave, the reverse of the leopard fur and not much fun. The whole thing covered the single bed in my mother's room where she did most of her crying when Stan Lindbloom didn't call, which was most of the time.

But why did she cry so much? How many tears do you have to shed before you realize a man is not calling you back? At a certain point you would think you would throw on some clothes and get some fresh air, far away from the source of your unhappiness. But it did not work that way. The few times my mother tried this approach, about the time she got her sweater on Stan would call and invite her to dinner or for a ride in his van, and off she went. I think he had a special pain meter and every time he sensed his numbers with my mother slipping below a certain point, he would call. He knew when. She never got out of the loop.

She liked to cry on top of the bedspread, not under it. She did not fold it on the end of the bed or push it to the floor. No, with her artistic eye, she knew that it was much more effective to stretch out on top of the leopard skin bedspread, where she reclined glamorously in her white satin bra and panties and elegant jewelry, than it was to curl up under a blanket. Why look a tangled ball of misery, when you could look like a spurned princess? Her pose was not unlike the famous paintings of Olympia or Venus, fellow beauties who had time to lie around staring at themselves in a mirror while the Stan Lindbloom of their time neglected to write or offer them a ride in his coach.

And like these nearly naked idols, she preferred to weep wearing as few clothes as possible. In particular, I remember a white brassiere, probably because it was at eye level. Her lingerie was typical of the time, feminine and lacy, yet mechanically sound with copious hooks and clasps. The balance of function and beauty was tilted to the practical side in those days, though my mother did the best she could in that pre-Wonderbra era.

I sat with her for hours and hours, right through junior high school, but I can't remember any single event that caused such misery. It was all left very vague. No details were offered to me, an eleven year old with little insight into the protocol of adult dating, but with great insight into what constitutes kindness. My sister and I tried to cheer her up. Madeline, two and a half years younger than me, took shots at counseling my mother and she and I came to the same conclusions about Stan Lindbloom: he was a meany, a dummy and a jerk. She should get rid of him. She ignored our advice and continued to sob because Stan didn't call her, or because he did call her but said the wrong thing. Whatever it was, she called him a prick, a bastard and a fuck at various times, worse names than she called my father.

She also cried because of Nancy. This was the other woman in Stan Lindbloom's life. I got the impression Nancy was of equal status to my mother, not more special or less, just another woman he dated at a time when the world was full of bachelors whose prerogative it was to date several women at once without telling any of them about the others. Nancy was like my mother; an attractive Riverdale divorcée—or maybe she was a widow—trying to look good in the 1960s.

My mother hated Nancy and sometimes she would report that she had seen Nancy on Johnson Avenue coming out of the Welcome Store Five and Dime, or pushing her cart up the dairy aisle in Gristedes. Now and then the unthinkable would happen and she would see Nancy in Stan's van as they bounced up Johnson Avenue and she would come home and tell me, "I saw that bitch with that prick." I don't remember what she would say after that, I only see a wet and teary blend of yellow fake fur and leopard skin and flesh.

Anyway, I had homework to do. I had geometry problems to solve and current events to sort out. At P.S. 24 they expected me to understand and explain the American system of checks and balances with what seemed to me, the nuances of a Supreme Court judge. I was supposed to have some grasp of the Viet Nam war, a tall order for anyone in those years. And then there were the 'ir' verbs in French to conjugate. That was just the school work. I also had my own personal matters to attend to like whether Mario, the object of my own romantic notions, would be at play rehearsal, and if so would I get a chance to talk to him before he was called away to some audio visual emergency, being the school's most indispensable AV monitor. I had my own life which had to take place elsewhere, away from the crying, away from the room with the leopard skin bedspread and from my mother in her white brassiere and jewelry, and finally, away from the wall phone.

For it was the telephone that seemed to be the catalyst for the bouts of weeping that took place in our apartment. This all happened in the years before multiple telephones in homes became as common place as flies. In the 60's you had one telephone and with a little effort, an extension phone, and that was as good as it got. There was nothing portable or modular, no cell phones, and you couldn't walk into a candy store and buy a phone in the shape of a Maserati, like you can today. Back then you had one or two phones and the phone company knew about all of them because they were wired right into the wall, and they all belonged to Ma Bell. A phone in the 60s was not taken lightly.

Our telephone was in the kitchen. We had a galley style kitchen, not much more than a hallway with counters, stove, sink, and the rest on either side. The phone hung on the wall just inside the entrance to the kitchen. When I wanted to talk on the phone I sat on a stepladder in the doorway or stood in the kitchen. My mother had the extension phone in her bedroom, always within her reach.

Since my mother was perpetually waiting for Stan to call, the telephone took on a charge, a force field of power. It could ring at any time, which meant at any time, everything could change. The phone might ring and on the other end would be Stan Lindbloom inviting my mother to go fishing.

The phone was a magnet, a being, a slot machine, a part of the household, a vibration, a pet. It was at the absolute center of things, though no one ever said as much. The phone was an inconspicuous household god, and it contained all possibilities in its plastic frame and rotary dial. The wall phone predicted the future.

I never spent much time on the phone because of this. I believed that through a chain of events, my presence on the phone connected to Stan Lindbloom and Nancy, and ultimately to the crying on the bedspread. If I were to stay on the phone too long or select the wrong moment to call a friend and review a homework assignment and Stan Lindbloom should call and get a busy signal, entire destinies might shift. Being on the phone was just too much responsibility.

This was the sixth grade for me. An atmosphere of general and constant disappointment, spent sitting on the bedspread asking my mother why she was crying, reasoning with her, trying to make her happy again. This was also the seventh grade, the fifth grade, maybe high school too. It seemed to go on like this for years. Tears. The telephone. Leopard skin. The white brassiere.

February

Sometimes she yells to the nurses, "Break out the martinis, gang!" and everybody laughs. She's always been a showman. The problem is, she can't hear anymore. Her hearing went so suddenly that she never had the chance to learn to modulate her voice. She says things at the top of her large, smoke-stained lungs, and her jokes and asides boom through the hall of the hospital. It's sort of funny. Like a vaudeville gimmick.

I was taking her back from radiation the other night—a Jamaican attendant did the actual wheeling—through the endless hallways of one of Memorial Sloan-Kettering's dingy subbasements. Sloan-Kettering, or as my family calls it, the Cancer Hospital, rises above and below New York City, its basement spreading beneath the avenues like a subterranean anti-hospital with gray halls that are the opposite of cheerful hospital rooms and lounges above. I felt like we were in a ship's boiler room only instead of steam engines, there is radiation equipment, heating systems, laundry rooms, and other mysterious workings.

As we wheel back to the elevators we talk about the technician who gave her the radiation dose that evening. He was a red haired pipsqueak, a little too curt for my mother's taste who felt she still deserved the respect due a New

York lady, even if she was in a thin cotton hospital gown with no makeup. As soon as we were away from the radiation department my mother said, "He's a real cocksucker, that one." She made this pronouncement in a voice that was loud and deep, and it echoed off the walls. No one heard because no one was in the corridor but my mother, her attendant, and me. It would have been all right if they did, and anyway, she was right.

When my mother wasn't busy crying over Stan Lindbloom, she liked to have a good time. In fact, there were long stretches of time before, between, and after Stan, when she just had fun. Why not? She was in her mid-thirties, the sexual revolution had arrived and there was no better decade to go out and have a good time.

She had a lot of friends, some married and some divorced, but all strong-willed and a little wild, all with children the same age as Madeline and me. They would meet in someone's living room, laugh a lot, and knock back martinis while the kids disappeared in the bedrooms to play board games and wrestle. One of her friends, Barbara, was a dusky blonde with a beautiful, round face who near the end of the sixties died of cancer and left my mother a Picasso painting.

Barbara wore bangs cut low with straight platinum hair hanging down on either side of her face like the girls in a A Hard Day's Night. She and my mother would talk about their exploits with men over brisket sandwiches in the local luncheonette on Johnson Avenue, unfolding their lives while the kids by their side explored the joy of blowing soda though a straw.

Like many Americans, when the sexual revolution hit my mother and her friends behaved as if they had just been let out after twenty years of hard labor. Everything that had been kept in check since D-day just blew. Women grew bold, donned bright colors, went back to school, canceled their beauty parlor appointment, smoked pot, flew to Mexico, or packed up their false eyelashes and moved to California. The white satin brassiere became a Pucci print of swirling sea green, sky blue and geranium pink. Adults started talking in hushed tones followed by mad bursts of laughter. Posters by Peter Max of long-legged figures in top hats striding across rainbows, stars and planets suddenly appeared everywhere, from library bulletin boards to dry cleaning stores, like a ubiquitous ad campaign for acid. The newspapers and television news may have been full of stories about Viet Nam and Cambodia, riots and protests at homes, and assassinations, but around me, in a day to day way, it was party-time.

Even those who cleaved to their semi-urban existences up in Riverdale, whose only concession to the 60s was to buy their husband a Nehru jacket, could not help but be changed by the turmoil and the rupture of the decade, by its optimism and bitterness. It happened from coast to coast; riots, violence, and tragedy mingling with money, parties, and sex. Women who only a few years earlier had been thinking of refrigerators and washer-dryers suddenly knew the name of the Secretary of Defense. Social upheaval met self-control, and self-control lost.

For a child in that era, New York City life offered constant stimulation. On a Saturday Madeline and I would jump into our mother's white Corvair and head downtown with her to the Guggenheim, and later in the day, to visit one of her friends in Greenwich Village where we had lived before our parents divorced. We stopped for a sundae at the ice cream parlor on Eighth Street, looked at posters and drug paraphernalia in neighboring head shops like the Postermat, studied the small store window off University Place that displayed buttons which said things like, "my karma ran over your dogma," wandered through Brentano's — a first-rate bookstore since replaced by a cheap clothing chain — then wrapped up the day in Azuma, one of the first shops to sell the magical knick-knacks of what was then called the "Far East."

The air in Azuma's was so thick with incense, you could almost see the Sandlewood. For an hour we would lose ourselves in exotic treasures, strings of unfolding paper daisies, vinyl inflatable pillows, origami paper, wind chimes, strands of Indian bells, mirror-covered clay elephants, incense holders, fans, Chinese finger puzzles, wooden snakes, painted yo-yos, sparking tops, inflatable animals, and magic tricks that all found their way to a shoe box in our closet.

Not only did my mother like to have a good time, I got the impression everyone then liked to have a good time, judging from all the talk about singles bars and weekend parties. Fun had to be out there somewhere for her to put all that work into an evening out; the bathing ritual, the tedious jigsaw puzzle of picking an outfit, the intricate job of putting on nylons, not to mention the sinister task of gluing on eyelashes. Her preparations took hours to complete, and when she was done we would go down to Barbara's apartment on the third floor to be dropped off with a baby-sitter who would look after Barbara's son, Madeline and me. Out they would go, the two women, a sense of urgency surrounding them as they gathered their coats and checked their bags one last time, bustling to the door amid our high-pitched yells and the sing-song voice of the Rumanian babysitter which mingled with the thin threads of children's voices.

Florence drifted towards the middle-aged, middle-class crowd who discovered divorce, freedom, and quickly afterwards, drinking and sex. In their late thirties and forties, many were children of the depression and they remembered or had even fought in World War II. For them life was looking up. The stock market was doing well, they were seeing a little money for the first time in their lives, they had their own apartments and then the ultimate happened—singles parties were invented. From the Upper East Side to the Miami strip, from the Hamptons to the Catskills, there were parties, junkets, balls, bars, and weekends.

I know Florence and her friends went to the hot spots. Not the underground, funky hot spots like Max's Kansas City or The Cafe Wah which I only learned about later, like most people, on the liner notes of record albums. No, Florence and her pals went to the spots patronized by single and divorced New Yorkers; lawyers, manufacturers, and stockbrokers among the men, teachers, interior decorators and divorcées among the women. They would meet at these original singles hangouts, arriving in pairs or threesomes to crowd the bar with their layers of hopes.

Florence and her friends went to Maxwell's Plum, one of the most famous singles bars, owned by a bon vivant named Warner LeRoy who seemed to believe you can't have too many potted plants or too many cocktails. Maxwell's was a fanciful place that created magic for its patrons night after night. There were other places—the bar at the Sherry Netherlands or PJ Clarke's—but Maxwell's was the place where you could always count on a party.

Singles went there for dinner, then moved over to the bar for the action. For a special treat, Florence would take my sister and me to dinner at this notorious place. It was always on a Sunday afternoon during the most benign hours of Maxwell's daily cycle. First we would pay a visit to Tommy, one of her pals who lived around the corner. Then we would head downstairs for an early dinner.

I remember the decor of the place perfectly, as well as the nagging feeling I always had that its jungle theme was just too wild for adults. It was an overloaded hodge-podge of bric-a-brac and antiques assembled with a uniquely sixties kookiness, a look that had found its way to 68th Street via Carnaby Street. Big glass animals hung overhead—tigers and lions, ceramic giraffes, monkeys, parrots—and an elephant stood in the corner with a potted palm on his back. Every inch of the place was filled with ceramic beasts and leafy plants; it was the culmination of free spirit repackaged for the professional crowd.

I was always embarrassed about finding myself in Maxwell's because I knew children didn't belong there. This place was for adults. An eleven year old and an eight year old could only cramp their style. I would look at the waiters lined up along the exposed brick wall with nothing to do at five o'clock on a Sunday afternoon, and feel their stares. I imagined they were signaling to us to eat and get out. I begged my mother to hurry up so we could end our intrusion. But no, this was a treat and we had to stay. In Maxwell's Plum I felt much the same way I felt in the gorilla house at the Bronx zoo; it was an interesting place, but bad things could happen there.

The sixties were not like today, when everyone goes everywhere, usually dressed in work-out gear. Today, babies go to bars, parents bring toddlers to parties. To be a kid in the sixties—a decade designed to be fun for grownups and teenagers—was to spend a lot of time figuring out where you did and didn't belong.

One evening, my mother came home with the news that she had seen Cary Grant in Maxwell's. "What an elegant man," she said. "He was so gracious. He waved to everyone and smiled. He's still gorgeous." By then, I was old enough to adore Cary Grant. The fact that my mother spotted him in Maxwell's Plum only confirmed the unparalleled superbness of grown-up life in New York City, where you could go out for a martini and see Cary Grant.

If it seems odd that a kid would love Cary Grant, remember that the era was not for children and throughout the decade, right up until John Travolta in 1976, there was a total ebb in production of teen movie idols. Things had just about died out with Frankie Avalon. For a brief moment, Hollywood was actually busy making good movies for grown-ups, and teens were left with free reign in the world of rock music, where they designated rock stars instead of movie stars for personal worship. If we wanted screen idols we had to opt for the ones that had been in service for years, like Paul Newman and Cary Grant.

So Florence would run around with friends and go on dates, at the same time work as a teacher and take care of two little girls. It must have been hard for her, but as a child I had no real sense of what was difficult for an adult.

Things shifted, Maxwell's closed, and anyone who remembers accordion-folding paper daisies is not a child anymore. The sixties have already cycled in and out of revival once, and more revivals lie ahead. A nationwide chain of coffee bars has appropriated peace signs and plasters them to the windows as if they were invented to sell espresso, and never served as instruments to protest the death and destruction in far off Southeast Asia.

Florence and I still sit together on the bed like we used to. And she is still crying, with me doing the comforting, only now it is a hospital bed. There is no leopard skin bedspread, just a white blanket, and she is not wearing the white brassiere and earrings or pearls, just a white cotton hospital gown with little blue diamonds on it.

A Conversation with John Updike

Barbara Probst Solomon

*I*n the spring of '91 Spain's main news weekly Cambio 16 asked me to interview Larry Rivers and John Updike as I was their New York correspondent. In May I interviewed Larry; like me he lived in New York, then, during the summer, I flew up to Boston to meet with John Updike. The Updike interview was way too long, so Cambio was only able to use a small part of it. I wanted to publish it in its entirety in the United States, but at that time I couldn't find a magazine to give me that kind of space, and I didn't want our talk to be cropped as though we had been exchanging media sound bites.

I had met John Updike once before our Boston meeting, in the 1950s. He had won the annual Dana Reid prize for the best piece of undergraduate writing at Harvard. Dana Reid had been on the Harvard Yearbook with my husband Harold Solomon; he had been killed in World War II, and his friends on the yearbook had established a yearly literary award in his memory. Though the dinner that year took place at our Central Park West apartment I don't believe I actually spoke to Updike — I was still a student at the Columbia School of General Studies, despite being married to Harold, I was intimidated by these tall people from Harvard in their casual well-cut jackets with leather patches who had been to war.

An interview, like a photograph, should reveal as much about the person doing the shoot as it does the subject. In rereading this piece so many years later I am more consciously aware of how much my earlier interview in the spring with Larry Rivers had intruded a sort of zippy slightly mysterious energy into my summer encounter with Updike. At the time Larry was finishing *What Did I Do? The Unauthorized Autobiography of Larry Rivers*, and when I went to his studio a quick tense, combustible attraction erupted between us — when he finished his memoir he dedicated it to me. I realize now that I must have had Larry on my mind when I interviewed John Updike. I think it accounts for the abrupt somewhat askew segue about art and writers and artists that crept into my questions to him.

On a cool summer afternoon John Updike and I met at the Ritz in Boston; it had been my idea to go there. I had flown up from New York, and he had driven in from his home in Beverly Farms. He didn't seem, at least that day, to like being in the Ritz, so, at his suggestion, we went across the street to the Boston Public Gardens. We sat together on a bench and watched the swans in the lake and talked. I felt embarrassed at paying so much attention to my SONY recording machine; I kept shoving it in his direction. I was afraid that the shrieks coming from a group of noisy children near us mixed with the street noises and birds chirping would prevent his voice from being properly picked up; he spoke in a low voice, and kept his head turned away from the machine. I looked at him. He was no longer the gawky student I had met in my living room, he had become a writer whose thick gray hair fell in the right way on his face, he had a nice way of moving his hands and his clothes hung on his body in the right way and he wore good shoes. Though he complained about his problems with skin allergies, his face looked right too; he had grown into looking like the writer he had from the beginning wanted to be. *A touch of his idol Fred Astaire, a touch of Harvard Yard.*

S.   Has Harvard and your undergraduate life there in the early '50s always been central to your definition of yourself?

U.   For many years I had begrudged Harvard the place it had in my life. I was delighted that they had accepted me. Because my mother had figured out that it was the place for writers to go. And so it was. It was a very literary place. It also was a very snobby place. I was so innocent about the various social levels that I didn't know what the finer clubs were. I didn't realize that in part they were an engine for perpetuating the Brahmin class of New England. I liked my courses and I liked that I did well in them. Everything worked out wonderfully, but I remained sort of sullen inside — I wanted to remain a Pennsylvania farm boy. But I married a Radcliffe girl and after a few years in New York moved back to within an hour of Harvard. And I've never really left. I lived within an hour of Harvard for the last thirty-five years. Not that I go there often, but I like knowing that it is there.

S. So Harvard was your chosen identity?

U. Yes. I can't imagine my life if I had gone to Cornell as I nearly did. I'd be a different person. Harvard still had potent literary ghosts around in those days. I wasn't smart enough to be one of the young modernist writers — in those days I sent the Lampoon funny stuff, or would-be funny stuff — but nevertheless there was a sense of confidence — a sense of hands on. T.S. Eliot and Wallace Stevens came and read. e.e. cummings gave the Norton lecture.

S. In one of your essays you remarked on what you felt was the epitome of New England fair-mindedness. In the chapel at Harvard opposite the great wall covered with the names of Harvard alumni killed fighting for the Allies, there is a plaque with the names of four German graduates. Do you remember what I am referring to?

U. That was in an article on New England churches. One of the churches I discuss is Mem Chapel, which has that little quite moving plaque over the corner commemorating the Harvard graduates who fought on the wrong side in World War II. It was lovely. Harvard had not forgotten its sons. *Non oblita est.*

S. I was struck by your reference to the German soldiers — in re-reading your work a certain music filters through. First you were a Pennsylvania farm boy, and after that you adopted a Harvard style. And you seem very drawn to certain kinds of European writers — you've written four essays on Knut Hamsun and you have also written on Céline. I am wondering about the German part of your heritage — it was on your mother's side?

U. Right.

S. How did it affect you? I felt that you seemed to mind that the First World War ended just before your father, who was in the infantry, could be shipped overseas and that you were very *mea culpa* about sitting out the Korean war on a student exemption and then not being drafted because of your bad skin.

U. I thought being a 4-F was a kind of weaselly thing to do, but I couldn't control that. But then I didn't try to sneak around and enlist anyway. I accepted the 4-F and I made a nice little life for myself.

S. Yet you refer to these things almost as though a sin was involved. And I am thinking, did the German part bother you? Growing up so soon after the Second World War? What is the sin?

U. Who knows? My mother's maiden name was Hoyer. They came here shortly after the Revolutions, so they weren't new German. And my mother never really admitted to being German, she always said that her father was Swiss and her mother Arab. She was rather fanciful about her past. When Europeans come to Berks County, or Lancaster County, they say it reminds them of Europe. So maybe that makes me interested in European writers. Or ask me if I'm interested in my fellow Americans, who all suggest a prairie to me. And their books are like prairies. Whereas German fiction and European fiction is sort of like a European landscape. It's tight and kind of green, and packed in. It's fun, of sorts. One of the reasons I've reviewed so many Europeans is to avoid sitting in judgment on my fellow Americans. I've reviewed Bellow and Vonnegut, but I basically have tried to avoid it. Once you get to know the writers it becomes harder to know what you think as opposed to what you want to think. So the Europeans, being distant, are comfortable and dead. That's doubly nice.

S. But you could have picked the British — you are definitely more in line with Europe than Britain.

U. With some exceptions the British novel is a tame thing. Talky. It doesn't get off the ground or into any other realm. I like the French. They do it with their heads. And the Latins. The Spanish and the Spanish-Americans do it with something more. It's exciting to see that happen. They are really trying to find a frontier in fiction. Whereas the British are content to work the old social plot.

S. I'm particularly fond of your novel *A Month of Sundays*. It has that kind of European passion and central drive. It's Nabokovian in a way.

U. I kind of loved that book when I was writing it. I described somewhere that after *Couples* I spent an awful lot of time researching James Buchanan, the fifteenth president of the United States, and I found a historical novel a very resistant form. Time was going by, I wasn't getting any younger, and I thought I must send a novel down to Knopf. The easiest way to write one fast is to have a man writing a kind of a journal. I took two writing days for each day in his journal. So he writes twice as quickly as I do. But it was my fastest novel. And also one where I could let go. Have some fun. Use what was in my upstairs.

S. I felt that you had some fun with the religious things.

U. I was very interested at that time in the differences between Karl Barth and Paul Tillich. The book is about a Barthian who becomes more Tillichean at the end. I was sort of frantic at the time.

S. You seemed to be arguing with yourself. In my reading of *A Month of Sundays* the novel at moments seemed to suggest that Christ just represented another mystery cult and was a megalomaniac. That would be hardly Barthian.

U. No, Karl Barth would not say that. The novel kind of laid an egg when it came out. One reviewer said are we any the better for knowing the Reverend Tom Marshfield. It struck me as an interesting idea, that the reader should be any the better for knowing a literary character. As you said, it is Nabokovian in a way. It is tricky. It is even trickier in the first version. I wanted the last chapter to be to be a blank page. But it was hard to tell that was what I was intending. So I had to put in a few words. The book was full of secrets. Ins and outs.

S. You mentioned Bellow earlier and you have written about what you consider the professorial element in his novels. But you, too, are known as a writer with a thinky mind. Do you think, by writing so many essays, you can keep the thinky part out of your fiction? Is this what you mean to do?

U. I don't have Bellow's passion for abstract thought. Or for European thought. He really is obsessed by it. It's in *The Adventures of Augie March* and continues in his later books. So I can't pretend to care as deeply as Bellow does about great ideas, but what interest I do have in them is vented in the reviews. With *The New Yorker*'s permission I'm able to make little essays. If I have something to say about civilization I can do it there, so I feel free not to have to do it in the novels.

S. So you do the intimate moment, that American moment, in the novel, and get rid of all these other ideas in your essays?

U. In the novel you are basically trying to represent things, the same as events, and not judge them. As Proust said, it's like finding hieroglyphs in oneself tracing them underwater. You're not trying to communicate like a professor or politician. You are trying to make a thing. There is a thingyness about a novel which we should respect.

S. Okay. As in Flaubert. But you have at times raised the question of politics and it seems to me that you view politics, the *idea* of politics, also as a sort of sin. As in your essay *On Not Being a Dove*. Almost as if you have a phobic repulsion toward it. In that essay, I find about ten different Updikean voices. If you merely had wanted to write about was why you were not part of the hysterical somewhat propagandist 1960s it seemed to me it would have been stated in a different way. Most people who were in favor of our involvement in the Viet Nam war didn't question whether they were patriots or not, which you anguished about. They took it for granted that they were. I'm not discussing one's point of view regarding that war. But it does strike me, much in the way that some writers overly resist seeing the sexual in a situation, which is not your problem, the political, in any form, seems to mean something very special to you. Something very sinful and dark.

U. Well, you certainly are right. That was a very squirmy piece.

S. I didn't say squirmy —

U. Well, I say squirmy because most people in the sixties took the attitude
that the men who were leading us — LBJ and then, Nixon — were kind
of insane killers ...and I thought they were certain men caught in the
predicament of being President. And so I was a little more sympathetic
to their basic situation. On the other hand I think I do bring some of my
childhood experience of local politics, and Harvard in the early fifties,
and I do look upon politics as something dirty and silly, and I can't
imagine why anybody first rate would want to get mixed up in it. I think
that is a prejudice which I am now confessing. We loved that in Adlai
Stevenson. Because he did seem to be wonderful. He was like us —
better than us. Bigger.

S. I feel when I read you that you sound like someone who as a kid who
had been hit over the head by politics. And so I think — where does this
trauma come from? I'm not making a commentary about the point of
view you expressed in that book, because most people who had that
point of view expressed it without fear. Look, my father was a Republican — but he wasn't traumatized by his views.

U. I was traumatized because I was raised as a Democrat, I had always been
a liberal. You're asking why did I make so much of this?

S. Yes — why was it expressed by you as a trauma, rather than, saying, I
simply disagree with these people?

U. I felt very traumatized by it, because by trying to see our full war position, I seem to be condoning this war, with dead on all sides, and when
you find yourself defending war it is very uncomfortable if you are a guy
who can't step on an ant. To suddenly seem to be cheering on the bomb-
ers in Hanoi while you are so squeamish in your own life seemed to me
to be a way into my own insides. An unpleasant way. But I thought
being a writer I shouldn't flinch from the unpleasantness of it and, yes, I
wrote that essay. For which I got very little thanks. It's done me nothing
but harm — people have forgotten what I thought and who cares really?

I care, apparently.

S. But you wrote it as though you had no awareness that other intelligent people might share some of your views?

U. No, I didn't know that. Were there some? I'd love to believe that.

S. Sure. That's what struck me. You wrote it like you were a man alone in the wilderness.

U. I felt alone. I felt alone with my kind of small town patriotism in an age that couldn't care less. That spat on it. Yes, I did feel alone. I don't know why I felt alone. There are a lot of Republicans in Ipswich. But my wife was not among them.   I've sort of erased the whole thing — I don't know why.

S. You wrote it like you were in shell-shock.

U. Yes, you're right. I don't feel so shell-shocked now that it has receded. And you can see now that the war must have been a mistake, or we would have won it. The results proved that the doves were right. I don't know why I got so heated about it — even now I get sort of hot about it. Because I'm cool about most things.

S. You felt about the Viet Nam war that you took an outsider's position — as though you were, so to speak, on the wrong side of history. I do feel that you confuse politics and history, they are not the same thing. It even crept into your essay about Proust and Céline.

U. I have to reread the essay. It's been quite a few years since I wrote it. As I remember it — I am not a great Céline reader — I suspect he is one of those writers who greatly benefits from the reader's knowing French. George Steiner is constantly telling us that. Steiner is constantly moved by the spectacle of men whose politics he can't fathom but whose style he admires. These European anti-Semites. And I was just going by what his book said, which showed that in addition to not just zany but murderous views there seemed to be also a kind of a sweet doctor. Is that true? Or untrue?

S. Well I don't think he was sweet, or not sweet. But I didn't agree with
    your analogy to him and Proust — because you said Proust was anti-
    Semitic. What he wrote about Bloch. And I thought Proust was doing
    no more than when you call Christianity a scandal, in your book *A Month
    of Sundays*. Proust, after all, was a fervent Dreyfusard, and there's where
    I began to feel that the political in some ways is so traumatic to you.

U. I think what I was trying to say is that there aren't any anti-Semitic
    portraits in Céline as deadly as Bloch in Proust. I may be wrong. But
    Céline's views didn't seem to carry over into his art. He didn't bother to
    give us caricatures of Jewish people.

S. This is taking things out of context. You would have to add that Proust
    became a Dreyfusard and that Céline —

Updike shifted his legs and gazed at the swans, and at the park. "Céline
would not have become a Dreyfusard?"

I too gazed at the swans. But I didn't want to pursue the subject. I sensed
that Updike felt constrained by the cassette machines — the interviewer has
the unfair advantage of being able with a change of a comma, or inflection,
to win all arguements, so to speak have the last word, and that sort of winning is a mug's game. I wondered if Updike thought of me as a wandering
reconnoiterer from the New York Jewish intellectual set to which he felt somewhat alien. I wondered if he comprehended that a girl, even a Jewish girl,
growing up in Manhattan could have been as ill-equipped to deal with the
snarls and smart heat of the "New York intellectuals", and as innocent as a
small-town boy from Pennsylvania. Well, like Updike, like Proust, I had had
childhood asthma. A bond. I wondered whether I should mumble that I had
been raised by a German Lutheran. Whether it was relevant. Then I didn't.
I decided to switch tacks.

S. This is interesting. The place of politics and history is something that
    you push away from. Just like Cheever maybe pushed away from certain
    aspects of sex.

U. Well, it could be. This is almost psychotherapy.

S. We could talk about something else — Art.

U. No, it's fine — I'm just trying to think about it. You had mentioned Knut Hamsen, who is another great writer who disgraced himself, and who I felt obliged to review repeatedly.

S. Four essays.

U. Yes, that's a lot of Hamsun. Because I became interested in his style. He has a kind of style that I don't have but that I like. Very dry, precise, sort of magical — what Donald Barthelme used to call the little nut-hard word. I seem to like that. I did get a couple of letters from Jewish fellow Americans angry that I would have anything good to say about Hamsen. I was surprised that after all these years they still noticed. I was shocked. Again, because you don't want to be in a position of seeming to condone Hitler, of coming out on his side.

S. No, no. I didn't think that. What interested me is that kind of interest, whether it's from Jews or non-Jews, usually comes from Europeans. Because they've been on every side they get enmeshed with the guy who ended up on the wrong side. So I was trying to figure out why so much passion about being on the right or wrong side from this person who had been this boy in this rather innocent American town in which these things were not at issue.

U. Well, it must have been a kind of insecurity — right?
Because if I had been more secure I would not have felt guilty about my patriotic reflexes.

S. Usually people have this kind of guilt over something like sex. It fascinated me because it seems to have come from nowhere.

U. It comes from my sense of myself as being a man who has chosen to be a certain way. I spoke of myself as being a farm boy, but actually we weren't that — I was really a small town boy who wanted to get out and become Fred Astaire or one of the Algonquin crowd or somebody like that. So that the sophisticated ideas were in my head from early on. So even then there was a kind of ambivalence. On one hand I was Johnny Updike in my knickers going down to the playground, and really having quite a lot of fun in my little environment. On the other hand I was starting to get out — in a way betray Shillington by getting out of it. And then I got a coating of Harvard on me and a coating of *The New Yorker*. I needed all these veneers to bring off my impersonation of a sophisticated knowledgeable person that I know down deep that I'm not. And the Viet Nam war somehow found me out. It said the real you is a little killer, flattening tin cans and wanting to bomb those poor gooks over there. Maybe that's why I took it so hard. I was trying to write a book about me and trying to find ways of writing about myself that interested me. I guess I was needing to find ways of talking about it, and about that one terrible lapse of mine in not having the politically correct, and therefore dismissible, view. Then Norman Podhoretz ran what I wrote in *Commentary*. It was my great rapprochement with him, he had never had much use for me or my work.

S. Oh, because *Commentary* ran the Alfred Chester review?

U. Oh, you remember that? It was a most vicious review — how can any-one attack *Pigeon Feathers*? Bad reviews serve a good purpose. They alert you to the fact that life is not an ice-cream stand. I was this small town kid. These small town bouquets must have irritated Chester — the Brooklyn kid, smart, probably kind of tough. But I was trying to say that this is kind of a life too. Most of my writing has been saying that. I write about Shillington or Berks County as if these conflicts and issues matter as much as what happens in Manhattan.

S. I was rather glad you wrote some nice things about O'Hara.

U. O'Hara knew a lot more about the actual power struggles in Pottsville than I did about my environment. What I saw, to which I bore witness, was domestic strife and confusion whereas O'Hara saw really a class-ridden society. So his Pottsville is more mappable than my Brewer. But on the other hand O'Hara had what Wallace Stevens, a native of that part of the world, called a willingness to celebrate. He just has this terrible itch to *tell*, and a belief that everything is interesting. Maybe this is a Pennsylvania quality — I suspect I have it in my way too. This wish to celebrate, and if you don't say it the first ten times, say it maybe five, ten more. O'Hara has faded fast, but some of his best short stories are lode stars to me of what good fiction can do.

S. You are so interested in art — do you feel at this point that more of our twentieth century autobiography is in art rather than fiction?

U. It's been more glamorous. And its avant gardism is much easier to trace. You can see things happening, can't you? If you've been to a couple of rooms in a modern museum you can see things that all the people are pushing a little harder against. Representation. Yes, I think it's the art of this century. Fiction takes too long to absorb, and people really don't have the time — the patience that it took to really read novels.

S. I feel envy. I feel envy towards the artist.

U. Of course very few become artists at the order we are thinking — of the order of Picasso and Matisse. You don't want to become a Jackson Pollock — that kind of a symbol. Also it seems to be more fun to paint rather than sitting at the typewriter. All the smells and the gooeyness of it all, and just the materiality of it is exciting. So I found museums, which I have written about, very consoling, inspiring places. Something you have seen there maybe you can do in words.

S. Would you have liked to have written on Balthus?

U. The guy who does adolescent girls in semi-masturbatory positions? Uh, I could do it if I had a room full of them to look at, but he's not some one who greatly moves me.

S. The way Ryder did?

U. Ryder sort of did. Certainly all that crust and crud on his painting was exciting. I'm sort of a fraud as an art critic, but I like the challenge in trying to write about a painter. And Ryder was interesting to me because he is very American. He is such an American mystic, that kind of reaching, that wish to go beyond, even though he doesn't have the tools. He still is working for something in a way that Europeans in that era weren't.

S.   What I meant by envy, is that when I think of what I am, of my journey and this place, then I think of art, or the movies, not fiction. They have expressed my autobiography, they have expressed my reality. And that makes me angry. Because I think of writing as what I chose to do, and yet I realize my head is somewhere else.

U.   The other things are much easier and they kind of blast you, but I'm not sorry that I'm a writer. I can do a lot more with it than I ever could as a painter. In writing there is always more to do. More to say. More to try.

S.   It strikes me that when you write about women — you are doing your painting.

U.   Really? Painting the women. A bit, maybe. How to make them attractive and poignant? Yes.

S.   You seem to do the painting with the women, and your theology with the men.

U.   That may be a limitation of my world view.

S.   I didn't say it was a limitation. I just wondered if you see how much you paint when it comes to women.

U.   No. Probably not, but I'll look for that now. Yes, it makes sense. Although I've tried to write from the insides of women now and then, in part because it's been pointed out to me that I don't do it much. And one should. But I suppose I'm male enough to be more excited by the outsides of women than their insides. I don't know. My mother was a very eloquent woman who was constantly offering to share her thoughts with me, and maybe I got an overdose of female thought early. There's a heat about female confidences, this tremendous female heat, and you sort of run backwards and try to find some guys to play a little softball with. But, oh, there's this sense of women being almost too much, too wonderful, too sensitive, and yet somehow wounded — wounded I suppose by their disadvantage within the society.

S. I wondered when I read your story *The Rumor* whether you were now trying to achieve that sense of art, of painting a portrait, they way you do with women, in writing about men?

U. Well, I was trying to do something a little different and it was fun to write about that gallery. I was trying to make use of something which did happen. There was a rumor that I had eloped with a young man. I don't know how many people it reached, but it reached me by several routes, and, uh, my wife looked at me. Was I really here? Which was she to believe? Me, or the rumor? There's some sort of idea there for a story, which I tried to use. And if you hear a thing often enough you begin to believe it, don't you? You begin to think Jojo isn't so bad, is he? He's sort of touching, Jojo, and that little scar.   And there were John Cheever's journals. Having known John before we knew he was a homosexual and then to read how homosexual he was has been for me mind-blowing. I didn't know him tremendously well, and I'm a pretty innocent guy, as we've established, but I began to get a glimmer in some of his late stories. There's one in which two men begin to roll around with their scratchy bald heads and their scratchy chins, and the guy says, "this isn't so bad". And I began to feel, well maybe there's something revealing here; but that was fairly late. It's — God, those journals! How do you feel about those? Oh no, you're interviewing me.

S. You can ask me anything you want, John — this is a conversation.

U. I was going to ask you how you feel about those journals appearing in *The New Yorker* in such bulk.

S. Well, I was very taken with them, and I also felt very sad. I felt it's hard to capture now that this is the way Americans lived then — we are living in such a different society, where this wouldn't happen in this way. I mean Cheever in a later period could have had an open life as a homosexual. It moved me because I thought, hey, we've forgotten that even Tennessee Williams didn't overtly write much in the early phase about homosexuals. We've forgotten our history in that sense. I felt the fact that Cheever did it that way is part of our history, our emotional baggage. I think that's what you said when you mentioned *I Thought of Daisy* or maybe it was *Memoirs of Hecate County*, how moved — or not how moved, how sexy you remembered Edmund Wilson's "two little nothing sentences" — I think it was a mention of a pubic hair —

U. It was very short — it didn't even have that, but yes, Wilson was franker than anything you get in Hemingway —

S. You said the Hemingway didn't talk below the waist.

U. Right. It wasn't below the waist.

S. But *Memoirs of Hecate County* blew our minds, right? I was struck by your bringing that up because it was so true for our generation. So when you ask me how did I feel about Cheever, about his journals, I think it was just hard for him and I feel sad.

U. I felt sad for him, that he wasn't having more fun out of his life because at that time, many thought, he was the best short story writer in the country. I thought he had it made. And everything was wrong with his life as he saw it. Not enough money, not enough wife-love, not *enough*. The journals are a miserable document about the condition of a man's soul. I guess it's justified by the quality of the prose — some of those old Cheever paragraphs.

S. He liked the way you wrote. He was a sort of mentor?

U. I never knew quite what he made of me. He put himself on record as having reservations about all those sexual nuts and bolts of mine. Well, maybe he had a point. And I felt when we were together in the fall of 1964 in Russia that I was rubbing him the wrong way without meaning to, or at least it emerged from some letters he wrote at the time that he found me a bit of a pill. But I imagine that we got fonder of each other, and he put me up for things. So it's hard to know. I don't believe there was an awful lot of room in John for admiration of other writers. I think his attention was so skittery that it's hard to picture him reading too many books, or if he did read them he read them very fast. He was an impatient man in the way I think alcoholics often are — they're really thinking about the next drink all the time. I was so innocent I was shocked by those Cheever stories of the late forties and fifties, that people could behave in this decadent, drunken way. I remember being shocked not by the explicit carnality but by the confusion and hanky-panky, and the unhappiness. Oh, some of those New York stories, when you read them now, are so unhappy, aren't they?

S. Yes, they are.

U. The grayness, and picking up kids at school, and being in love with some other kid's mother, and going to little rooms above restaurants. It's all very New York, and very period, in a way. Men wore hats still.

S. You have a very nice short story that I thought about recently which is about a couple and their problems. And they go to the analysts.

U. "The Fairy Godfathers." Right.

S. And when the analysts leave they take the interesting part of their patients, of their patients' lives, with them. When I read the newspaper accounts about Anne Sexton and her problematic analyst, I thought of your story. Isn't that, in a way, what you were trying to say — that the analysts can become over fascinated with their patients?

U. It's not about seduction, but it is about the way in which an analyst, a good analyst, seems to possess a larger part of ourselves than we ourselves do. The couple quarrel, and as they discuss their adulterous romantic plight, the analyst becomes more interesting to them than one another. But we're lonely. We have a terrible need to make contact, Katherine Mansfield said somewhere. We'll put up with almost anything to make contact. We'll pay a hundred dollars an hour to sit in a creaky chair. We'll get battered. People are hungry for other people. It puts us in a lot of fixes, but how else could you do it? How else could you organize the human race? I only went to one, and I didn't go for very long, but you do get the illusion that this person loves you. If he said "sleep with me" you probably would think twice before you'd say no — I don't know if I'd say no if it was a woman. I don't know how you'd get around it. I've seen it said that Anne Sexton actually was never healthier mentally than when she was sleeping with her psychiatrist, which goes against all of the principles of the Psychiatric Association. She was a very needy woman. Have you read her letters?

S. No. She once stayed at my house.

U. Oh, well, then —

S. No, I didn't really know her. I think I was just part of the convenient scenery. She arrived with the poet Caroline Kizer and all her pills in an orange evening dress. It was all so far out of my ken I just watched.

U. I think she looks pretty good now, looking back on the poets of that era. She wasn't as subtle as some, or as striking as Plath, but in a way there's more human stuff there. I'm sorry she had sunken so much she had to do away with herself.

S. I also think that being "crazy" then was sort of more stylish than it is now. It's a bad word, crazy, but —

U. No, it's okay. You're not as aware of crazy writers now as you were then, are you? There were lots — Roethke, Plath, Lowell, Berryman.

S. But do you notice how it suddenly stopped.

U. Yes, it stopped. What do we have instead? A lot of dull healthy people who write too much. That other generation were terribly modernist, weren't they? Terribly passionate about what they were doing. They had the sense that this is the boat to immortality. This is the way to Valhalla, to write wonderfully well. It makes you frantic if you think about that day and night.

S. It did make them frantic.

U. It made them frantic.

S. But that's not what is going on now.

U. No. I don't know what is going on now in poetry. A lot of women are telling how it feels, and that's good. We need to know that. Not too many men, although there was a very good column in *The New Yorker* last week. It's a poem by the English poet John Ash, and it ends with the image of the century as a battered wife who comes into a bar. A battered woman. And says that she did it falling down stairs. And the bum asked, "How could you do that falling down stairs. Somebody did this to you. Who?"

I laughed. John was getting hoarse, so was I. Over an hour had passed — we had been talking non-stop. The summer light in the park was getting less harsh. "It does seem to me that in your deepest self, the territory you use is Chekhovian. Well, not quite Chekhovian, but that Chekhovian moment of intimacy that sort of wafts away. I don't know how to quite say it. I'm just not a very coherent person."

U. How could you be more coherent? You'd be too coherent if you were any more coherent. What gives me satisfaction when I look into my own short stories are the little moments when there's kind of a *lock*, and you really get a sense of a space, of a little complicated space, like inside a lock, that I've done with words, that shows the quality of the moment or a relationship. Yes, I'm after the little moments which add up.

S. You always write great last paragraphs about men and women and love and nostalgia. I think, when I read you, *hey, that's what happened to me in that kitchen — why didn't I write about it?* That's what I think you are essentially about.

Updike got up and stretched. He stared at the swans, at the children playing near the pond. "I'll buy that. That sounds nice. It's a nice way to think of me. That's the way I think of myself, probably. I think it is." He paused. "I probably ought to get my body into that car before the rush begins." He stretched again. "Can you stand up?"

I stood up and packed up my two cassette machines and I watched him as he walked taking long steps in the direction of his car; he was heading back home to Beverly Farms. Then I went to a Boston Hertz office and rented a car and drove to Cape Cod for the weekend.

Outsiders on the Inside

Hats for Alice

Julián Ríos

MOBY DICK

*H*at first, tale afterwards?, said the Mad Hatter to Alice putting a weird toothed mitre down on her, Then listen to me carefully, he added, because I won't repeat twice what will happen to you only once. Right. Once there was...Or do you prefer once upon a time? Anyway, it's all going to be the same to you. It's a sunny summer afternoon on board of the ferry-boat *Moby Dick*, that sails the Havel in Wansee (Berlin), teeming with tourists. Call me Dick, an obese albino will say to you in German, as he sits beside you with an old leather briefcase (covered with hotel labels from many parts of the world) on his lap. But you can also call me "Moby Dick" if you like, as my friends do, and then he guffawed in such a way that his whole frame shook. Do you like to know what's in here? he asked you when he saw that you were staring at the labels from all those hotels, and without even giving you a chance to utter a word. he opened his briefcase and took out and unfolded a jaded bishop's mitre that he pulled down on your crazy little head. Close your eyes and think where you'd like to go, because this Saint Barandan's mitre will take you there in no time, wherever you want in either time or space. And then suddenly you found yourself on a quiet beach, at night, with a naked man lying by the shore. Call me Jonah, he said to you. and opened his eyes wide; then you felt you were inflating like a balloon, your head became similar to a big fish's and your mouth opened to swallow Jonah down. Aha, the obese albino next to you said, this time you won't let him go. And then you ran to the gunwale, with an urge to vomit, and your mitre fell into the water and disappeared into the foamy wake like a fish. "Do you feel well, Miss"? the obese albino asked with a gleam of strangeness In his eyes, as if he saw you for the first time.

Fez Number 5

Try this one on: it is an upper-crust fez, the hatter said to Alice, and you'll see what's good for you. You are at the top of Berlin's Viktoria Park, in Kreuzberg, at sunset, next to a young Turkish flower seller with large black eyes and long limbs, who holds you and stands tightly crushing your back as you two watch the waterfall hurl noisily from above, looking as if it streamed down Grosbeerenstrasse until it disappears from sight. The dusk colours the mountain red, and the cascade is already black when the flower boy covers your eyes with his hands smacking of carnations, and, with a light touch of his silky fingers, as if he was winding up a watch, he makes you see a terraced truncated pyramid, covered with blood, up the steps of which you climb, gravely, dignified, arms crossed on your chest, ready to be sacrificed by the priest with the shaved skull that will drive the stone knife into your drumming heart at the very moment in which the flower boy touches your eyelids to make you see — second vision — a scarlet tower in a burning desert in which you are imprisoned, and all through the years you manage to knit a ladder with your hair, the one that the man of your dreams will climb to rescue you; eyes half-closed, you imagine him again, and from far away there comes, quick as lightning, a dust cloud: no doubt it is him on his horse: but the flower boy touches your eyes once more and then you suddenly see yourself in Xemaa-el-Fnaa, Marrakech, beside a giant wearing a leopard-skin loin-cloth and a fez with a long tassel, who commands you to follow him to his master's house. You obey and walk through a maze of alleys in the old town, and in the yard of a terraced house, coloured in red from the blood-shot dusk, a little moustached man, wearing a tux and a red cape makes a gesture and shows you how the terraced house grows until it reaches the clouds, and from the top of that red tower flows a black river murmuring incomprehensible sounds. The wizard in the tux is about to make another gesture, but the flower boy lightly touches again your startled eyes and you find yourself in a room with red curtains — fourth vision — kneeling naked with your back to the boy who is stroking you as he whips you with a bouquet of red roses. Blood covers you like a burning cape, and your hair flows black down to your feet. You are about to shout, from pleasure or pain, but the flower boy once more strokes your eyes and — fifth vision — once more you are at the top of Viklona Park, completely alone with that strange fez in your hands, that I have just made for you, so that you won't believe what your eyes will see.

SAINT VALENTINE

This hat of hearts — the Mad Hatter said to Alice — will remind you of that freezing February 14th when you met (or recognized, perhaps) your eternal beloved in Gramercy Park. Everything's possible in New York. You and the elegant old man with the white temples dressed in black were the only hotel customers who fancied walking in that private square on such a cold morning. As you tried to call the squirrels attention, he came along side you and said: I knew you would keep our appointment on such a special day.

Did you feign surprise?

I didn't expect you would be so young this time, he added with the same ease, but the fire in your eyes remains the same. Now (the roles are reversed), he murmured with a distracted air. At our last meeting I was in my early twenties and you were over fifty, though you didn't look it. London. February 14th 1941. Do you remember?. The truth is that you were already trying to remember. On the following night, when I went to see you again, the old man continued, a heap of fuming debris was all that was left of your place. But I retrieved that blue shred, also red from your blood, from the mattress we had put on the kitchen floor during the previous night's blitz. The house trembled to its foundations while you died of love wrapped in my arms. Do you remember? This is our chance, he said earnestly. We won't wait fifty years more before we meet again. And perhaps with very different ages. I have been studying the astral charts. Should we now reject this death in life, we'll have a chance to be born again in the same period, with no great age gap. Like in Paris 1789. Do you remember? But the expression on your face shows that you don't. Everything's been taken care of in my room, the sleeping pills will help us to wake up to a better life. Your frightened expression startled him and made him see that you hadn't been with him in London in 1941 or in Paris in that revolutionary time. His only reaction was to turn around and run away. Stung by curiosity, you inquired about him at the hotel, you gave his desciption to the Latin American porter and it turned out that the gentleman in black had left the hotel hurriedly that same morning. But now this Saint Valentine's hat, the Mad Hatter said with a nostalgic smile, will bring back the memories of eternal love to you.

Bichat Hat

Try this yellow hat on. the Mad Hatter said to Alice, and you'll see how you get a temperature in less than no time. You can see yourself as a night sister in the Zurich Red Cross Hospital on that January night, when you had to wipe away the sweat and tears of a man, a bony foreigner, suffering from fever after being operated on for peritonitis. You took as good care of him as you were able, but it was hard for you to understand him. Was he speaking foreign tongues? Frankish, pidgin, biche-la-mare, night slang... In the incomprehensible words he spluttered in a railing stream, you thought you heard him constantly repeating in English, "Is there anybody here who understands me?". You bathed his temples again, and he seemed to fall asleep Sitting in the semi-darkness, at his bedside, you, too, began to feel sleepy. He mumbled in he sleep something by Bach, and the crystal-clear music transported you to a lengthy white corridor that you knew for sure was in a Paris hospital. And you were about to cross the threshold to a room where a painter burning up in fever kept spreading the sheet over his face. Bichat, or something like that, he said looking at one of the sheet's corners. And then he began to doze. In dreams, he said something about Molly, or maybe he said démoli, demolished . . .

You were about to take his temperature but stopped in time, not to wake him up, when you understood in a sudden fraction of a second that the Zurich Hospital, the babelian raver who talked about Bach, and yourself, with a yellow beret adorned with thermometers were a fragment of his delirium.

La Fanciulla Del West
Or the Fair Maid of the West

Wear this three-thousand cornered hat, the Mad Hatter explained to Alice, and you'll see that no cactus grows without thorns. She used to sing lusty ballads and show off her legs in a nervy way in a Denver saloon. The bride of the West, that striking red headed, green-eyed girl was called, the one a card sharp with long fingers fell madly in love with. On a day he felt good the gambler decided to turn in his cards for a plough, start a better life, or so he thought, on a small ranch near Phoenix, Arizona, and he proposed to her to follow him as his bride of the West. But the saloon beauty hesitated. Said that she would have to think it over. The luckless gambler rode away. As he rode across the Grand Canyon, a group of Navajos, mad from the fire-water, attacked him with arrows and darts and slashed his throat without pity. The following morning, in Denver, the bride of the West understood that she couldn't live without her gambler and left on the first stagecoach to Phoenix. The stagecoach stopped on the spot where the heinous carnage had taken place and the bride of the West instantly recognized her beloved, his body slashed by all the spears and arrows. In desperation, she ran to him and fell on his body pierced by the spears and arrows as she passionately embraced him. Both of them were buried there, and, instead of a cross, there stands a cactus plant, that grew strong, maybe from so much blood. The bride of the West the cactus is called but the lovers of the West would be a better name, both bodies pierced by the same arrows.

Captain Spider

You won't be able to remove this one from your head easily, said the Mad Hatter to Alice. and neither will your captivating Captain Spider. You met him, not long ago, in a Berlin café, the *Strada* in Potsdamerstrasse. and he has been drilling your mind with the innumerable exotic trips you are taking together. At last the moment comes and he takes you with a little luggage to the Tegel airport. He tells you that you will decide in the last minute the destination your destiny is taking you to, you will be inspired by chance and will fly on the wings of imagination. He will take you through the Tegel airport, stopping in front of many desks and at every gate open to a different departure. Amsterdam wouldn't be bad, he tells you in front of departure gate number one, but it lies too near. I think number two, here, would be better, Abidjan, but after going on in detail about some aspects of the Ivory Coast he drags you towards the gate leading to Bangkok, and you think that at last you will be flying free as birds heading towards such an exotic destiny, but the sly man. who is now going on with the risk of AIDS in the region, would rather choose a civilized European city like London, here, on gate number 4, and just as he is making you hear the rustle of the leaves in Holland Park he is actually taking you to gate five, Buenos Aires, *Mi Buenos Aires querido*, my beloved Buenos Aires, he exclaims, and then he is dragging you down Corrientes Street with undertones of nostalgia, almost to the tune of a tango, like the night when he tangoed you, in the twilight of love, in the Variété Chamäleon, but Buenos Aires has lost a lot lately, he complains, and now he is suggesting another city that will keep on changing until he gets to Madrid,

Mad Madrid, he exclaims, this time, it seems, with greater conviction, and in the last minute, he purchases a ticket for you for the city of the bear and the madrona. From Heaven to Madrid he exclaims enthusiastically, and he tells you to cross the gate and wait for him while he goes to change a ticket he had for Amsterdam. The moment to embark comes and you begin to get restless as he's not coming. But your hopes aren't lost until the moment the plane takes off, when you come to realize that, in going to and fro around the Tegel octagon, you have fallen into Captain Spider's net. That's a point, you say sadly as tears put a veil to your eyes, while you follow the dots and trace back your own steps.

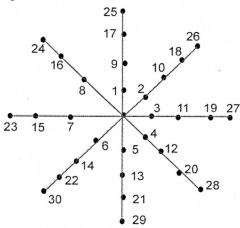

IBERIA

If you'd like to take one more step, then nothing better than this helmet, the Mad Hatter said to Alice, it will also make you take flight. It is the Iberia flight 525, that will take you from Berlin to Madrid this warm midday at the end of December. Shortly after taking off after twenty minutes delay at 12:55, you are in the clouds already and from above you see, half-asleep, a big grey eye that is one of the Tegel lakes. The plane is not full, and a smiling stewardess — who is also called Alice — asks you if you don't mind if a passenger sits beside you, a man in mourning or perhaps with just a gloomy look. The passenger in black sat beside you and opened that morning's *Berliner*

Morgenpost. On the front page the picture of a plane that crashed yesterday near Heidelberg struck you, it was a DC3: *25 passagiere tot*, and that 25 dead passengers is a dreadful but faceless figure, then the lugubrious man said "Dreadful, it was dreadful," and then mentioned a hill in the mist. I told the travelling businessman from Frankfurt beside me, the man in mourning, he continued, but he thought it was a macabre joke and he didn't believe I was the air's Angel of Death and that I had to visit that dump of a museum for airplane fans that Sunday morning. But now it will be even more terrible, and he sighed, on this one, the "Isaac Albéniz. Can't you hear the music?" he asked as he took his headphones off. "Binary air...." he said, and repeated it several times, mumbling. "Can't you hear the Corpus procession in Seville,"— he asked, amazed, "can't you hear Iberia's very Spanish music?" But all you heard was the old Christmas carol y beben y vuelven a beber.... when the captain announced that the "Ciudad de Badajoz" was about to land on the Barajas airport, "Ciudad de Badajoz" she asked with glee. Then this is not my mortal flight and she burst out laughing. The passenger next to me is mad, you told the other Alice, and her face, the stewardess's, showed the same amazement as you. Which passenger? When both of you looked at the empty seat. Only you couldn't account for the *Berliner Morgenpost* on the next seat —*25 Passagiere tot.*

HOOK

This swimming cap here, the Mad Hatter said to Alice, will make you dangle in the hook. You went to that solitary hotel by the beach to recover from a hapless love affair, it was on Sào Miguel island, in the Azores. In those November days the hotel swimming pool is dry, and instead of coming down to the black beach you can see from your balcony, you prefer to have a stroll to the nearby fishermen's village, Caloura, on top of a green cliff, and to plunge bravely into the white foam that gathers around the pier. The small white and red lighthouse at the wharf's end is becoming smaller, and the white boats with red and blue stripes become tiny dots. And your head, with the blue swimming cap is hardly a spot in the foam. Are you going to drown? At the wharf's end a man with ruffled white long hair waves at you, nervously, shouting something that reaches you only like shreds brought by the wind until eventually you understand "Beware of the boulters" and, seized by a sudden panic, you swim boldly towards the shore, fighting against the waves, until the last takes you safe and sound beside the boats, stranded on the wharves. The old man with white hair and beard in a gray tweed, very pale, maybe from the scare, reproaches your imprudence. There the sea drags you further and further and also it is full of boulters, he told you. Then added: "that's how my wife died." And next he told you the tragic story. He was one of the many people from Azores who moved to the States, in his case for further education, and, after years of being a lecturer on comparative literature in many American universities, he retired to his native island with his very young wife, who, people said, had also been his favorite student at his last university, in Madison Wisconsin, where he retired. "My wife's name was of Celtic origin and as beautiful as she, it meant 'white wave,'" he continued, "and here I come every evening to watch that white wave, always the same, one could say, that breaks yonder by the black rock. She was like so many American girls of the same age, fond of sports, dynamic, and like you preferred to swim among (or against) the waves instead of the calm waters in the beach near our house. On the day she discovered Caloura, she almost drowned, entangled in a boulter, but, thank goodness, a young and brave fisherman named Pio, on his way home in his boat, managed to rescue her, with great care he disentangled all the hooks that had been. caught in her swimming cap and in her long blonde hair. In spite of the incident and all the dangers of the Caloura waters, she stubbornly kept on bathing in that port of death and desolation. On a gray November evening like this, the old man in gray said with a lump in his throat, "she went and drowned over there, where the whitest wave breaks. And good Pio, who tensely watched how she bathed every day in those traitorous waters, didn't hesitate for an instant and bravely braved the streams to try and save her. It was useless, and both of them died in the midst of that swell, shaken, carried to and fro by the growing tempest, and those cruel waters only brought back shreds of their clothes, her swimming cap..." And so, please understand my emotion — he added with strangled voice — when I saw you swimming there, by the whitest wave. A few days later you'll hear a perversion of the same story in a fisherman's tavern in Villa Franca. The bodies did not appear because they had something better to do than float on those troubled waters. Evil tongues said that the lecturer's very young wife and the fisherman were madly in love and prepared the double drowning so that they could escape freely, maybe to America, from where she came, and there was even someone who insisted they lived in a fishermen village in New England. You don't know what to believe, but a chill runs through you as you swim towards the white wave that is already towering before you.

THE THREE-CORNERED HAT

Depending one's mental orientation, the Mad Hatter said to Alice, you will see, or listen to, different stores to be told by this peaky bat with the gift of gab.

Peak number one will remind you of a terrible ascent to the Aneto peak, in the Pyrenees, under a snow storm, that has already hurled your climbing companions and only you remain, looking at that lofty peak that's firmly fixed in your mind until your strength leaves you and you pass out and sink in the snow while an increasingly languid torpor takes you — corner number two — to a castle near XV Century Florence in order to watch a 24 year old youth with curly blonde hair, diligently writing on a desk a treatise on human dignity, *De dignitate hominis*, and you stand there staring at that sheet filled with Latin characters that strike you as utterly incomprehensible as the stains on the wall of the dingy room where you lie — corner number three — with a syringe piercing your left arm, spread on your side.

PROMETHEUS

This is a promising Prometheus indeed, the Mad Hatter told Alice, he's bound to become bantam weight world champion. Which is something to chuckle about. Especially for a Puerto Rican boy born and brought up in the Bronx, made for street brawls and the law of fists ever since he was a child. In spite of his name, the idea of a self-taught godfather, travelling encyclopedia seller, the bronze promising kid (bets indicate clearly that he will win tonight) surely never heard about the Titan who stole the fire of the gods in order to give it to men. It is also unlikely that he's heard about a rock in the Caucasus where the Titan was chained so that a vulture would eternally devour his liver as an eternal punishment. But, like all the Prometheus's that went before him, he will be lucky (or, rather, unlucky) enough to meet his tempting Pandora with a perfect body. Our Prometheus couldn't resist temptation, your tempting charms, and the box you are offering him is a bank's safe. Together with your tinselled love. That is why you are sitting in the first row of the Madison Square Garden, next to the ring, so that you make sure that he will keep the promise you wheedled out of him, at the end of a night of love: there will be a fix in that fight that he could have easily won, and he will let himself be knocked out in the sixth round. In need of a predator, the rival increasingly more self-assured, has been hitting him in the liver, the blows are taking their toll, and finally the last one forces him to bend his knee, as the referee begins to count: ONE

You see yourself being seen in your mink coat as you parade your beauty in front of the jewelry display windows on Fifth Avenue.   `
TWO

With the money from the fix, you'll be able to buy a bungalow in Florida, and you warm to the caress of the sunbeams, as you lie by your pool.

Bella

Michele Tolela Myers

*F*or a long time I lived with my parents in Aubagne, a working-class suburb of Marseilles. One of these little towns like so many gray old unromantic stops on route 8. This one claims Marcel Pagnol, the writer who created Manon des Sources and Jean de Florette. There are some beautiful old houses, and I liked it because the working men always told colorful stories. I met them at the cafe where my mother was a waitress. They came in their blue overalls, stood by the counter, drank their wine in the morning or *pastis* in the afternoon, and talked in their mellifluous singing accent. *Pastis* accent I called it. Like Jojo, who was not a young man any more. Wiry and angular, he drove trucks to Menton and back to Marseilles. He always stopped at the bar to eat something, he took huge bites of his food, washed them down with gulps of red wine and kept talking, his mouth always full. He railed against the cops whose presence en masse on their fancy motorcycles that day slowed the traffic to a grind, had no use for the tourists nor for the goddamn women drivers who did not know their right from their left. Women ought to stick to their cooking and babies and stop *emmerder le monde,* bothering the shit out of everybody. I loved his jocular and slangy language which infuriated my mother precisely because I would hang on to his every word. He would wink at me and rail some more, knowing he'd get a rise out of her. "Jojo, for God's sake, watch your mouth in front of the kid," my mother harangued him. He would pay no attention and I would giggle. Jojo always fussed, but he was funny and feisty and left good tips. My mother having grown up in Paris refused to speak *Marseillais.* Nor did I, because she corrected me all the time.

She was a petite woman, all muscle, all speed, darting here and there, waltzing with her tray full of dishes or glasses among the tables of the crowded *Bar des Platanes.* Talking to people, laughing, happy, weary by the end of the day. She would sink on a chair, stretch her arms over her head and sigh "Good

God," sounding almost surprised to be in one piece, to even feel anything at all, even exhaustion, after the numbing pace of the day, the mindless lifting of trays full of food she did not eat, wine she did not drink, the endless bits of conversations, being in them but not of them. She was dark-skinned and did not do much with her bushy, unruly brown curly hair except wash it and run her fingers through it as it dried on its own. No rollers for her, no hairdresser, having neither inclination, time, nor money. She wasn't exactly what you'd call a pretty woman, but her eyes sparkled and she seemed undaunted by the teasing familiarity of the mostly male clientele of the bar. She insisted I come there after school so she could supervise my homework. On the days I was sick I stayed home with my father. The men at the bar were used to me, and George, the owner, did not mind my being around. I sat quietly at one of the tables with a ginger ale, doing my school work, listening and looking, reading mostly without getting in my mother's way. I waited for my father although he seldom came to the bar, and when he did the local men and the truckers didn't talk to him. He sat at the table with me, sipped on some rum, ignored every one, and we waited for my mother to be done.

"Bella, tell *tu madre* to hurry up, I am hungry, famished, dying of starvation, and I will eat you if she does not come NOW!"

He made me laugh. "Mommy, hurry or Cardo's going to eat me," I repeated with fake fear in my voice. My mother pretended not to hear but she moved faster and eventually shed her large apron and appeared, bag on the shoulder and casserole dish in hands, ready to go home and feed us.

"All right, Isabelle Martinez, hang on to this gorgeous man here who's too weak to walk by himself and let's help him go home. George, I'm off. See you in the morning."

"Yep," was George's response.

He was beautiful, my father. Stunning, the sort you could not take your eyes off. I looked like him, I was told, and beamed with pleasure every time someone made the comment. I loved him then, mesmerized by his voice. Deep, slow, penetrating, as if everything he said had weight. His strong Spanish accent gave the impression he was singing. Isabella, Isabella, Bella, Bellissima, he cooed, and rapt I listened to the inflections of his words, my eyes locked in his as if his language were meant only for me and I alone could understand him.

Born in Valencia, the commercial port on the Mediterranean coast, Ricardo Solis Martinez, Cardo to me, had been a young man during the

Spanish Civil war, which he fought full of hopes and ideals until he was caught and tortured by the regiment his father commanded, and then released. He fled to France to avoid prison, he explained in an elaborate story that had him hiding in a fishing boat and making the journey to Marseilles knee deep in fresh fish. I never knew when to believe him. He always exaggerated everything, and with him trivial events became either tragedies or outrageous comedies. He was fun, often horsing around as when he swept me off the ground to sit me on the bar counter and, without my mother looking, sneaked the seltzer bottle and started spraying me in little spurts until I giggled so much that my mother heard and tried to grab the bottle from him. He sprayed her too.

"Two kids I have, TWO! " she cried in mock exasperation running behind the counter for cover. He put the bottle down, bent over and kissed her. But in truth, my mother was the other child, the freshness and newness of her love giving her a lift the daily dreariness of her exhausting work could not squelch. She was in love, with a childlike sense of awe and wonder, the certainty and abandon of a first love, awakened to a surprising capacity to enjoy a part of her she had had no idea was even there. She was never again so giving and free. Not her grueling job, not her child, not her learned inhibitions could keep her away from Ricardo. She never had enough of him. At first caught up in her excitement, delighted by her needs, he obliged and they made love often, openly, noisily, without restraint and with little concern for the toddler who slept in the room next door. Two children they were, playing with matches. I watched.

He was an artist. He painted tormented pictures of his war which did not sell. There was no market then for a Spanish painter whose violent images turned the sacred into horror and sex into a weapon. His colors screamed, reds, yellows, blacks, torn breasts, women's sexes plain to see, blood, distorted ugly faces painted upside down bunching up in the corners of the paintings as if they were sent away to die but could not leave the scene. Assaulting images reflecting a raw rage right under his skin which burst on his canvasses unbound, uncontained, and untamed. He painted all day long while my mother worked. Very tall and thin, dark, with shoulder-length straight black hair which he sometime gathered in a ponytail, unlike any of the men I saw in Aubagne, he towered over his easels, his eyes burning, a sorcerer's apprentice.

I hungered for him when I was little, found reasons to sit on his lap, hug him, touch him. He responded always with his big hands cupping my face, kisses all over my bare arms, tickling me until I could not stand it any more and wiggled out of his arms. I often observed him paint when he was oblivious to my presence. I watched a man possessed whom I longed for and whose touch filled me with ecstasy. My mother's kisses when she put me to bed at night never evoked the dreams a single smile from my father brought on. I wanted him, I played to him, I made myself beautiful for him. I danced around him shamelessly begging for his attentions, and he obliged. "Bella, Bellita, Bellissima, beautiful Bella, come here for a thousand kisses. Is that enough?"

"I want as many as fit in the whole world. Can you, Cardo?" He could. He did.

We lived in a small farmhouse, just on the edge of Aubagne. It belonged to a cousin of my father's who worked in Marseilles. We lived in it for free. On a small street, *11 rue des Pinedes,* our house was flanked by a bakery shop and a shoe repair store. The sweet smell of dough mixed with the pungent smell of leather. An arresting hot and cold combination which permeated our house early morning, at noon, and then again in the evening. While the bread and pastries smells dominated, the leather smell was never absent, a juxtaposition which bound for me the harsh pounding on shoe soles and the soft, slow kneading of dough. The image never left me.

Across the street was a small church which my mother and I attended every Sunday. I loved everything about it — its small square tower with one bell which rang precisely at noon and at six every day; how quiet, dark, and cool it was, a place to rest; the smell of wax, the lights from the candles, the feel of the hard wooden pews, the singing. Women came in to pray during the day in their black dresses, wearing dark scarves on their head. I saw them from the window of Cardo's room. Walking fast in rapid small steps, looking straight ahead of them, talking to nobody, edging their way in through a small opening of the heavy front door, as if they wanted no one to see them talk to God. On Sunday, the church was full but Cardo never went. It was with my mother I learned prayers and hymns, the only times I felt attached to her, bound by the powerful feeling which came from making the same moves, the same gestures, uttering the same words, singing the same notes. Once a week she felt transported by the glory of Christ which she genuinely felt reflected on her and made her life overcome its smallness, its numbing repetitiveness. She sang her heart out, in a clear, untrained but powerful soprano voice. You could hear her over most of the others, and I felt proud, goose bumps all over my arms. She took the Church at face value, never questioning its discipline. She went to confession, burned candles, recited strings of prayers on her rosary, and taught me Bible stories at night when she put me to bed. We recited prayers together. "Bless Cardo, God, and please little Jesus, keep him for me forever. I love him and I love you, Amen." When I was older and could take communion, I loved the idea of being clean and receiving the body of Christ.

Often sick when I was a child (something to do with my lungs), I missed a lot of school. I did not care about school and felt much happier at home watching my father paint. He had appropriated a spacious room with two large windows on the second floor of the house. You could see the church across the street and beyond it a field of poppies. He had several easels up with at least two or three paintings in progress. There was a good sized farm table that wobbled, or perhaps the floor was uneven, with junk all over it — paints, brushes, newspapers, rags, turpentine, jars of white paste he used to prepare his canvasses. An old red upholstered armchair in which he flopped, read, and sipped his rum sat in the middle of the room. Old newspapers littered the floor. A divan took up a corner of the room, and he slept there when he worked late at night. When I was sick I stayed on that bed with blankets all over me because he always kept the windows open. "You need to let in the sky, Bellita *mia,* let in the sky, and then fly....." He'd stand by the open windows, dreamy-like, and I had no idea what he was thinking about. He sang Spanish melodies in his sensuous bass voice when he painted, and I closed my eyes, happy to be near him. Women came in the afternoon, sometimes the same one for days, sometimes different ones. They always took their clothes off immediately and he drew them sitting on a stool, on the floor, their legs parted, or lying down on their stomach. They talked all the time and I fell asleep.

Cardo and I had rituals when I stayed in his big room. I made coffee in the kitchen, dark and strong as he liked, filled almost to the rim a small blue cup which had lost its saucer. I added a little rum, took two sugar cubes and a tiny spoon, found a small tray and carefully managed to take it and its load upstairs without a spill. There were seventeen steps to the second floor and I counted them each time, on my way to the coffee ceremony. Seventeen and I was there with him, seventeen, the magic number, and he appeared. I set the tray on his table and sat on the floor by the red chair. He stirred one sugar cube in the coffee slowly, dipped the other one slightly so I could see the white cube turn slowly brown. He then came and sat on the red chair and held the piece of sugar in front of my mouth for me to suck. He didn't let it go until it was about to crumble. I hungrily licked his fingers so he'd let the cube loose, and with one wet finger he brought in little specks of sugar which had strayed on the side of my mouth and gathered them carefully on my lips where I licked them clean. I loved these little specks of sugar mixed in drops of saliva which he caught on his finger and returned to my tongue. We repeated the ceremony many times the days I spent with him upstairs.

Sometimes he dressed me up. He had a collection of old hats, his contributions to my costumes, and I went downstairs and rummaged through my mother's clothes and picked a blouse, shoes, belts. Cardo had a red paste to color my cheeks and lips. I paraded in front of him, danced, pretended to be a queen or a fairy and he was not supposed to touch me then. He tried, I escaped, he tried again, I ran, until he finally grabbed my belt and pulled me to him, sat me on his lap facing him, and kissed my face over and over again. The room got dark. I heard nothing.

When my mother came home at night, she always brought food from the bar which she warmed up for dinner. I took a bath while she was getting things organized. Cardo had been the one to bathe me when I was little until one evening, already undressed and shivering in the bath room, I called him.

"Isabelle," my mother exploded, "for goodness' sake, you're old enough to wash yourself. Get on with it at this minute, and leave your father alone."

Her tone was sharp, exasperated, having meant to say this before many times. Cardo said something I could not hear, but my mother's voice thundered.

"Leave her alone, Christ almighty, leave her alone Ricardo, she's too old now."

I remember crying in the tub, hating her and missing the games Cardo played, like the mountains he made of my hair on top of my head, full of white suds.

"Bellisima Bella, look what a pretty queen you are. I must obey you, now. What is your wish? Shall I pull on your nipples a little?"

He gave them both a sharp tug.

"Or bite your earlobes?"

He bit one earlobe until I pulled away.

"Or shall I just tickle you all over."

He stood me in the tub, dripping water and shivering and tickled me until I laughed so hard I coughed and coughed.

"Shush, darling, or your mother will come and make us stop. You're beautiful like my mother, *mi amor.*"

He never talked much about his family, but had shown me a picture of his mother and father which he kept in his billfold. Tattered and yellow, it was the picture of a tall and strikingly beautiful woman in a long black skirt and white blouse at the arm of a handsome officer. Isabel and Eduardo Muñoz Martinez, my grandparents. Doña Isabel looked like a queen. Regal in her bearing, haughty, a confident smile on her lovely mouth, her gloved hand holding a closed fan, and the look of someone entitled to be wooed, courted, and loved. I traced my finger on her face and Cardo traced his finger on mine. "*Cariño, cariño,* my love." He then took the picture, carefully put it back in his billfold and gave me a full kiss on the lips.

The doorbell rings.

"Get it, *cariño.* It's Mireille. Tell her to come up and while you're downstairs make me some dark coffee, I can use it."

Mireille is an eighteen year-old who works at one of the Casino shops, the local grocery chain. Every once in a while, George's wife, Madeleine, hires her as an extra in the kitchen at the *Bar des Platanes.* Her boyfriend Lucien has no idea she comes to pose for Cardo. Mireille won't tell him because he wouldn't let her if he knew. Cardo hasn't paid her in a while but she keeps coming.

"Hello, Mr. Martinez," she says out of breath. She has run all the way from the Casino store on her lunch hour. She immediately takes off a blue knit cap which comes all the way down to her dark eyebrows. Her long black hair is tied with a rubber band in a simple pony tail. Her tiny little eyes are constantly on the move. She sheds her coat, her scarf, and she looks at Cardo.

"You look funny today."

"Funny?"

"Yeah, like you're waiting for something. It's my day, isn't?"

I hate it when they talk as if I am not there. I sit on the floor in a corner of the studio, knees up to my chin.

Mireille kicks her flat shoes off, starts wiggling out of her black tights uncovering long thin legs, still tanned from the summer sun. Cardo watches her. She slowly unzips her skirt which falls to the floor. With one foot she catches it, aims at the red chair, and kicks. The skirt falls just short of the chair.

"Shit," Mireille giggles, but she does not move. She keeps looking at Cardo. "Where do you want me?"

"Right here. Sit on the stool. Don't take anything else off."

I go downstairs to make the coffee and later appear in the room carrying a small tray with one blue cup of dark hot coffee, a faint smell of rum trailing. There is a small spoon and a few scattered sugar cubes on the tray. My thick hair falls to my shoulders, my bangs almost covering my eyes. I'm often told my cheeks are translucent like porcelain, but now they are flushed. I wear a pleated navy blue skirt and a dark sweater, dark blue knee socks, no shoes. Cardo smiles, my serious face breaks into a grin.

"Leave the tray on the table, *cariño*, and it's time for your nap in your room. I'll come for you when Mireille goes." Cardo dips one sugar cube in the coffee and offers it to me. I close my eyes, eat it, turn around and leave. But I crouch outside the door, watching.

"Weird, she's a weird kid," Mireille shakes her head. "She's creepy." She helps herself to a sugar cube from the tray, dips it into the coffee and chews it.

"Enough, Mireille, enough. Be quiet." Cardo drinks his coffee almost in one gulp, puts the cup back on the tray, takes a sugar cube in his mouth and sucks it slowly. He looks at Mireille who sits immobile on the stool, her shirt opened enough to hint at breasts unsupported by any bra. She catches his look and slowly unbuttons the blouse which finally lays open revealing dark and taut nipples, small round breasts which Mireille touches softly, a smile on her face, her cheeks slightly pink.

Cardo comes closer, and with his finger traces over her shoulders and her breasts, lingering.

"*Chica*, you are beautiful and you know it. I could eat you up, darling, but we've got to work. Sit there just like this and don't talk." Cardo moves back and begins to draw. For an instant Mireille frowns, her mouth in a slight pout, fleeting sign she wished Cardo's hand had played with her breasts longer.

Cardo bites his lips when he draws, and he talks softly in Spanish, as if someone else were in the room who could hear and understand him. Mireille is used to it and knows not to talk to him until he is ready. Later he will let her get off the stool, and only then will he come to her, slowly take her blouse off and lead her to the divan. He sits and she stands facing him, her breasts right by his mouth. He slowly licks her nipples until they are so firm and hard she will be numb to the pain of his bite. Her hands move to his belt and begin to undo the buttons on his fly. She kneels, helps him out of his trousers and shorts, hurrying now, and she takes him in her mouth. He sighs "*madre mia*" and does not move until moments later he grabs her by the shoulders and, as he lies on his back on the divan, brings her on top on him. She straddles him, slides him in, and her eyes wide open, a smile on her face, she looks at him and starts moving, slowly at first. His eyes are closed, and he says "*madre, madre*" over and over again, until he jerks her away from him, moves her brutally under him, gets in her and furiously, his face contorted, pounds her until he just stops.

"Ricardo, you shouldn't do it in me. What if I get pregnant?"

He looks like he's going to say something, but he doesn't and closes his eyes. When he opens them again, I am there. Looking at him. Mireille is sitting on the bed naked.

"What are you doing here, Bellita? You are supposed to take a nap."

"I'm not sleepy, Cardo. I want to watch you draw."

He brings me to him and kisses me. "You know *querida* that you can watch all you want. Let me get dressed and I'll show you what I've done."

Mireille shakes her head and starts putting her clothes on.

I am not sure when it began, but Ricardo and my mother spent all their time arguing at night. I could hear them from my room. They argued mostly about money; there was never enough. About work; wasn't it time for Ricardo to get real work?

What I remember most about those times was the noise. Ricardo shouted, banged doors, threw chairs around in his big room, knocked the paints off his table in a fit of rage once, kicked his easels, and swore at the top of his lungs in Spanish and in French. She was a whore, couldn't get enough of it with him, had to fuck every one in town. He'd kill her, he'd teach her, cunt, *puta*. I heard the blows, the words, the cries, the rage and buried my head in my pillows or went to the second floor on Cardo's divan to escape, frightened of what they might do to each other. I was petrified that my mother would leave, take me with her, and I would never see Cardo again. There were times I wished her dead. Just me and Cardo. I would make him happy and with me he would not get angry. And at other times, I felt a rage that burned my chest, my belly, and I groaned feeling uncontrollable panic, burying my head in my pillow hoping to kill off the last sounds of their dying love, hating them both, hating myself.

I live in Paris now. My Parisian friends say to me, Bella, how charming. How picturesque. To have grown up in a tiny town near Marseilles. The sun, the accent, the colors. And I am silent. All I think about is black, white, and cold. A dance: precise, rhythmic, fake. My childhood in Aubagne.

A Novella

Hello Herman

John Buffalo Mailer

*H*ERMAN: I got real close to his face. He was like bigger than me. I said to him "Spare some change?" And he said "What?" And I said "I'M THE ONE ASKING THE QUESTIONS NOW, ASSHOLE! So, can you spare some change?" I put the gun to his nose as I said it. He started fucking with his pockets but he was so scared he couldn't get his hands in. I said "Not fast enough," and pulled the trigger.

INTERVIEWER: This was Michael Ray?

HERMAN: Yeah, Michael Ray.

INTERVIEWER: What went through your mind as you pulled the trigger?

HERMAN: I thought there would be more blood.

INTERVIEWER: You look disappointed.

HERMAN: No, I wasn't disappointed. I mean, his nose came off his face but it held on by a string of skin at the top and fell back into place before he hit the ground. That was pretty cool. I guess I just thought there would be more blood.

INTERVIEWER: Why did you shoot him?

HERMAN: He was an asshole.

INTERVIWER: What had he done to you?

HERMAN: He was always making fun of me, especially in front of girls. He was just a dick.

INTERVIEWER: Do you think he deserved to die because he was just a dick?

HERMAN: Everybody dies whether I think they deserve to or not.

INTERVIEWER: That's true, but most people, even dicks, live until they're old and then die naturally.

HERMAN: Naturally? Not Michael Ray.

Washington Post
10/26/99

Herman Howards, a sixteen year old student at Broome High, a public school in Broome, Iowa, shot twenty-four of his classmates, two teachers, and three police officers before he was apprehended yesterday at 11:40am. Twenty of the children were DOA, four made it to Paul Blake hospital where two died. The other two children are listed in critical condition. Two of the police officers were killed, the third is in intensive care. One of the two teachers shot, Nathaniel Phelps, died on the way to the hospital. The other, Sharon Cribb, is listed in critical condition at Paul Blake.

Howards was described as quiet, a loner. His classmates said they always thought he was strange, but never imagined him capable of this carnage. When asked, his mother said that Herman is a happy, healthy teenager with a promising future; she can't understand why he would do such a thing.

New York

Lax Morales received the call from his agent around eight o'clock in the evening. *Query Magazine* wanted to offer him an exclusive interview with Herman Howards. They were in position. Howards' mother was ready to sign the contract. An arrangement had been made with the guards and the Warden at Iowa State prison; Lax would be escorted in past the press with no hassles. He would have two days to talk to Howards.

"Lax, this is the follow up to Georgia you've been waiting for. Do you know how many strings have been pulled to get you in there?" his agent urged.

"How many, Marty?"

"This story is a journalist's wet dream. 'LAX MORALES interviews HERMAN HOWARDS!' Big money, baby. The right move."

Los Angeles Times
11/3/99

While parents of the formerly peaceful community of Broome, Iowa grieve the tragic loss of their children, parents all over suburban America are wondering if their town will be next in what seems to be a series of copycat crimes started by the Littleton, Colorado massacre. "Bloody Broome", as it is now being called, is the tenth highschool in two years to have incidents of students bringing guns into class and opening fire. Never before has the carnage been this bad, and the death toll as high as Bloody Broome. Twenty-five were killed in all, four remain in critical condition.

The most disturbing fact remains that there is no clear motive for the killing. What has become very clear is that today's teenage culture has become destructive and dangerous everywhere.

Senator John Cox (Rep.) issued a statement to the press saying he will make a plea to the grand jury that Herman Howards be executed. He also plans to make a plea for the execution to be televised so that "...these kids can see first hand what happens when you disregard the value of life".

I've agreed to write this article on Herman Howards. It most likely will boost my career even higher than it has already gone. I feel scared. Not sure what of, but scared. I don't want to meet Herman Howards. I don't want to meet him because I think I understand him. I think I know why he did it. Makes me want to kill him. A darkness festers inside of me, and I'm afraid Herman Howards might bring it out.

When Lax Morales landed in Fort Dodge Regional airport he was not in a good mood. The airline had messed up his first class reservation and he was bumped down to coach. Surprised and pleased to find the two seats next to him unoccupied, he prepared to have a comfortable trip and had just begun to take out his research on Howards when the stewardess reopened the doors for an extraordinarily large woman with two children. She was directed to his seats and by God if she didn't fill up two of them. All through the ride he was forced to listen to this woman's stories of numerous husbands who had left her because she was too fat, or because they weren't man enough to raise her kids with her. She had gone through three husbands. She was about to go through number four. She had three kids aside from the two on the plane. "Future Herman Howards," Lax thought to himself.

Had Molly McPeterson known what kind of flight Mr. Morales had had, she might have been more careful about what she said, but as she did not, and as she could not always help herself from being overly honest, her first words to him were "My God, You're just a kid! I expected you to be much older." It wasn't that he had never heard those sentiments about himself, he was admittedly young for such a respected journalist, however he hadn't expected to hear it from some country bumpkin hired to drive him around.

"Golly," he said. "I know exactly how you feel, I was expecting you to be young and somewhat attractive. But, people surprise you." And he smiled.

"Yes they do." Coldly.

Molly had been called late the night before by the editor and chief of the Des Moines Gazette, Carl Lipsburg. Apparently he had gotten a call from his good friend, Marty, in New York who told him Lax Morales was coming to Broome to do an article on Herman Howards. And Morales had access. Could she pick him up at the airport and drive him to Dayton where he would transfer to a prison van? That way he could enter the prison without being seen by the wolfpack of reporters outside. She would also be there to supply him with any local background. This would be a good chance for her to make a solid connection with a famous journalist from New York.

She had heard of Lax Morales. Something to do with the busting up of a large skin head gang down in Georgia. Real undercover stuff. Maybe he could get her in to see Howards. Then she could do an article for the Gazette on the experience. Help her to move to the Chicago Tribune.

By no means was she a beautiful girl, but undoubtedly not ugly. She had chestnut hair cut in a bob and quite a nice figure. Thirty-seven, divorced once, and her facial features were slightly bland, but she made up for that with strong personality and a good amount of lipstick which did draw nasty comments from the girls at the Gazette. Yes, she was really looking forward to meeting him. But Lax Morales turned out to be such a prick. They did not talk.

INTERVIEWER: Now, what went through your mind when you woke up that morning?

HERMAN: The morning I did it?

INTERVIEWER: Yes.

HERMAN: That was a Monday. I hate Mondays. I had a test that day.

INTERVIEWER: Are you saying that if you didn't have a test, you wouldn't have murdered your classmates?

HERMAN: Don't put words in my mouth. What I was saying is I might not have done it *that* day. But there is no way in Hell those people weren't gonna' get what they deserved.

INTERVIEWER: You feel no remorse.

HERMAN: (pause) I didn't want to kill Mr. Phelps.

INTERVIEWER: Why not?

HERMAN: Because he was an all right teacher. He gave a shit.

INTERVIEWER: It sounds like you liked him. Why did you kill him?

HERMAN: He got in my way. I hadn't finished yet.

INTERVIEWER: Did you finish before you were apprehended?

HERMAN: No.

INTERVIEWER: So there's more people you want to kill?

HERMAN: Yes.

INTERVIEWER: What are you going to do about it?

HERMAN: Kill them.

INTERVIEWER: How are you going to do that in prison?

HERMAN: I think I better not talk about it.

INTERVIEWER: Why not?

HERMAN: Next question.

INTERVIEWER: What did you do when you got to school?

HERMAN: I waited until everyone was in second period, then I went around and put chains with locks on all the exits. It was easy. Second period is when the security guards take their lunch break. Then I went to the computer lab and told my friend Tim to send out a different message of the day on the hallway monitors...

INTERVIEWER: Did you get that idea from Harris and Klebold?

HERMAN: You're good. Only my idea was brilliant. I didn't give any warning. I sent out a mandatory pep-rally message instructing all the kids to skip their third period, go to the gym. Tim thought it was a great prank, I told him to make sure he was there. (laughs) He said he wouldn't miss it for the world. Then I went to my locker and got the guns and pipe bombs.

INTERVIEWER: Where did you get the pipe bombs?

HERMAN: I made them.

INTERVIEWER: Was it easy?

HERMAN: It was easy once I got the instructions off the net. All I needed was to go to a hardware store and get half the ingredients, then go to another and get the other half. No one had any clue what I was up to.

INTERVIEWER: Where did you get the guns?

HERMAN: A friend of mine works at the WALMART in Council Bluffs, he sold them to me.

INTERVIEWER: Don't you need to be eighteen to buy guns in Iowa?

HERMAN: Do you have any idea how many people own guns in Iowa? I tell you it scares me. There are more ways around being under eighteen and getting a gun than I can count. Everyone and their brother has a gun.

INTERVIEWER: You mean everyone and their mother.

HERMAN: What?

INTERVIEWER: Everyone has a mother, not a brother. That's the saying — "Everyone and their mother".

HERMAN: Whatever.

INTERVIEWER: You are aware that everyone has a mother, right?

HERMAN: Jesus Christ you're asking stupid questions. I thought you were supposed to be some kind of hot-shot reporter, that's why I agreed to do this. This is a very important story, you know. I don't think you'll ever have one bigger.

INTERVIEWER: Okay, let's cut to it. Did you ever think of the people's mothers or fathers or loved ones while you were shooting them in their faces?

HERMAN: No.

INTERVIEWER: You never thought that maybe these kids had people who cared about them, would miss them?

HERMAN: No.

INTERVIEWER: Why not?

HERMAN: Because I'm obviously fucked up. Lax, do you think a normal person goes into school and shoots everyone? What can I say? I'm special.

INTERVIEWER: How do you think your mother would feel if you had been killed?

HERMAN: It would have taken her a few days to realize I was gone.

INTERVIEWER: Oh, come on.

HERMAN: No, Lax. Sometimes I would go two, three, four days without seeing her.

INTERVIEWER: How is that possible?

HERMAN: It's not like me and her have a lot to talk about. She goes to work all day, I go to school all day. At night, she has her life and I have mine. We don't interfere with each other. She's very good about giving me privacy.

INTERVIEWER: Yeah, but your life consists of playing video games and making pipe bombs. Didn't she have a clue?

HERMAN: She's a busy lady.

INTERVIEWER: What about your father?

HERMAN: He lives in Chicago with his girlfriend.

When Herman was thirteen, his little sister, Loretta, got into an accident on her bike. She was ten at the time and a car with out-of-state plates clipped her in a hit-and-run outside of her own house. Herman was home and paused his game to go to the window and see what all the hubbub was about. A crowd of people were gathered around and someone was yelling about calling the cops. Shortly an ambulance arrived. Herman saw his sister strewn against the sidewalk, blood pouring from her head. He watched the men put her in the ambulance and drive off. The crowd dispersed, some people knocked on the door, but Herman didn't open the door for anybody, not even neighbors. Perhaps he should call his mother at work. He refilled his Coca-Cola, then looked at the number on the wall next to the phone marked: MOM. He dialed and got her secretary, Rose.

"Hi, may I talk to my mother please?"

"She's in a meeting right now, I can have her call you back just as soon as she's done."

"You can't get her, it's kind of important?"

"Hold one moment, I'll see what I can do."

Gale Howards was sealing the deal on what was possibly the biggest merger the company had ever seen with Ventucom Corporate when Rose buzzed on the intercom.

"Please excuse me for a moment." She said as she hastily picked up the phone. "Yes, Rose, I'm in the middle of a meeting."

"I'm sorry to interrupt, Miss Howards, but your son is on the phone and he says it's kind of important." Rose sounded unsure of herself and probably realized that she should not interrupt Miss Howards in a meeting for something that was "kind of important".

"I'm sure it's not as important as this. I know my own son, Rose. Tell him I'll call back when my meeting is over. No more interruptions please," she said with an anger slightly too visible for the people she was meeting with. Herman went back to his game. It was three-forty-six.

Gale did not think to call her son until she was on 35 North heading home at five after five. She tried her cell phone, but the damn thing wasn't charged up. "Nothing is easy," she thought. "Well, if it is important, he'll tell me when I walk in the door." And with that she let it slip into the back of her mind.

She entered her house at five-fifty-three, Herman was sitting on the floor playing one of his video games. She never could tell one from the other.

"Hello," she said. "Mom's home."

Herman did not respond, but rather sat there about one foot from the set, transfixed by his game.

"Don't sit so close to the television, dear. It's bad for you."

He scooted back a few feet without letting his eyes drop from the screen. She went upstairs, drew herself a bath, and poured a glass of white wine as she did whenever she had a good day at work. After her celebration ended, she went down and started thinking about what she would make for dinner. Herman was still playing his game and she asked him if he had finished his homework. He gave a slight shrug which indicated neither an affirmative nor negative response. His eyes never left the screen.

"Where's your sister?" She asked after it dawned on her that aside from the constant gunfire emitting from the screen the house was quiet.

"She was out riding her bike."

"This late?"

"I dunno'."

"What was it you called about before, when I was in my meeting?" An eerie feeling crept over her.

"Nothing important." He said with no emotion.

"So, why did you call?"

No response.

I knew it, she thought. It was nothing. God, he can be inconsiderate. The eerie feeling did not go away.

Los Angeles Times

Lax Morales, well respected journalist, famous for his work with the FBI down in Surville, Georgia, has been hired by *Query Magazine* to interview Herman Howards. Morales was not available for a quote. His agent, Martin Shift, told reporters "America will have a better understanding of the boy when Lax is through with him. What we have here is the good voice of youth culture vs. the "Bad." It will make for some exciting stuff."

Many people are wondering if one of the causes for all these copy-cat crimes of late is the amount of press attention given to the criminals of these crimes.

The addition of a well known name like Morales is sure to raise the price and the

attention given to Howards' story. The T-
shirt worn by Howards ("Y2K Blows" on the
front, "But I Dig Blow" on the back) is
becoming a popular item among Los Angeles Teens.

"He's not that unattractive", Molly thought as the corn fields passed by
them on both sides. She and Mr. Morales still hadn't said a word to each other
since they had gotten the car, but she had sure taken him in. His eyes were
a deep green and he had neatly combed, straight, black hair, a little button
nose and nice sharp chin bones. He wore octagonal, steel rimmed, glasses
that seemed to accentuate his eyes. Yes, quite good looking. He was wearing
an odd tie. Little birds in a line down the middle of it, but not beautiful birds;
big, awkward, ugly birds. The kind of birds Dr. Suess would have drawn if
he were into horror. A really off-beat tie.

Molly knew that if she was going to be remembered, she would have to
make an impression now. She needed something to break the ice and the ice
was thick with this guy. Perhaps being a celebrity in a profession which no
longer had many, got to his head. Maybe he was just young. She decided to
take a gamble and said, "So, why is it exactly that you think your shit smells
like ice cream?" He was shocked for a moment, then something cracked and
he let out a pearly smile.

"I'm the youngest journalist ever to win the Pulitzer Prize." he said.

"What for?"

"Journalism."

"That's cute. What did you write about?"

It was then that he decided he almost liked this girl. "I went undercover
into a sect of Neo-Nazi Skinheads in Surville, Georgia. They had some gran-
diose plans of killing every Nigger, Spic, and Ash in all the state. I helped
the Feds get enough evidence to bust them up before they could do too much
damage, and I still told their side of the story without prejudice. So they gave
me the Pulitzer."

Well, Molly thought, *it ain't a half bad reason.*

Lax was noticing that with nothing but corn on both sides of the highway for miles on end, one could hardly tell that they had moved forward. The
rows upon rows of corn almost put you into a strange sort of internment. It

gave the feeling you might never reach the end. Hell, he thought.

"Morales is a Spanish name, but you don't look like you have any Spanish in you. Is that your professional name?" Molly intruded.

"No. I'm one sixteenth Mexican."

"A sixteenth!? Honey, I'm a sixteenth Cherokee, but I wouldn't go around calling myself 'Writes With a Vengeance'."

"Like I said, I didn't choose that name, it's been in my family for more generations than I know about. My great-great grandfather grew up in Mexico and ran across the border when he was sixteen. Back in 1886. He married a white girl and had my great grandfather. My grandfather married a white girl and had my father, and my father married a white girl and had me."

"No daughters?"

"Not one. Each man got married once and had one son."

There was a silence. They were nearing Dayton.

"You must've seen some ugly things when you were in Georgia, huh?" She was still trying.

"You can't imagine."

"It couldn't have been that bad."

"Forget it."

"What did you do?"

"I told you, forget it."

"Did you go out bashing 'Niggers, Spics, and what else did you say?'"

"Ash. That's what they call Jews."

"Did you go out bashing?"

He gave a laugh of full dismissal.

"Did you bash anyone, Lax?" Again an uncomfortable silence.

"It looks like we're here," he finally said. They were. A guard came up to the car and told him to get in the back of the Transpo Van.

"Well thank you for the ride, Molly. I'll see you around." He started to get out.

"Lax, did you bash anyone?" grabbing his arm.

He paused for a moment with his back to her, half in, half out. Then with one sudden movement he turned around and was so close she could smell his breath. In a numb voice and a face without emotion, he answered, "Not in any way." Then got out of the car and into the van.

New York Magazine: KID CULTURE IN THE BIG CITY.

NEW YORK MAGAZINE: What do you think of Herman Howards?

KELLY GRAHM(16 years old): I'm just glad he's like not a Goth kid, cause Christian America would have crucified us. Like he was just this ordinary kid that flipped out. He like didn't have anything to do with Goth culture, and that's good. I mean it's not good that he killed all those people, it's just good that he wasn't a Goth. I mean it would have been worse if he always wore black or something. You know what I mean?

NYM: I've heard that some Goths practice self mutilation. Have you ever tried anything like that?

KG: I did once, but I don't want to talk about it.

NYM: Why don't you want to talk about it?

KG: Cause like it was just this stupid thing that I did.

NYM: Why did you do it?

KG: I don't know.

NYM: Do you regret it?

KG: Yeah. I do.

While waiting in the little prison room for Herman Howards, Lax was thinking back to the night in Riddleville when he took a bat to a fifteen year old black kid. He hadn't wanted to. He received no pleasure from the act. But he had proven to himself that he was capable of doing it. Now it was in him. What was it that had numbed him to that point? Was it living with the skinheads for nine and a half months? Hate and violence so strong reality became nonexistent. He beat the poor kid, oh, Jesus, ruthlessly. Ruthlessly. Of course if he hadn't, his own blood would have been spilling to the floor. Was that enough justification? The real question was what had he paid for it? Hell, he'd been rewarded. A Pulitzer. What would they give him for Herman Howards?

The door opened and a guard escorted Herman to the seat at the far end of the six foot table. Herman wasn't as tall as expected, maybe five seven. He had stringy blond hair that came down to the top of his ears and was then cut short in a buzz. His chin was too small which gave his face a beakish quality. Eyes as blue as the sky in New Mexico. There was a blank look in the kid's face, but his blue eyes held something else in them, something recognizable from Surville. Hate. The raw kind that no one is born with. You have to acquire it.

"Hello Herman, I'm Lax Morales."

"How much money do I get for talking to you?" he said.

"That's up to your mother. She's the one who signed the contract with *Query*. I don't have anything to do with that…"

"How much?"

Pug-faced little bastard. "I'd guess for a story like yours, the standard would have to be at least one hundred grand."

"There is no standard for what I've done." Herman said.

"True. No one as young as you has ever killed so many people during a time of peace."

"What do you mean during a time of peace? No one has done something like this ever!" He was getting frustrated already. Lax was thinking that it might be easier than he anticipated to get under this kid's skin.

"When Hitler was running out of troops toward the end of World War II, he had to enlist children about your age, a little younger, into his army. Those children killed thousands of soldiers, but they were doing it in the name of their country. They were in battles. Why did you do it?" The tape recorder was running.

"What the fuck is that stuff on your tie?"

"Dodo birds."

"Why are you wearing a Dodo bird tie?" Herman said with disgust.

"Why were you wearing a tee-shirt that said 'Y2K Blows' on the front, 'But I Dig Blow' on the back?"

"Why not, it's true."

"You dig Blow, Herman?"

"Sure." Lax noticed a patch of scruffy yellow hair under Herman's chin. Goofy looking.

"Did you get picked on a lot at school, Herman?"

"Why do you have Dodo birds on your tie?"

"Because they look stupid, but they're really smart."

"Okay, that's cool."

"Sounds like the seal of approval. May I interview you now?"

"Why not?"

"Did you get picked on a lot at school?"

"Everyday."

"Elaborate."

"The jocks called me names cause I'm small. They'd give me wedgies and push me around. Stuff. One time I was at one of the urinals and two asshole hockey players came in and pushed me up against it. I got piss all over my pants. They laughed. I wanted to cry but I sure as Hell wasn't about to let them see that. I just sat there on the floor looking up at them. Then one said, 'Spare some change?' I didn't have any, so he kicked me in the stomach. They walked out and left me there. I had to wait for the bell to ring so everyone would be in class and I could run home."

"What's with 'Spare some change.'?"

"It's MTV. They were doing this show about kids who leave home and go to live on the streets in New York. They ask people if they can spare some change, and if the person says no, or ignores them, they beat him up."

"The kids are big enough to beat up adults?"

"Yeah, they're like seventeen, eighteen."

Lax took a sip of coffee, he could feel Herman loosening up. "Why don't they just get jobs if they're healthy enough to kick the shit out of people?"

"Why get a job if you can make just as much begging? Especially after that show. People all over were scared to say no to them. That's why people around here do it, they want to be like the kids in New York. If someone around here asks you that, and you don't give them anything, you'll get jacked up."

"Have you ever heard of Eric Harris and Dylan Klebold, Herman?"

"What do you think?"

"Would you have ever thought to do what you did if they hadn't done it in Colorado first?"

"But they did."

"I know, Herman, pretend they hadn't."

"I guess I might not of thought of it, but come on, they became real famous afterwards. Everyone knows who they are. They put my generation on the map. I just took it one step further."

"You look at them as heroes, Herman?"

"Yes."

"Why?"

"Because they said Fuck You to the assholes. After Colorado, nerds started getting respect. Now that I've hit the scene, they'll be running the schools."

"So you feel like you started a revolution?"

"You'll see. All over the country, kids are going to start doing what I did until all you assholes finally realize that we are here. We matter, Lax."

"What about the twenty-four kids you shot and killed in cold blood, Herman? Are they not part of your revolution?"

"Fuck them. They grouped me in with the nerds. They thought I didn't count." He chuckled.

"Well, Justin Martin was considered a nerd and you killed him anyway."

"I did that fat bastard a favor. Look, I didn't say I wanted to be grouped with losers. Those asshole Jocks grouped me in with them. I didn't have shit to do with those nerds. I'm an individual! Don't forget that! You think that just anyone could go into school and do what I did? No sir. There's only one Herman Howards, and now history will remember me!"

As Lax watched, he could almost swear that Herman's eyes turned from blue to red. His face certainly had. It was time, Lax decided to change pace.

"Have you ever played 'DOOM'?"

"Of course."

"What would you say is the goal of the game?"

"To shoot everyone up and get lots of points."

"Now, how about 'POSTAL', have you ever played that game?"

"I own it." He said with pride.

"Explain it to me, Herman. I haven't had a chance to play."

"You're a postal worker. You go into the office one day cause you've had enough of people's crap, and you shoot everyone up 'til they're all gone."

"It sounds easy."

"Well, you've got time limits, and you get more points for hitting people in the face than in the stomach or the legs or the back of the head."

"Do you 'shoot up' women and children too?"

"You get less points for them."

"That's nice." Lax felt serious anger starting to brew in him. "Your mom supports you in playing games like POSTAL?"

"I don't think she knew anything about it."

"But she bought it for you?"

"No, I downloaded it off the web."

"Would you say that playing these games has numbed you to violence?"

"I don't get your question."

"Would you say that playing these games made it easier for you to go into your school and kill your peers?"

"Of course it did. How do you think I got to be such a good shot? At one point I was getting ready to kill this little prick, Eddie, who had back from the jocks. This girl started running for the door. She was about fifty feet from me, but I clipped her right in the back of the head and her face exploded and landed all over some kid." Herman started to laugh.

"You think that's funny?"

"You had to be there. I mean here was this girl that thought she was home free because she was so far from me, and she's running, about to get to the door when all of a sudden, 'OOPS! THERE GOES MY FACE!' and lands all over this tiny little kid in glasses. I mean, can you imagine what that kid must have been thinking when that happened? Jesus, that's gotta' be worse then getting shit on by a bird! Sucker! I mean, what are the chances?"

"Do you even know the girl's name, Herman?"

"She was background. Not a key player."

"It was a game, wasn't it?"

"It's all a game, Lax. Wasn't it a game when you bashed that nigger's head in with a bat?"

"What did you say?"

"Down in Georgia, when you bashed that nigger's head in with a bat. Did that seem real to you?"

"Never happened." He tried to laugh it off.

"Well, all sixty four people that were there say it did."

"How do you know?"

"WWW.KKK.COM, Georgia faction. When you won the Pulitzer, they had quite a few things to say about you, Lax."

He remembered hearing something about that, but never paid it much mind. Perhaps it was that he knew behind the lie there was an ounce of truth. An ounce was enough for him to avoid visiting the site. *How could I ever be affected by something that's on the KKK website?*

"You make it a habit to surf hate-sites, Herman?"

"I have respect for anyone that's willing to stand up for themselves. Besides, you can learn a lot about people from their websites. That's where you really learn stuff, Lax. Lax Morales. It sounds like you're Puerto Rican or something."

"Mexican. I'm a sixteenth Mexican. Does that make you want to kill me too, Herman!?"

"I just think it's funny, that's all." He looked a little hurt, like up to now they had been getting along. Starting a friendship. As a journalist Lax should have liked that. He didn't.

"Why don't we stop here today? You've given me a good bit to digest. I'll come back tomorrow."

"Whatever."

Day Two

Herman was waiting in the room when Lax arrived. He had an ugly grin on his face.

"Morning, Lax."

"Hello Herman."

"Hey, that sounds like a TV show. 'Hello Herman!' starring Lax Morales and Herman Howards…Or should I get top billing? I mean it is my story."

"Let's get one thing straight, Herman. I'm not here to turn you into a rock star. I'm not here to make you look like a tragic hero. You're not. Personally I think you're just a psychopath who got off to an early start. The reason I'm here is because there's a world outside that thinks you're a monster. They think you should be electrocuted on national television and cable. That's a story. I'm here in case they do it."

"Fuck you, Lax!"

"Fuck me? Herman you have no idea how far from being fucked I am. You, however, are sitting closer to death's gate then you can imagine. Cherish this time you have with me, Herman. Even if they don't execute you, the moment they transfer you to Population, someone's going to get you."

Herman was looking at him with his blank eyes. He had a grin wide enough to upset your soul.

"They will never transfer me to population. I'm too important."

"Yeah, you're important, but you're worth more to them dead than alive, kid."

Herman was still smiling. "We better get on with the interview."

"When you were thirteen, your sister was hurt in a hit and run, right?"

"Right."

"Then she died a few months later."

"Yep."

"Were you close to her?"

"We had our moments."

"You want to tell me about one, Herman?"

"It's not nice to talk to strangers about dead people who you cared about."

"So, you did care about her."

"She was my sister."

"Were you home when it happened?"

"Yeah."

"It happened right outside your house."

"You've done your homework, Lax."

"Did you go out and help her?"

"No."

"Why not?"

"Because I was thirteen, there wasn't a whole Hell of a lot I could have done, now was there?"

"Did you call your mom?"

"What?"

"Did you call your mom when you found out what had happened?"

"Did it feel good when you took that bat to the nigger's head?"

"I'm asking the questions, Herman."

"No."

"No what?"

"No, I didn't call my mom."

"Why not?"

"Because it didn't occur to me. What would she have done, anyway?"

"I imagine she would have rushed home."

"You really don't get it, Lax."

"Tell me about your relationship with your father."

"What about it?"

"Was it a good one? Did he play ball with you as a small child? Or did he molest you and your sister? Tell me about it."

Herman laughed. "He was all right. Just a dad. He left when I was ten. I haven't seen much of him since."

"What's the most memorable thing he ever said to you?"

"Make your mark, kid."

"When did he tell you that?"

"Right before he got in the car and moved to Chicago with his girlfriend."

Outside the prison, the reporters looked like masses of ants who have had their hole closed up and don't know what to do with themselves. There was much milling and seeding and sharing of false tips. Some of the press were going around to different survivor's homes trying to get exclusives. Others were at the high-school talking to the guards who had been at lunch during the shootings.

NEWSWEEK: Did you know Herman Howards personally?

SCHOOL GUARD: Yeah, I knew him. He was all kinds of fucked up...Can I say fucked up?

NEWSWEEK: Yes.

SCHOOL GUARD: Yeah, he was *fucked* up! It's a damn shame that no one saw it coming. I don't know what's wrong with that boy's mama, but it's something for her not to see the signs.

NEWSWEEK: What signs would those be?

SCHOOL GUARD: The kid had no friends. How can a boy grow up with no friends and be a normal kid? Will you tell me that? Every kid, no matter how strange they are, has friends. Not Herman. He'd eat his lunch alone in the cafeteria and listen to the kids laugh about him two tables away.

NEWSWEEK: Did you ever sit with him at lunch?

SCHOOLGUARD: We don't sit with the kids, and besides, child psychology ain't my field of expertise. I could tell, though. The kid was going to snap. Shit, anyone with a set of working eyes should've been able to see that. Those kids could've been nicer to that boy, maybe all this shit wouldn't have gone down.

NEWSWEEK: You were on your lunch-break when it happened, correct?

SCHOOLGUARD: What of it?

NEWSWEEK: Just trying to clarify.

SCHOOLGUARD: Now you want to blame me for this shit?

NEWSWEEK: I was not implying that, sir.

SCHOOLGUARD: All you fools looking to blame someone. Blame the games, blame the music, blame the school-guards. Go blame yourselves.

"What's your favorite movie, Herman?"

"That's a hard question."

"Don't tell me *Natural Born Killers*."

"That's an awesome movie. But I guess my all time favorite is *KIDS*."

"Tell me about it."

"Well, for one thing, that's really what it's like. Kids are doing some things that parents don't have a clue about. That's why that movie got so much shit."

"What sort of things?"

"Fucking without condoms, smoking pot, drinking forties, taking X, getting into fights, that sort of thing. Straight shit. Parents want to close their eyes and pretend that it's still 1955 and everything is hunky-dory. It's just not like that."

"But that movie was about kids growing up in New York. Are you saying Iowa is like that?"

"After the movie came out, it got a lot closer."

"So, what you're saying, Herman, is that because kids around here saw that movie, they were so impressed they started to live that life. I have a hard time believing you. I saw the movie. It does not have a happy ending. It doesn't give off a positive image."

"When the theaters wouldn't show it, and parents forbid their kids to see it even on tape, they automatically made it cool. If the parents won't let them see it, then the kids will do what is done in the film. It's the nature of rebellion; always do what they think you're incapable of doing 'till they notice you."

"So, you think the parents should have sat down and watched it *with* their kids?"

"Sort of."

"Sort of?"

"Yeah, kind of."

"Well, Herman, I think we may agree on something."

"I think we see eye to eye on more than that, Lax." He stared at him and let out his chuckle. "But that's not why it's my favorite movie."

"Why then?"

"Because the main kid says what's up."

"What's up, Herman?"

"He says that when you're a kid, you have to find something you care about and stick to it, cause that's all you got."

"What's the one thing you care about?"

"I don't know, I'll tell you when I figure it out." Herman started laughing, hard. After he cooled down, he looked up at Lax and said; "You know what I really miss, more than anything?"

"What?"

"My Nintendo sixty-four. Man, if I could just get one more game in, I'd be happy."

"Is that really what you miss most after being in jail for a week?"

"Yeah, ain't it fucked up?"

"Do you follow politics, Herman?"

"What for?"

"Believe it or not, politicians change the world."

"How do they do that?"

"They make the rules. They break the rules. They change the rules. Do you know who your governor is?"

"No."

"Do you know your mayor?"

"No."

"Do any of the kids in Iowa?"

"They know who I am."

"I guess they do. What's your fondest memory of childhood?"

"I'm not that old."

"Early childhood."

"Shit, I don't know. Maybe…I guess there was this one day when my family took a trip to the beach in New Jersey. My dad had relatives out there. I guess I was five, my sister was two." A smile appeared on his face. Innocent. He actually looked like a normal kid. "Me and my dad kept trying to get my mom to go in the water, until finally he picked her up and put her over his shoulder. He was much bigger than her. He walked out to his belly, and threw her in. My sister started crying because she thought he was hurting her, so my mom got out and picked my sister up and told her it was all okay, that daddy hadn't hurt her, and then we all started laughing because my dad got bit by a crab and started howling in pain."

Frank Howards was coming home from work early to surprise his wife and kids. He had told them he had to work late that night, and would not be home until after dark. When he walked in the house at noon, he was greeted by cheers and hoorahs. His ten year old son came running up to him and jumped in his arms.

"Dad's home! Dad's home!"

His daughter was roller-skating around the house and he told her to get some shoes on because they were going to take a family trip to go see John Wayne's birthplace, near Winterset. Everyone was excited and Frank felt like the man of his house, until the phone rang and as fortune would have it, Herman answered.

"Dad, there's some lady on the phone for you. She's crying a lot."

Frank took the phone and went into the other room. After a few moments, he came back out and told everyone that an emergency had come up at the office and he didn't know what time he would be back. He would try to make it in time to still go to Winterset.

Two weeks later he packed his bags and moved to Chicago. Herman never did get to see John Wayne's birthplace.

"Tell me more about the day you did it. You had rounded up all the kids in the gym, then what happened?"

"A couple of teachers had come in also, I guess to see what was going on. It was Mr. Phelps and Ms. Cribb, the phys-ed teacher. After I saw them come in, I knew I had to lock the doors quickly. I put the last two chains on and threw the keys under the bleachers. Then I went to the top and took out the UZI. Fired a couple of shots in the ceiling and told everyone to get down on the floor. They didn't know what the Hell was going on, but they heard the shots. They got down. I called up Paul Shrewber, the captain of the football team. 'Paul! Paul Schrewber! Today is your lucky day, Paul! Because you are so *valuable* to our school, you get to live! Now, come on up here, take a bow and get the fuck out of my gym, Paul.' He slowly got up and started walking toward the door. When he got a little closer he began to run. 'PAUL!' I yelled. 'You forgot to take a bow.' He kept running, so I shot him in the knee. He fell down and I could see his bone was shattered and hanging out of his leg. I took one of the pipe bombs out and told the crowd that the first person who moved without me saying so, was gonna' get a pipe bomb up their ass." Lax could see Herman transporting himself back to that day. It was, yes, it was the happiest moment of his life.

"I walked over to Paul. He was crying and screaming. I told him to shut up and shot him in the gut. Mr. Phelps came walking toward me slowly telling me there was still time for me to stop this madness because I hadn't killed anyone yet. I told him to sit the fuck down, that I didn't want to kill him, but he kept walking toward me. I had to shoot. He would have grabbed me if I didn't. I shot him in the collar bone and it splintered everywhere. He started to kind of fall toward me, so I shot him in the eye. He looked so stupid with nothing but red for his right eye and no collar bone. I almost started laughing, but like I said, he was an all right teacher so out of respect I didn't."

Nathaniel Phelps was walking down the hallway when he saw two kids from the football team push Herman Howards into the boy's bathroom on the third floor. It was fourth period and he had been going to see if Ms. Richards wanted to go for a walk and share some Fig Newtons and milk as they often did on Thursdays during fourth period.

When he walked into the bathroom he saw the two boys holding Herman out the window.

"What the Devil do you boys think you're doing?" he said to them in his quiet voice. The two football players instantly pulled Herman back into the bathroom and looked at the floor.

"What are your names?" he asked. They told him in sheepish voices. "Is that their real names, Herman?" Herman had a blank look on his face. "Do you boys have any idea how dangerous what you were doing, is? Herman could have been killed for Godsakes! Killed! Do you understand that? Now you two get out of here and go to the principal's office and tell him what you've done. I'll be up shortly to make sure that you tell the truth." Just before they were out of the door he said one more thing to them. "You two should be ashamed to call yourselves Broome students, picking on a boy half your size."

When they had left, Nathaniel took Herman to his office and had a quick chat with him.

"You're a freshman, right Herman?"

Herman nodded.

"I remember when I was your age, the older boys would treat me the same way. But don't worry about it, Herman. In a few years, things like that will all be fond memories of high-school. You'll probably be friends with those boys next year. I know it sounds crazy, but some of the greatest friendships start with fights. Take me and my best fri..."

"Mr. Phelps? Can I go now?"

"Yes. Yes of course."

"Thanks." Herman walked out with his head hanging low and that idiot blank expression Mr. Phelps had noticed on so many kids in recent years.

"Poor little guy," thought Nathaniel. "He'll always be a nerd."

"I asked if there were any other teachers in the room, even though I knew Ms. Cribb was there. No one came forward, so I called up three kids who were sitting on the floor near me. That was Susan, this fat girl who no one really liked, James Hankley, the editor of the school paper, and Marsha, the fucking hottest girl in school. I asked again if there were any other teachers in the room, and could they please come forward. No one came.

"I took out the .45 and walked up to Susan. 'Oink.' I told her. She didn't get it. 'Oink! Like in *Deliverance*. Squeal.' She tried, but she was crying too much. Then she gave up and began to say something like 'Jesus, please protect me.' Over and over again. I started to laugh. 'Not today' I told her and I shot her through the cheek, but up, at an angle so the bullet could go through her skull and blood would splatter all over Marsha."

"Why did you want the blood to hit Marsha?"

"To show that bitch that her shit wasn't all that! She walked around those halls like she owned the place. And why? Because she was a nice looking piece of ass? You think that's gonna' fly in the new order?!"

"What new order?"

"The next millennium, Lax. Shit's going down. Being some sweet piece of ass ain't gonna' cut it. It's the ones like me that are going to run the show."

"How do you figure?"

"Do you know what the largest generation is? Mine. We have more than the Babyboomers. I heard so on MTV. There's more of us than any of you other fuckers. You don't stand a chance. We're gonna' do a Hell of a lot more than 'Rock the vote'. More and more kids are going to realize that this is the only way to make you assholes pay attention to us. When they do, watch out. I made damn sure to kill more people than they did in Colorado. You know why? Because you have to reset the precedent. Sure, the precedent was set in Colorado, the nation freaked out. But people didn't freak out when that kid brought a gun into his school in Georgia, T.J. Solomon was his name. You know why people didn't freak out, 'cause he only wounded six students, he didn't even kill anybody. How can you expect the world to take notice when you don't up the ante. People looked at that incident and all they said was 'At least it's not as bad as Columbine.' Not with me Lax. I wasn't about to settle for some rinky-dink shit, oh, no. I blew that fucking fat bitch's head off and made sure a little got on James Hankley as well. But I was never going to kill him. I wanted him to live, so he could write about it in his precious paper. Marsha on the other hand, she didn't have a chance.

"Before I could waste her, though, Ms. Cribb came running up to the front crying and begging me to stop. I shot her right in the mouth from about twenty feet away. Shut that bitch right up. Really tough shot. I would've gotten like two-thousand points if it were POSTAL. I don't even think she died. Isn't she at the hospital or something?"

"Intensive care."

"Have you seen her, Lax?" He was eager.

"No, I haven't seen her."

"But you heard something?"

"They had to amputate her lower jaw. What was left of it. She'll have to be fed intravenously"

"Awesome! She deserved it."

"Why?"

"That bitch gave me a C- for gym class. Can you believe that? A C- in fucking gym? Unreal. Lax? Lax, you still with me?"

"Yeah, I'm still with you. Listen, why don't we take a quick break? I need some coffee."

"Whatever."

Lax got up and knocked on the door twice. The guard opened it and let him out. He went to the bathroom and splashed some water on his face. Then he lit up a cigarette and thought to himself "My God, not human." One tear rolled down his face. He took out his notepad and started writing.

When Europeans first came to America and systematically extinguished the Indians, we were at least able to say that we, like the Indians, lived off the land and worked hard for our food in small farming communities. When we had multiplied enough to create the demand for it, we built The City. Big giant slabs of concrete land with little or no nature. One lived removed from nature, but at least it was interesting. The architecture was stimulating, artists from around the world would come to these cities, it was a microcosm of Society. It was action.

Then, as the world became more and more corporate, humans wanted a place to live that wasn't dangerous or exciting or stimulating. They wanted to be near enough to it that they could work there in their nine to fiver jobs and their gray suits. They wanted the convenience of a city with the peacefulness of the country.

Neutrality. Suburbia. No real crime. No real danger. Utopia. Now they're learning that you can't have it both ways. Neutrality kills the soul.

Who's paying? The kids. The kids with their numb souls are paying for three generations of living in the suburbs. They're going insane and suburbia is as much a reason why as everything else. Living in neutrality means there's nothing real to live for.

I don't know that I have it in me to kill. All I know is if I do, suburbia would bring it out.

Lax looked at it for a moment and then ripped it up. He knew the magazine would never print it.

After composing himself, he got a cup of coffee and prepared to go back into that room. Herman was laughing when he came in.

"What's the joke?"

"I don't think you would find it very amusing."

"Try me."

"James Hankley is one of the smartest kids in school, right. He's head of the paper, gets really good grades and all that."

"And?"

"When I blew Susan away, some of her brains landed on him." Herman started laughing hard.

"What did you do next, Herman?"

"Next? Oh, I told James to take his clothes off. He did and then I told him to sit down. Marsha was still up there covered in blood."

"You let James live because you wanted him to write about the day?"

"Yeah." No pause at all. "Do you have a cigarette?"

"No."

"I can see the pack in your shirt pocket?"

"No, Herman."

"That's a shitty thing to do to a fellow smoker."

"What happened next?"

"I'd be able to think a lot clearer if you gave me one of those cigarettes."

"Forget about it. Those things will kill you."

"Think I'm afraid of dying, Lax?"

"Yes."

"Why say that?"

"Because you weren't man enough to do yourself in like your buddies Eric and Dylan."

"Hey, I was prepared to pay the price for what I did. That takes more balls then just offing yourself."

"You don't believe in karma?"

"I don't know much about it."

"Well, Herman, in your language I think the closest translation would be 'what goes around comes around'."

"What, I'm gonna' pay for my deeds in the after life?"

"Something like that."

"You know what I think? I think that when you die, it's game over. Nothing. Blackness."

"What about 'reset', Herman?"

"When you hit reset, the game you played before doesn't have shit to do with the next one. All the characters come back to life."

"That's not how it works in reality. Once a kid is killed, he doesn't come back to life."

Herman didn't speak immediately. His face changed. It was as if he was beginning to worry.

"What are you thinking about?" Lax finally asked after the silence had gone on too long.

"I haven't been able to sleep well." The blankness in his face returned.

"Why not?"

"Nightmares."

"What sort?"

"I dream they come back."

"Who?"

"Those assholes. They come back, and I shoot them again. They come back again. I keep shooting them. I have unlimited bullets, and they have unlimited lives. We keep going and going. No reason. No goal. We just keep going."

"You don't think they're haunting you?"

"How can dead people haunt your dreams?"

"Ask them next time when you go to sleep."

"You want to hear what else happened? Or not?!"

"I want to hear, Herman. I want to hear."

"Where was I?"

"Marsha was covered in blood."

"Right. I, uh, I told James to take his clothes off…"

"You already said that, Herman."

"Shut up! I'm fine! I don't remember what happened next. I think I started firing into the crowd…No, that happened after the police came to the door. Yeah, that's how it happened. The police came to the door and all the kids began to scream because I threw a pipe bomb into the middle of the crowd and a whole bunch of people scattered. It got crazy. The kids ran towards the door, the police ran into the gym, and I was just running around shooting people left and right. There were only three cops at first, and I was able to pick them off right after they stormed the gym. The idiots only got one door open, so with all the kids trying to get out, no more cops could get in. It was anarchy. Awesome.

"I ran up behind Marsha and put the .45 in her back. 'Ready to die, prom queen?' I said to her. Then I shot someone who was running right next to her. She screamed and fell to her knees begging me not to kill her. Isn't it funny, she never would've even talked to me before that. Now she was practically spreading her legs for me. I shot her down low, where it counts, bashed her nose with the butt of my gun, and left her there to bleed. I hope she survived."

"Why's that?"

"Because I want her to learn what life is like when you're not the prettiest girl in school."

"You're a teacher?"

"People needed a lesson."

"What did they learn, Herman?"

"Maybe they learned to be a little nicer to each other."

Lax paused before he spoke. "Maybe they will be. Maybe we all will be."

"I doubt it. The world's gonna' see more kids like me before they finally get it. That's okay, they will."

"They'll finally get it?"

"No Lax," he grinned his yellow grin. "The world will see more kids like me."

People Magazine:
Interview with Brian Green, survivor of Bloody Broome.

PEOPLE: Did you ever think that something like this was possible in your school, Brian?

BRIAN: I don't think anyone believes that it could happen in their school, but it can. No one is safe from these nerds.

PEOPLE: Do you consider yourself a jock?

BRIAN: I play sports.

PEOPLE: Did you ever have interactions with Herman Howards?

BRIAN: I used to rib him a little, but no more than any of the other kids. He's evil! I hope they fry him.

PEOPLE: If they do execute Howards, do you think it should be televised?

BRIAN: Absolutely.

"Are you ready to spend the rest of your life in jail, or would you rather be executed, Herman?

"It really doesn't matter. Jail has been all right so far. I don't care if I die. It's gonna' get harder if they transfer me to population, though. I heard today it could happen down the road."

"Yeah, it's going to get harder." Lax was starting to wrap up.

"Look, if I can blow away twenty-nine people, I think I can handle myself in prison. I've seen Oz, I know what to expect."

"I want to ask you one more time, do you feel bad in anyway about what you did?"

"Is this between you and me?"

"Off the record." Lax stopped the tape recorder.

"I'm scared. I don't want to be in a cell for the rest of my life. I don't know what they're gonna' do to me in State, but I'm damn sure I won't like it. Sometimes I even wish I could take it back. You know, hit reset. But I guess I can't."

"No, Herman. You can't. I think I have all I need here. Thank you for your time."

"My pleasure."

Lax put the rest of his papers in his brief case and got up to leave.

"Hey, Lax?"

"Yes, Herman?"

"Do you think those nightmares will ever go away?"

He thought about what he should say for a moment. "No, Herman. I don't."

"Yeah. Me neither."

"Good bye, Herman."

Herman did not respond. He just gave Lax a look. Blank and scared.

Molly showed up to the bar she had told Lax about at around eleven thirty. He had called her half an hour before, obviously drunk, and asked if there was anyplace they could meet for a drink. She wasn't sure she wanted to go. Lax sounded deranged on the phone. In her mind his words were circling like airplanes with no place to land.

She walked into the Pit Stop and saw him sitting at the counter. The Pit Stop was a tough bar mostly for bikers, but it was open late. Molly immediately noticed some of the boys were looking Lax up and down.

"I didn't think I'd see you again." she said.

"I was hoping you'd show up." He was close to slurring his words. "What are you drinking?"

"I'll take a Bud."

"BAR KEEP! One Budweiser for the pretty lady next to me. Please." The bartender stared at him for a moment before getting the beer.

"What did you think of Herman Howards, Lax?"

"You're such a reporter. Always cutting to the chase. I like that. BAR KEEP! Another Gibson. Onions this time. Please."

The two guys at the table were blatantly staring now. They wore spiked chains and had on Harley Davidson shirts, both of them.

"What did you think of him, Lax."

"He's a kid. I don't want to talk about him. Let's talk about you, Molly. What do you think of him?" He laughed as if this were the best joke he'd heard in years.

"I think he's a product of today. The world's getting to be a cold place."

"THE WORLD'S GETTING TO BE A COLD PLACE! Did you hear

that gentlemen? We're living in a cold world." He might be drunk, but he knew right through the drinks that he was close to crossing the line.

The bartender came over with the Gibson and told him to keep it down. Was he testing him, Lax wondered. It wasn't a Gibson. It had an olive with a toothpick sticking out.

"Sorry." Lax said. "I'll try a little harder."

She took his hand. "Lax, why did you call me tonight?"

"I wanted to ask your advice on something."

"My advice?"

"Yeah, I fly out tomorrow and I wanted to know what you think of my piece."

"I haven't read it, Lax."

"No. No one has. I have the only copy right here." He pulled it out from his pocket, crumpled and hand written. "Wanna' take a look?" He finished his Gibson. She took it from him and unfolded it. She had to smooth parts of it out, it was nearly illegible.

Crossroads by Lax Morales

Kids today are taught by mass media that life is not precious. Even the ones that don't go into their school with a TECH 9 and shoot up all their classmates are still mean to each other. A few are inhumanely mean. These kids in the height of their hormonal teens, are learning that the only way to prove you exist is by becoming dangerous.

Or is it that they just don't see anything wrong with blowing each other's heads off? Since they do it in Cyber-reality, they can conclude that it could be as much fun in real reality. "I mean like, what is real-reality anyways?" Sometimes I don't know anymore. I'm twenty-two years old and I feel I belong to a different genera-tion. I didn't grow up on-line. We had to try a little harder to find things out. Occasionally, we even asked our parents for the answer.

Those days are done. Kids aren't going to ask their parents questions anymore. Why would they? The Internet can not only give them an answer, but won't scold them for asking. The Internet has an answer for everything.

If we stay on this track in which our technology evolves faster than we do, in which our capabilities are far beyond our compassion, eventually we'll all be plugged into the Net. Entirely. No real contact with real people in real space. We won't need it. We'll be no more alive then the computer screens we study.

I don't blame Herman Howards entirely.   Herman thought he was a character in a video game.

She finished reading and looked up.

"What do you think?" he asked.

"It's true."

"They'll never publish it."

"Why not?"

"You're so naive. How can you be so much older than me and be so naive? This is stuff," he said with great drunken dignity, "that comes straight from the heart and· *Query Magazine* doesn't want to pay for that crap. Heartfelt crap. They want a story that's going to put Americans' minds a little more at ease. They want the picture of a little hick monster who's a throwaway. Not some story written by a twenty-two year old punk that tells them they're shitty parents. They don't want to hear that."

"At least you didn't blame the music."

"Good point, Molly."

"I mean, like what is real-reality anyways?"

They laughed a bit after that. Lax gave Molly an open invitation to come to New York whenever she felt ready, and Molly gave Lax a kiss before they said goodbye. He got on his plane and flew home.

Query Magazine refused to accept the article, but legally they owned the rights to the interviews. They hired Archibald Skinny, who, for enough money was willing to write any piece, any Goddamn piece, and he gave them a write-up to go along with the interviews. The issue broke the record for the magazine's sales. Lax's name was plastered right next to Herman's on the cover. He knew he would be associated with the boy forever more.

New York Post

Two years after the Broome High school massacre, Herman Howards was put to death at seven thirty this morning. His execution was the first to be televised in the United States. It was the highest viewed event in television history. An estimated sixty-seven percent of the country had their sets on while Howards was strapped down to the electric chair.

Outside the prison, protesters surrounded the area holding up signs while they chanted, "Killing people does not stop people from killing people!"

Lax Morales was invited to the execution but declined to come.

Iowa Senator John Cox (Rep.) stated: "This boy's execution is long overdue. America will be watching and they will see today that the government will not allow their children to be in danger anymore. Killing people may not stop people from killing people, but seeing the execution sure as heck will. Thank you."

As more than half the nation sat with eyes on the screen, Howards was asked if he had any last words before they flipped the switch.

"Yes," he said. "I'd like to tell the viewers at home, that while you may not like me, one thing's for sure; you'll never, never, forget me. Goodbye America. Good luck."

CONTRIBUTORS

Lionel Abel, known as a playwright and literary critic, won the first Obie award for his play *Absalom*. His books include *The Intellectual Folies and Important Nonsense*. His new book, *Tragedy and Metatheatre* will be published this year.

Linsey Abrams is the author of three novels, most recently *Our History in New York*. *Living Pictures* is an excerpt from her novel-in-progess. She is co-director of the Graduate Writing Program at Sarah Lawrence College.

Madison Smartt Bell is the author of eight novels and two collections of short stories, including *Waiting for the End of the World* and *Dr. Sleep*. *All Souls' Rising* was a finalist for the National Book Award. This excerpt is from *Master of the Crossroads*, to be published by Pantheon in the fall.

Peter Bush, the Director of the British Center for Literary Translation at the University of East Anglia, won the Cervantes Institute's 1998 Ramón Valle-Inclán Prize for his translation of Juan Goytisolo's *The Marx Family Saga* published by City Lights.

Elizabeth Chakkappan received her M.F.A. in fiction writing from Sarah Lawrence College. She lives in Brooklyn, and is a teacher and freelance writer. She is working on a collection of short stories.

Stanley Crouch's books include *The All-American Skin Game, or The Decoy of Race,* and *Notes of a Hanging Judge*. He is a columnist for *The New York Daily News* and Artistic Consultant to Jazz at Lincoln Center. His novel *Don't The Moon Look Lonesome* will be published by Pantheon in April. *L'Imperiale at the Georges Cinq* is an excerpt from a work-in-progress.

Avi Dressner is an American-Israeli author based in New York City. His poetry and fiction have appeared in Promethean and the Israeli literary journal Omphalos. *Where the Lightning Was* is an excerpt from a novel-in-progress.

Stuart Engesser is currently working on a collection of essays, of which "Tales of the Blue Mazda" is one, and on a screenplay. He teaches in the English department at Montclair State University. He lives in his car.

Juan Goytisolo, considered Spain's leading writer, has written twelve books including *Count Julian, Juan the Landless, Makbara, Quarantine* and *The Marx Family Saga*. His essays have appeared in literary journals throughout the world. Until Franco's death he lived in voluntary exile in Paris and Morocco, and now lives in Morocco.

Kenneth Koch's most recent books of poems are *Straits* (1998) and *One Train* and *On the Great Atlantic Rainway* (1994), for which he received the Bollingen Prize for Poetry. "To Jewishness" is part of *New Addresses*, a collection to be published by Knopf in May 2000.

Don Maggin is the author of the biography *Stan Getz — A Life in Jazz*, and is currently working on one of Dizzy Gillespie. His other books include *Bankers, Knaves and Thieves*. His work has appeared in *The Christian Science Monitor* and other periodicals.

John Buffalo Mailer grew up in Brooklyn and will graduate from Wesleyan University in the Spring of 2000. *Hello Herman* is his first published story.

Daphne Merkin is the author of *Enchantment*, a novel, and *Dreaming of Hitler*, a collection of essays. Her critical essays and fiction have appeared in *Commentary, The New York Times Book Review, Mirabella, Partisan Review* and other publications. She is a staff book critic and columnist at *The New Yorker*.

Mark Jay Mirsky is a founder and the editor of *Fiction* magzine. He edited the English edition of Robert Musil's *Diaries*. His eleven published books include fiction and essay collections. *The Absent Shakespeare* was nominated for the NBCC award.

Yvonne Murphy is finishing a Ph.D. in Literature and Creative Writing at the University of Houston. She held the Wallace Stegner Fellow in Poetry at Stanford. Her poems have appeared in literary reviews. She, her husband and cats, live in Manhattan.

Julie Obaso was born in Kisumu, Kenya, in 1968. She is a graduate student in the Creative Writing Program at City College. She is working on her first novel. She lives in Riverdale, New York

James Purdy is the author of sixteen novels, including *Malcolm* and *Eustace Chisholm and the Works*. His new book *Moe's Villa and Other Stories* will be published by Arcadia Books in London later this year. His two short plays, *Dangerous Moonlight* and *Down the Starry River*, will be presented later this year off-Broadway.

Larry Rivers: His art is in the Metropolitan Museum of Art, MOMA, and major museums and private collections here and abroad. He has written poetry, is a jazz saxophonist, a composer, has his own group, The Climax Band, and is the author of *What Did I Do? The Unauthorized Autobiography of Larry Rivers* with Arnold Weinstein.

Michele Tolela Myers is the president of Sarah Lawrence College. She grew up in Paris and spent all her childhood summers at her grandparents' home in Marseilles. She has lived in the United States since 1964, when she came to graduate school.

Cara Prieskorn grew up in Michigan and now lives in the Hudson Valley. She attended the University of Michigan, Vassar and Sara Lawrence. She is single, but if you know anyone . . .

Julián Ríos's sixteen books including the novels *Larva, Poundemonium, Kitaj: Pictures and Conversations* and *Loves That Bind* (Knopf) have been translated into several languages. He contributes to many journals and lives in Paris and Madrid.

J. Schwartzman is the author of *I, Grace Note* (Aventura Books). *When They All Went to Maxwell's* is from her work-in-progress, *Flo*. She graduated from Yale College and lives in Brooklyn. She won the 1990 Mademoiselle Magazine Short Story Prize.

Barbara Probst Solomon's six published books of fiction, memoirs, and an essay collection include *The Beat of Life, Arriving Where We Started* and S*mart Hearts in the City*. She has written for *The New York Review of Books, The New Yorker, The New Republic* and *Doubletake*. She is correspondent for *El País*.

Maria Solomon, a graduate of Sarah Lawrence College, studied Slavic and Yiddish Linguistics at Columbia University. She is a psychiatric social worker at the Presbyterian Hospital/Payne Whitney Clinic in NYC. She is working on an essay collection.

Carl Watson was born in Indiana and now lives in New York City, where he works as a freelance writer. His published books include *Bricolage ex Machina,* and *Beneath the Empire of the Birds*. His novel *Hotel des actes irrévocables* has been published by Gallimard.

ABOUT THE TYPE

Some of the most widely used typefaces in history are those of the sixteenth-century type designer Claude Garamond. Robert Slimbach visited Plantin-Moretus museum in Antwerp, Belgium, to study the original Garamond typefaces. These served as the basis for the Adobe Garamond romans, the face used for the body of this book. Running heads are Formata.

The
Cathedral
Church
of Saint John
the Divine

1047 Amsterdam Ave.
at 112 Street
New York, New York

For information
call: 212 316 7540

Join us to hear authors from *The Reading Room* read selections from their works.

Date: 9 May 2000
Time: 7:30 pm

The event is free and made possible through the generous support of the Aubrey Cartwright Foundation.

LETRAS LIBRES

Editor-in-Chief
Enrique Krauze

The leading intellectual and artistic journal of the Spanish-speaking world.

One year's subscription (twelve issues): $49.90

Subscribe by internet at

www.letraslibres.com

An die Musik

oboe, string trio & piano

Robert Ingliss, *oboe*
Frank Almond, *violin*
Richard Brice, *viola*
Daniel Rothmuller, *cello*
Constance Emmerich, *piano*

*F*ounded in 1976, hailed internationally for its fresh and innovative programming built around its unusual instrumentation of oboe, strings, and piano AND its unique collaborative story-telling projects with painters, writers, and composers, **An die Musik** has inspired audiences with its "ardent impetuosity, musical integrity and fiery instrumental brilliance" *(N.Y. Times)*, attaining a place in the foremost rank of world-class chamber music ensembles today.

Join us for our concert series at Merkin Hall on **November 12th, 2000** and **March 25th, 2001**. Performances will include works by Beethoven, Shubert, John Deak (original music for *Rapunzel*), Mozart, Tschaikovsky, and Brahms.

For more information please contact:
MERKIN CONCERT HALL
129 West 67th Street • (212)501-3330 • (212)831-8331

LINCOLN PLAZA
CINEMAS

Six Screens

63rd Street & Broadway
opposite Lincoln Center
757-2280